Language and Politics

Loyola Lecture Series
in Political Analysis
Richard Shelly Hartigan
Editor and Director

Language and Politics

Why Does Language Matter to Political Philosophy?

By
FRED R. DALLMAYR

University of Notre Dame Press
Notre Dame • London

Nachtvacht by Rembrandt used by
permission of Rijksmuseum Amsterdam

Library of Congress Cataloging in Publication Data

Dallmayr, Fred R. (Fred Reinhard), 1928–
  Language and politics.

  Bibliography: p.
  Includes index.
  1. Languages — Philosophy. 2. Languages — Political
aspects. I. Title.
P106.D24   1984   401   83-50744
ISBN 0-268-01270-9

Manufactured in the United States of America

FOR MY WIFE

Qui invenit mulierem bonam
invenit bonum; et hauriet jucunditatem . . .

Diu minne ist der natur, daz si
den menschen wandelt in die dinc,
die er minnet.
(Meister Eckhart)

Contents

Preface

The present study originated in a series of six lectures held at Loyola University of Chicago in the Spring of 1981. The framework for the lectures was the annual Loyola Lecture Series in Political Analysis, a program directed by Professor Richard S. Hartigan and sponsored by the Department of Political Science at Loyola. I am sincerely grateful to Professors Hartigan and James L. Wiser, Chairman of the department, for the opportunity to prepare and deliver the lectures and for the general hospitality extended to me during my stay at their institution.

The invitation came for me just at the right time: at a moment when I was deeply troubled by questions of language. Aware and convinced that twentieth-century philosophy and thought had become inextricably embroiled with language issues, I was perplexed by the diversity of approaches and the different accents and dimensions of the so-called "linguistic turn"; as it seemed to me, prominent conceptions of language were not only not complementary but often diametrically opposed to each other. The perplexity was for me not simply a general intellectual dilemma but one fraught with distinct political implications. If, following the Aristotelian tradition, man was defined as a "language creature" or a "being endowed with language" (*zoon logon ekhon*), the contemporary Babel of tongues about language carried confusion and disarray into the meaning and status of "man"; given the close linkage in the same tradition between notions of "language creature" and "political animal" (*zoon politikon*), the same confusion rendered imperative a reconsideration of the meaning of politics and of man as a political agent.

The Loyola lectures offered me a welcome occasion for sorting out my thoughts in this area and for bringing a semblance of coherence into the heterogeneous manifestations of the "linguistic turn." My endeavors along these lines were greatly aided by the faculty and students at Loyola University whose probing questions sharpened my perception of pertinent issues. My intellectual indebtedness, of course, extends beyond the immediate confines of the lecture series. The reader of this study will

ix

quickly notice the pervasive influence of such Continental philosophical mentors as Martin Heidegger, Hans-Georg Gadamer, Paul Ricoeur, Jacques Derrida, and also Karl-Otto Apel. In addition, I have benefited over the years from discussions with numerous American philosophers, inluding Calvin Schrag, Richard Bernstein, William McBride, Michael Murray, and John Searle. Among practitioners in the field of political theory whose arguments have provided me with a continuous source of reflection I want to mention particularly Hwa Yol Jung, Michael Shapiro, William Connolly, John Gunnell, and—last but by no means least—Hannah Arendt.

The usual caveat regarding final responsibility for shortcomings obviously applies also in the present case. On the whole, the study preserves the general structure of the original lecture series—although some portions have been expanded or fleshed out and others shortened. The one major alteration concerns the sixth lecture which was broken up into two chapters dealing respectively with poetry and with the general assessment of the language-politics relationship. The study also maintains the internal structure of individual lectures, in the sense that each chapter combines a descriptive exposition with critical exegesis and rejoinders. Regarding the typing of the manuscript I gratefully acknowledge Patricia Flanigan's competent and reliable work.

The study is dedicated to my wife, Ilse, without whose encouragement and loyal support neither this book nor any of my other undertakings would be conceivable. The dedication is particularly fitting in view of the room accorded in the study to poetry and literary interpretation—areas in which I have learned so much over the years from her knowledge and sensitivity. Beyond this topical range, however, the fittingness extends to the general tenor of the book which, as the reader will discover, is in a sense an homage to love.

August 1983   F.R.D.

Series Editor's Foreword

Since man first perceived his uniqueness from other living species, and in turn perceived that he possessed the ability to reflect upon that uniqueness, he has attempted to define himself. These definitions of his specific "nature" have ranged far and wide with the animal describing himself variously at extremes as benign, aggressive, cooperative, competitive, material, spiritual, rational, instinctive, or combinations of these and other characteristics. Indeed, some have even speculated that man's singularity of nature is best identified as the capacity to attribute uniqueness to himself in the first place.

Whatever the truth of these attributions may be, in whole or in part, one fact about man is inescapably true; he is nature's most formidable communicator, he is the master of language.

As apparent as is this truth, so too is another; the initimate relationship between language and politics. So crucial is this phenomenon that, as the present author points out, Aristotle's definition of man, the political being, is fully understood only in conjunction with his second definition of man as a living being capable of speech. It is to this relationship of human communication and behavior, with its myriad implications, that the present volume is addressed.

Language and Politics is the outgrowth of six lectures which Professor Fred R. Dallmayr delivered in the spring of 1981 at Loyola University of Chicago. His was the seventh presentation of the Loyola Lecture Series in Political Analysis. Inauguarated in 1968 by Loyola University of Chicago's Department of Political Science, the series has provided a critical forum for the ideas of a distinguished number of contemporary political philosophers. Subsequent publication of the revised and elaborated lectures has fulfilled a second goal, that of making these scholars' works available to as large an audience as possible.

Those associated with the Lecture Series are pleased that its previous publications have been so well received, but they are especially proud to present Professor Dallmayr's contribution. His work over the years has been consistently marked by an enormous depth and breadth of scholarship, a tradition maintained in his *Language and Politics*. In addition, we are deeply grateful to him for his personal warmth, extended cooperation, and continued friendship.

Richard Shelly Hartigan

1

After Babel:
Competing Conceptions of Language

Mors et vita in manu linguae . . .

The aim of the present inquiry is to focus, and perhaps shed some light, on language and politics and their reciprocal relationship. Such an aim does not seem to deviate perceptibly from typical modes of conceptual analysis. As in other instances of conceptual pairing, one might think, the simplest manner of tackling the theme would be to offer a definition of terms—a procedure which, if properly performed, should directly yield the desired correlation. Despite its plausibility in some contexts, I shall not follow this approach here for a number of reasons. For one thing, it is by no means clear that our key terms—language and politics—are amenable to a straightforward definitional settlement, if by "definition" we mean the identification of fixed substances or conceptual essences. On a prima facie level one cannot rule out the possibility that our terms belong to what are sometimes called "contestable" notions—notions whose very meaning implies disputes about formulation. Moreover, even assuming the success of a definitional strategy, the settlement would be effected only on a plane of abstract, invariant categories—a plane insensitive to the historical changes in the language-politics correlation and, above all, to the particular timeliness which the theme has acquired in our century. For these and other motives I prefer to pursue a more phenomenological or (if you will) maieutic course, by surveying initially the terrain in which our terms are situated and against whose backdrop they acquire their varying contours.

Language and Politics: Some Views

To begin our survey, we may wish to start from a view of correlation in the sense of a relatively accidental or random assortment. As everyone knows, students of politics deal with a wide range of diverse phenomena; in fact, there is hardly any topic which cannot somehow be brought within the purview of political analysis. No compelling reason exists to exclude linguistic phenomena from this purview; in this manner, language can be placed as one item on the long list of conventional subject

1

matters which includes, among other things, electoral behavior, pressure tactics, and governmental decision-making and its effects. To the extent that language is seen as a structured domain cultivated by professional specialists (linguists, grammarians, philologists), its relevance may be construed in terms of an interdisciplinary relationship; from this vantage point, the language-politics correlation is treated on a par with other pairings of disciplines such as politics and medicine, politics and psychopathology, or politics and literature. No doubt, much useful information can be gleaned from such comparative investigations. In some cases, the relationship has the character of reciprocity, making possible the study of each partner's influence on the other. Thus, in the second pairing, one can distinguish and compare the politics of psychopathology—meaning the organization and policies of psychiatry—and the psychopathology of politics, referring to psychic disorders manifest in political actors or in the political structure at large. Likewise, one can juxtapose the politics of literature to the literature of politics, with the first phrase denoting the policies of professional writers and critics, and the second phrase the literary expressions of political thought and action.

Going beyond random assortment, language may be accorded a prominent place within the broad domain of politics itself seen as an empirical process. Under the impact of advances in electronics and the expansion of mass media, many students of politics in recent decades have stressed the importance of linguistic or (more generally) symbolic "communication" for the maintenance and regulation of political communities or systems. As viewed by spokesmen of this outlook, communication signifies basically an ongoing flow and exchange of messages, that is, a continuing transmission of "information" between various senders and receivers in society, in such a manner that all social elements ultimately coalesce into a complex communications network. On the level of political decision-making, proponents regard communication as vital both for the initial articulation and the subsequent implementation of policies, arguing that the former requires a flow of information—frequently termed "inputs"—from the population or pressure groups to relevant public authorities, just as implementation demands an "output" flow from authorities to the respective political clientele. In more technical terminology, political communications analysts tend to study the "fidelity" of channels, the general "noise level" of a network or the extent to which information is transmitted from unit to unit without loss of relevant detail, the "selectivity" of receivers, the complexity of "coding" and "decoding" devices, the adequacy of "feedback" flows, and similar matters.[1] To the extent that it coincides with communication, language from this perspective plays a functional role with respect to the larger political framework, a role whose performance can be empirically measured;

metaphorically speaking, it operates like a currency or (better still) like an electrical current ensuring the cohesiveness and viability of political life. By translating "function" into a means-ends relation, one might describe language here as a cognitive tool or an instrument for maintaining the proper information level in society.

The political relevance of language, however, may not only be tied to this kind of functional role. Instead of serving as vehicle for the dissemination of (presumably factual) knowledge, language can also be enlisted in the pursuit of practical-political goals: looking beyond its cognitive potential, politicians or public agents may seize upon it as a means for the promotion of their aims and ambitions. Seen under practical auspices, the objective of linguistic communication is not so much information as rather persuasion; the concern from this angle is less with a well-integrated network than with the effects of public speech and rhetoric. To the extent that political life encourages reciprocity of speech, interaction takes the form not of a simple exchange of messages but of public argumentation and debate. More commonly, public speech consists in the promulgation and inculcation of partisan views and preferences—sometimes of compact platforms or ideological doctrines. Students of public speech or rhetoric (using the latter term in the slightly tainted sense it has acquired in recent times) typically focus on the personal style of speakers, on the occasion and setting of public pronouncements, and on the attunement of chosen idioms to targeted audiences. Where speech operates as a technique of mass propaganda, the assessment of personal aims becomes blurred and submerged in more empirical types of analysis concentrating on the statistical frequency of words and symbols in official statements.[2]

The connection of speech and propaganda brings into view an aspect of our theme which points beyond a straightforward means-ends relationship. When backed up by political power and broad ideological precepts, language functions not as a mere cognitive tool nor as means for particular aims, but rather as a cast or grid for an entire way of life, that is, for preferred manners of thinking, speaking, and acting. This molding or constraining character of political language is well-known from totalitarian and authoritarian regimes where customary speech patterns tend to be progressively suffused and corrupted by officially sanctioned jargon; to a lesser extent, social-economic classes and political subcultures are usually welded together by the prevalence of a distinct linguistic idiom or mode of symbolization. In the American context, no one has more vividly portrayed the political impact of language—or better the politics of language—than Murray Edelman. In a string of publications ranging from *The Symbolic Uses of Politics* over *Politics as Symbolic Action* to *Political Language: Words That Succeed and Policies That Fail*, Edelman has drawn attention to the pervasive structuring or architectonic role of political language. Thus, focusing on the style and symbolic content of official pronouncements, the first-mentioned study made a compelling case for the thesis that political authorities or elites are able to shape the attitudes of people in their dealings with the government, while disguising the unequal allocation of opportunities and disadvantages behind the veil of public-spirited rhetoric. Subsequent studies further corroborated and expanded this thesis by delving into the domains of mass psychology and social status. Examining in greater detail the issue of social-economic disparities, *Political Language* tried to show how official statements and public symbols generate beliefs, assumptions, and perceptions in such a manner as to facilitate widespread acceptance of chronic poverty and inequality.[3]

The pervasive and architectonic role of language, however, is not only — perhaps not even primarily — tied to political domination and exploitation. In a sense, elite manipulation only accentuates and intensifies the language-politics correlation which is bound to prevail wherever political life finds linguistic or symbolic articulation. In an overt or subterranean fashion, the politics of language always accompanies or is associated with a given language of politics — to the extent that the latter phrase denotes a prevailing public idiom. Thus, in the transition from the late Middle Ages to modernity, political conflicts between church and state and between elites and nonelites were fused and mingled with debates regarding the respective merits of Latin and the *lingua franca*. In our own century, similar or comparable controversies have surfaced in many "developing" countries, sometimes taking the form of language clashes or riots. A well-known case in point is the Indian subcontinent. In emerging from British rule, the subcontinent initially was torn by a rift between several competing vernaculars, primarily between the Indo-European Hindi, spoken mostly by Hindus, and the more arabized Urdu, favored by Moslems; subsequently, after the establishment of separate nation-states, the officially recognized status of Hindi in India was challenged by a number of regional and local languages (such as Telugu in Madras and Kanarese in Bombay), a challenge which invariably implied a political test of national unity. At the same time, Pakistan experienced a protracted period of violent confrontation between the Urdu-speaking population in the West and the champions of Bengali in the East. Examples of this kind could readily be multiplied in African and Asian contexts; however, the problem is not restricted to the developing world — as is evident from frictions between English- and French-speaking communities in Canada and between French- and Flemish-speaking groups in Belgium.[4] What renders the mentioned cases and experiences intriguing is the peculiar political saliency and even explosiveness of linguistic idioms:

rather than being incidentally or instrumentally involved in contested issues, language itself at this point seems to be the bone of contention, as a centerpiece in public discourse and in the quest for a meaningful way of life.

The saliency of language for individual and collective self-understanding is not a novel discovery—although its full implications have been explored and elaborated mainly in our century. For some time, students of the human sciences have tended to portray man as *animal* or *homo loquens,* that is, as a creature whose distinctive quality or humanity resides in the capacity for language and speech. In the modern era, the idea of *homo loquens* was extolled with particular fervor by Wilhelm von Humboldt, in his wide-ranging studies of indigenous cultures and vernacular languages. In Humboldt's judgment, an understanding of indigenous cultures presupposed a grasp of linguistic structures and speech patterns which, in turn, reflected the mentality and historically grown world-view of a people. On a more ontological (and less man-centered) plane, the notion of *homo loquens* can be traced to classical antiquity, and especially to Aristotle's famous definition of man as *zoon logon ekhon,* that is, a creature endowed with "logos"—a phrase which has commonly been rendered as *animal rationale* or "rational animal," despite the fact that the Greek "logos" designated not only thought or thinking but also (and above all) language and speech. If Aristotle's phrase is joined with his other, equally famous definition of man as *zoon politikon* or political creature, one catches a glimpse of an essential (or ontological) linkage between language and politics where both appear as requisites for a properly human life.[5] Yet, mainly due to the dominant preoccupation with cognitive rationality, the linkage has tended to remain submerged or embryonic throughout much of Western history.

Among contemporary philosophers, the importance of language and the cogency of the Aristotelian formulations have been eloquently stressed by Hans-Georg Gadamer (who in this respect followed up leads in Heidegger's writings). Western philosophical thought, Gadamer observes at one point, "has not placed the nature of language at the center of its considerations"— mainly because of a fascination with reason and consciousness which obscured the Aristotelian insights. Actually, in the Western tradition, the definition of man as a creature with "logos" became "canonical in a form which stated that man is the *animal rationale,* the rational being, distinguished from all other animals by his capacity for thought." In this manner, the term "logos" was identified with "reason or thought," despite the fact that "the primary meaning of this word is language." According to Gadamer, however, the Aristotelian phrase has crucial implications for individual and collective human life. Due to the endowment of "logos," he states, man "can make what is not present manifest through his speech, so that another person can participate in this view." More importantly, "it is by virtue of this ability to communicate that human beings alone share a common meaning, that is, common concepts and especially those through which a common human life is possible without murder and mayhem—in the form of social interaction, a political constitution, an organized division of labor." In this sense, he adds, language can be seen as "the true core or center of human life, provided it is placed in the context which is properly its own: the realm of human togetherness, the realm of common understanding and of an ever-renewed common agreement—an agreement as indispensable to human life as the air we breathe."[6]

Gadamer's views are echoed or seconded by a number of contemporary political thinkers, foremost among them Hannah Arendt. In *The Human Condition* Arendt forcefully underscores the language-politics linkage by noting that "wherever the relevance of speech is at stake, matters become political by definition, for speech is what makes man a political being." Like Gadamer's arguments, the study relies explicitly on the Aristotelian formulations of the key characteristics of the human species. "Aristotle's definition of man as *zoon politikon*," we read, "was not only unrelated and even opposed to the natural association experienced in household life; it can be fully understood only if one adds his second famous definition of man as a *zoon logon ekhon* ('a living being capable of speech'). The Latin translation of this term into *animal rationale* rests on no less fundamental a misunderstanding than the term 'social animal' " (as a rendition of the first formula). Arendt's study also draws attention to the central ingredients of the *bios politikos* or "political way of life" in the Aristotelian frame of reference: "Of all the activities necessary and present in human communities, only two were deemed to be political and to constitute what Aristotle called the *bios politikos,* namely action (*praxis*) and speech (*lexis*), out of which rises the realm of human affairs." As she continues, the classical view of political life was in large measure indebted to pre-Socratic and Homeric conceptions—to the extent that the *polis* "grew out of and remained rooted in the Greek pre-*polis* experience and estimate of what makes it worthwhile for men to live together (*syzen*), namely, the 'sharing of words and deeds'."[7]

Puzzles of Language

As discussed so far, the contours of our theme are still quite hazy and elusive; although backed up by the testimony of leading philosophers and political thinkers, the linkage of language and politics is at this point at best a broad conjecture or road signal. To learn that man is a creature endowed with language is surely an important insight—but an insight insufficiently instructive as long as the meaning of "language" remains doubtful. Questions or doubts regarding language, however, quickly spill over and affect the meaning of "being human" as well as the sense of politics. Actually, at a closer look, language emerges as a complex, multifaceted phenomenon whose diverse layers or dimensions are by no means readily compatible. In fact, instead of blending into a harmonious fabric, the relations between the various dimensions appear in many ways deeply paradoxical or enigmatic—a situation which, in turn, reverberates in the *bios politikos* seen as a distinctly human way of life.

Little effort or reflection is required to realize that language—in one of its many dimensions or guises—is not simply a phantasm but a concrete-real entity or process, inserted in numerous ways into the fabric of empirical reality. People not merely seem or pretend to communicate, but actually do exchange greetings, warnings, exhortations, and pieces of information. Moreover, the messages exchanged are not fleeting images, but are composed of strings of distinct sounds (or else of written marks or symbolic notations). In light of this undeniable concreteness or factuality, language and speech can be—and have been for some time—the targets of a variety of empirical-scientific investigations. One feasible approach is to concentrate on the linguistic data themselves, that is, on phonetic units, morphological characteristics, and their combination in words and sentences; integrated into a coherent framework these topics are the subject matter of empirical linguistics. However, the concreteness of language is not confined to its constituent elements. In order to be articulated in speech, language requires the assistance of various physiological processes and mechanisms—aspects which are studied by speech science and speech pathology. In addition, the same articulation is commonly associated with complex mental and psychological dispositions and occurrences as well as with prevailing cultural patterns and modes of socialization—features which provide ample research material for the disciplines of psycholinguistics and sociolinguistics. As previously indicated, the rise of electronics and cybernetics has spawned the emergence of a field of empirical political linguistics, concerned with communication processes in political systems and with the technical-instrumental role of language in the dissemination of information. The same field also encompasses empirical research in the domain of public speech, especially quantitative "content analysis" of ideological or propagandistic pronouncements.

While yielding important findings in matters of detail, however, empirical research can never account for the status and significance of language in human life. For, how can strings of sounds or letters on their own ever manage to produce warnings, greetings, or condolences? And how can physiological processes and psychological sensations, even when combined with social-cultural influences, coalesce into a medium of individual and collective self-understanding? For these and other reasons, students of language sometimes shift the accent from empirical linguistic data to an underlying cognitive faculty or an innate linguistic endowment. Particularly in the modern era, descendants of Descartes—philosophers and grammarians alike—have tended to postulate the operation of a deep-seated competence or invariant matrix capable of integrating linguistic data into a coherent fabric. Seen from this perspective, language coincides indeed with "logos," but in the sense of reason or consciousness; according to proponents of the view, there is a cognitive potential prior to experience, an inner language or speech prior to actual linguistic performance—in other words, an a priori grid antedating and structuring concrete phenomena. Yet, although correcting the defects of empiricism, Cartesianism conjures up new quandaries and dilemmas. For, how can an invariant cognitive grid provide the basis for the multitude of actual languages and for the diversity of actual speech patterns? Moreover, even assuming an invariant and universal endowment, why would human self-understanding require intersubjective articulation and communication? The latter dilemma has been keenly pinpointed by Hannah Arendt. Under the auspices of the rationalist position, she comments at one point, what men have in common is not a shared world or experience but "the structure of their minds, and this they cannot have in common, strictly speaking; their faculty of reasoning can only happen to be the same in everybody."[8]

Given the difficulties besetting both empiricism and rationalism, it may seem advisable to regard language neither as sense object nor as cognitive grid but rather as an event or a practical performance accomplished by concretely situated speakers or human agents. From this vantage point the emphasis is less on man as *zoon logon ekhon* than on *homo loquens;* in the terminology of Ferdinand de Saussure—the founder of contemporary linguistics— the preoccupation is chiefly with *parole* or speech rather than with *langue* seen as a structured system of sounds and letters. There are several advantages deriving from this shift from epistemology to a more practical or pragmatic outlook: prominent among them are the enhanced sensitivity to linguistic innovation and diversity and the greater attention given to the genesis of meaning in human speech. However, despite these and similar merits, the change of accent again carries a price—mainly the price of a potential new instrumentalism, in the sense of a reduction of language to a means of human self-articulation and self-expression. Evidently, expression is not an entirely self-sufficient enterprise; even novel or idiosyncratic modes of articulation presuppose an existing linguistic arsenal for their purposes.

The issue is not only or not so much that we have to adapt speech to intended meanings, but that—to use Stanley Cavell's formulation—we may be constrained to "mean what we say"; differently put: the difficulty is not only for words to capture intentions but for intentions to catch up with words, that is, with the implications of a given linguistic idiom.[9] In a sense, what reasserts itself here behind the back of speech is again the "logos"-dimension of language—the dimension of logical syntactical properties and also of conventional rules of meaning inherent in "language games."

Yet, the dilemma at this point exceeds the conflict between intention and convention or between expression and rules; for, without further elaboration, resort to cognitive or else factual rules merely revives the noted rationalist and empiricist quandaries. As it appears, language precedes speech not only on a logical but an ontological plane: the most perplexing puzzle resides in the circumstance that somehow "language itself speaks"—in a manner which overarches and gives sense not only to intentions but to general rules. It is on this plane that Gadamer locates the real "enigma of language" which he associates with the latter's "unfathomable unconsciousness of itself." As he notes, in speaking a language or about a language we seem to have a firm grasp of our medium or subject matter—a grasp which is undermined by its prior availability as a condition of speech. To be in charge of language implies that we consciously extricate ourselves from its sway. The problem, however, is that "we can never really do this completely; rather, all thinking about language is always already overtaken by language. We can only think in a language, and just this inherence of our thinking in language is the profound enigma that language presents to thought."[10] Gadamer is not the first to have sensed and articulated the mentioned enigma or—if one prefers—the implicit vertigo of language. Almost two hundred years ago, in 1784, Johann Georg Hamann wrote a letter to Herder which contained these lines: "If I were as eloquent as Demosthenes I would yet have to do nothing more than repeat a single word three times: reason is language, *logos*. I gnaw at this marrow-bone and will gnaw myself to death over it. There continues to remain a darkness over this depth for me; I am still waiting for an apocalyptic angel with a key to this abyss."[11]

Basically we, too, are waiting in the same manner. The present study certainly does not pretend to hold the key which would unlock the riddles of language. My ambition here is more modest: on the whole, the inquiry will have served its purpose if it induces us to hover less comfortably—or with greater self-awareness—over the dark abyss mentioned by Hamann. The study's objective is limited in other respects as well. Although dealing broadly with the correlation of language and politics, the chief focus of the inquiry is on the theme's import for philosophical reflection, and especially for political philosophy. Several consequences follow from this limitation. Without questioning their general significance, the presentation does not seek to emulate the procedures, or recapitulate the findings, of contemporary sociolinguistics or empirical political linguistics; likewise, no effort will be made to delve into political rhetoric and the concrete methods of mass persuasion. Rather, the emphasis will tend to be on the philosophical underpinnings of particular approaches or vantage points and their relevance for political thought. Thus, in the field of empiricism, the concern will be with theoretical implications of an empiricist or behaviorist treatment of language; still in the same broad area, attention will also be given to empiricist epistemology, more specifically to an empiricist or referential semantics in which language serves as tool for the investigation of empirical data. Similar considerations apply to the discussion of phenomenological, structuralist, existentialist, and "ordinary-language" approaches to linguistic phenomena; in all such instances the richness of concrete descriptions and analyses will in large measure have to be bracketed.

Initial Objections

The attempt to treat the language-politics theme in the indicated manner—from the perspective of philosophical reflection—may provoke a number of immediate objections which probably should be addressed without delay. Critical reservations may spring from purely philosophical or else from more mundane-realistic and political motives. The focus on language, even a reflective focus—one line of argument holds—is bound to jeopardize philosophical reasoning itself, by eliminating or obscuring from view the genuinely "great" or "perennial" questions, such as the issues of justice, goodness, and truth. Descending from the plane of essential insight, another line of criticism chides the same focus for bypassing or shortchanging the autonomy of empirical reality, including the forces operative in political life. Although prompted by different considerations, the two objections are not entirely discordant or incompatible: both concur in assigning a relatively subordinate role to language, while questioning the correlation and interpenetration of language, politics, and thought.

The first type of criticism has frequently been leveled against Anglo-American "linguistic philosophy," mainly because of a certain antimetaphysical posture commonly associated with this perspective;[12] however, the thrust of the reproach exceeds geographical boundaries. In his *Nihilism: A Philosophical Essay*, Stanley Rosen extended the charge of antirational bias to a broad spectrum of contemporary views—particularly to the school of "ordinary language analysis" deriving from the teachings of Wittgenstein and Austin, and to Heidegger's "fundamental ontology" of language. As used in the study, the term "nihilism" was basically a synonym for irrationalism and the arbitrary, nondiscursive indulgence in whims; in this specific sense, the term was first "defined by Nietzsche, and subsequently elaborated by Heidegger," but its repercussions could also "be found in the teachings of philosophers like Wittgenstein and his various epigones." According to Rosen, it was imperative clearly to differentiate between language, on the one hand, and objects and rational ideas, on the other, because only such segregation permitted a discursive justification of propositions. By contrast, an excessive preoccupation with language was bound to undermine discourse and the exploration of basic philosophical questions, including the Platonic theme of "the good"; this subversion, in turn, could only end up in reducing "reason to nonsense by equating the sense or significance of speech with silence"—an outcome which was at the core of the "contemporary crisis of reason." The application of the term "nihilism" to the Wittgensteinian school, the author realized, was unconventional and perhaps overdramatic in view of the relatively modest aims of its proponents in comparison with recent Continental thought. As he observed, however: "In order to engage the attention of those members of the philosophical community who regard nihilism as a literary neurosis imported from continental Europe, I believe it is useful to spell out the nihilistic consequences of a mode of philosophizing that prides itself upon its rigor and Anglo-Saxon sobriety."[13]

Rosen's argument is surely not entirely misguided or unprovoked; students of twentieth-century thought cannot fail to have encountered at some point samples of unimaginative and unenlightening linguistic inquiries—inquiries almost deliberately purged of theoretical relevance. Yet, as a general indictment of recent language philosophy, I find the charge of irrationalism and nihilism vastly excessive; in a sense, the charge can itself be seen as a strategy of avoidance—to the extent that it muffles or sidesteps problems beleaguering contemporary discussions about language. Moreover, it is entirely conceivable that some of the so-called "perennial" issues can be reformulated—perhaps even require to be reformulated—in the idiom of present-day language philosophy. An example may illustrate this point. In one of his writings on language theory, the philosopher-sociologist Jürgen Habermas observes that "pure intersubjectivity"—or what he calls an "ideal speech situation"— "exists only when there is complete symmetry in the distribution of assertion and denial, revelation and concealment, prescription and conformity, among the partners of communication." These three symmetries, he adds, "represent, incidentally, a linguistic conceptualization of what are traditionally known as the ideas of truth, freedom, and justice." Here one can hardly claim that philosophical topics are ignored. Generally speaking — and excepting such terms as "resolve" or "dispose of"— I tend to agree on this point with Hilary Putnam when he states: "If philosophers have become very interested in language in the past fifty years it is not because they have become *dis*interested in the Great Questions of philosophy, but precisely because they *are* still interested in the Great Questions and because they have come to believe that language holds the key to resolve (or in some way satisfactorily dispose of) the Great Questions."[14]

In comparison with Rosen's metaphysical preoccupations, the second criticism has a more down-to-earth flavor and also a concrete polemical edge: the concern is not so much with timeless issues as with a presumed disregard of empirical reality as well as the harsher aspects of political life, including experiences of corruption and oppression. The most spirited attack along these lines has been launched by Ernest Gellner in his *Words and Things*—a book concentrating on British "linguistic philosophy," but whose arguments have a potentially broader reach. According to Gellner, the accent on language peculiar to linguistic philosophy fosters a narrow-minded and myopic posture; thus, the chief objection to its enterprise resides "in the vistas and ranges of interest which it suggests." In effect, its scope "excludes almost everything that is of genuine interest and that properly should be the starting point of thought: science, and the social and intellectual transformation which mankind is undergoing." Prominent among the problem areas excluded by linguistic analysts is epistemology construed as a theory specifying the linkage between thought or language and empirical objects; a central trademark of the entire movement, in Gellner's view, can be found in "the replacement of the epistemological viewpoint, of the critical evaluation of what we know, by an anti-epistemological outlook, which denies such a possibility." As a conception of language, he noted, this kind of outlook "denies that language is, in fact or in principle or in some hidden way, a mirror of reality, a mirror such that, from the nature of the basic constituents of *language*, one could infer the basic constituents of *reality*." To the extent that much of traditional philosophy revolved around inference or reference in this sense—linguistic analysts hold—"this was *the* crucial error of past philosophers, and the fact that the human mind is given to this type of error is the basis of all or most (past, mistaken) philosophy."

Apart from mounting an epistemological critique, *Words and Things* also probed the intellectual and social-political conditions buttressing the rise of the linguistic movement. Among those conditions the study mentioned: "a predisposition to see problems in terms of logic and language; an exclusion of transcendental possibilities; a conservative and formalist

spirit amongst philosophers, springing from a deep alienation from substantive and committed thinking; an organization and ethos in teaching
institutions favoring a lack of historical and social awareness; the existence in sufficient numbers of philosophers, favorable to scholastic, minute
and idiographic studies." Contrary to Rosen, Gellner saw the chief peril
or vice of linguistic analysis not in nihilism or a supposed "corruption of
youth"—although he did find the outlook saturated with irrationalist
premises and propositions. In terms of political implications, the emphasis of the study was on the movement's "neutralist" stance, epitomized in its dedication to pure conceptual analysis—a stance readily
compatible with conservative or traditionalist leanings. Whereas logical
positivism was still a "revolutionary doctrine" in that it "undermined
many of the traditional ideologies," Gellner observed, recent linguistic
philosophy is basically "conservative in the values which it in fact in-
sinuates." Without endorsing an explicit conservative program, the
movement "refuses to undermine any accepted habits, but, on the contrary, concentrates on showing that the *reasons underlying criticisms* of
accepted habits are in general mistaken." In this manner, linguistic
philosophers (and, more generally, students of language) "have shown
that, contrary to what Orwell thought, a cult of *oldspeak* can muzzle
thought at least as much as an invented *newspeak*."[15]

Again, as in the preceding instance, this line of criticism cannot lightly
be dismissed. No doubt, there are examples in the literature manifesting
the kind of linguistic myopia or self-indulgence (sometimes termed
"lingualism") denounced by Gellner; students of politics, in particular,
are likely to be apprehensive about a theoretical posture suspected of formalism or a lack of "substantive and committed thinking." On the
whole, I am thus quite willing to heed the realist rejoinder—provided it
is not itself a subterfuge or the outgrowth of antireflective bias. Surely,
politics or political reality cannot be grasped independently of language,
especially if one takes into account the latter's architectonic role—its
noted saliency for human self-understanding and for a properly political
way of life. Regarding the relationship between "words and things" or
between language and the world, as seen from a Wittgensteinian vantage
point, I find plausible Cavell's observation that "the philosophy of ordinary language is not about language, anyway not in any sense in which
it is not also about the world. Ordinary language philosophy is about
whatever ordinary language is about." In a somewhat broader frame of
reference, a similar point is made by Richard Rorty in his *Philosophy and
the Mirror of Nature*. "It is one thing to say (absurdly) that we make objects by using words," he writes, "and something quite different to say
that we do not know how to find a way of describing an enduring matrix
of past and future inquiry into nature except in our own terms." While

"almost no one wishes to say the former," to affirm the latter is "just a way of saying that our present views about nature are our only guide in talking about the relation between nature and our words."[16]

The Linguistic Turn

The preceding comments are not meant to settle or lay to rest the mentioned objections, but only to indicate possible responses and alternative vistas (which will be fleshed out subsequently). What the sketched debates indicate, in any event, is the prominence enjoyed by language in contemporary philosophical discussions—a prominence which leaves room for a great variety of accents, approaches, and favorable or unfavorable attitudes. To this extent the exchanges illustrate, if only obliquely, the thesis of an enhanced stature of language in twentieth-century philosophy, a thesis supported by impressive evidence and frequently summarized under the label "linguistic turn." At this point I would like to explore this thesis somewhat more closely, by examining the concrete manner in which the "turn" to language has occurred or manifested itself in different philosophical contexts. The claim is sometimes advanced that, to the degree language has risen in stature, the change is confined entirely to Anglo-Saxon or Anglo-American thought; a closer look, however, shows this claim to be unwarranted. Actually, linguistic topics feature as important concerns in a multitude of philosophical, literary, and social-theoretical perspectives cultivated mainly—though no longer exclusively—on the Continent. Without trying to be exhaustive, I intend to highlight both the pervasiveness and the complexity of the change by concentrating on a limited number of formulations taken from diverse settings.

Among British and American philosophers, the shift of attention antedates the emergence of ordinary language analysis or "linguistic philosophy" in the narrow sense; moreover, the change was by no means immune from Continental influences. The phrase "linguistic turn," it appears, was first coined by Gustav Bergmann, a logical empiricist and member of the so-called Vienna Circle;[17] however, its wide circulation and popularity seems mainly due to a volume published by Richard Rorty in 1967, under the title *The Linguistic Turn: Recent Essays in Philosophical Method*. In his Introduction to the volume, Rorty linked the turn in question closely (perhaps too closely) with the tradition of logical empiricism in our century; in his usage the term "analytical" or "linguistic philosophy" encompassed the broad time-span and intellectual spectrum stretching from the "logical atomism" of Bertrand Russell and the early Wittgenstein, over the rise of the Vienna Circle and its program of linguistic "constructivism" (or "constructionalism"), to the ascent of ordinary language analysis in the postwar period. The common denominator of these phases or trends was found in the effort to overcome speculative metaphysics and to facilitate empirical-scientific inquiry through close scrutiny of linguistic concepts and categories. "I shall mean by 'linguistic philosophy' the view," Rorty wrote, "that philosophical problems are problems which may be solved (or dissolved) either by reforming language, or by understanding more about the language we presently use." As a synonym or offshoot of logical empiricism, linguistic philosophy in his view was motivated primarily by epistemological and methodological considerations—in the sense that language served mainly as a tool or instrument in the investigation of empirical facts. To perform this task properly, the Introduction indicated, language had to be either "reformed" and even remodeled, or else be better "understood" through clarification of current conventions. The first alternative could take the form either of an attempt to uncover the inner logic or "logical syntax" buried under the "historico-grammatical syntax" of a given language (a strategy characterizing "logical atomism") or else of a deliberate "constructivism" leading to the design of an "ideal language" (an option favored by the Vienna Circle). The second alternative, on the other hand, was the aim of ordinary language analysis as inaugurated by the later Wittgenstein, Austin, and Peter Strawson. The shared premise animating these alternatives was typically that language "plus science" would somehow be "adequate to describe and explain everything that there is."[18]

A large portion of Rorty's essay was taken up by a discussion of the controversy between constructivists and ordinary language analysts—a debate whose details are not directly pertinent in the present context. Regarding the overall results or accomplishments of linguistic philosophy, especially in light of its epistemological aims, the Introduction noted only very meager success. The "relatively pessimistic conclusions" reached in his review, Rorty stated, "entail that linguistic philosophers' attempts to turn philosophy into a 'strict science' must fail." This verdict prompted him to inquire about further prospects: "If linguistic philosophy cannot be a strict science, if it has a merely critical, essentially dialectical, function, then what of the future?" In reply to this query, the concluding section of the essay enumerated "six possibilities for the future of philosophy"—all of which implied distinct attitudes toward language. In the order listed, Rorty's scenario included these options: first, Husserlian phenomenology, based on a rejection of "methodological nominalism" and of empiricism as such; secondly, Heideggerian ontology, pointing beyond philosophy as an "argumentative discipline"; thirdly, a redefinition of philosophizing along the lines of constructive "world-views"; fourthly, a transformation of reflection into a therapeutic enterprise, as recommended (perhaps) by the later Wittgenstein; fifthly, a development of linguistic analysis in the direction of descriptive accounts yielding ultimately a "lexicography pursued for its own sake," as advocated sometimes by Austin; and lastly, the pursuit of a "transcendental" linguistic inquiry aimed at uncovering the "necessary conditions for the possibility of language itself," as envisaged by Strawson.[19]

For all practical purposes, the mentioned options were presented in random sequence, without any hint of a rank order or preferential scheme; while indicating respective advantages and disadvantages, Rorty managed to hold his own judgment carefully in abeyance. The final paragraph, however, added the following startling comment (for which the essay had scarcely prepared the reader): "I should wish to argue that the most important thing that has happened in philosophy during the last thirty years is not the linguistic turn itself, but rather the beginning of a thoroughgoing rethinking of certain epistemological difficulties which have troubled philosophers since Plato and Aristotle." The noted epistemological difficulties were linked by Rorty to what he called the "spectatorial account of knowledge," an account predicated on the possibility of a direct visual access to reality unmediated by language. According to the dominant epistemology of the past, a conception still reverberating in logical empiricism, he noted, "the acquisition of knowledge presupposes the presentation of something 'immediately given' to the mind, where the mind is conceived of as a sort of 'immaterial eye,' and where 'immediately' means at a minimum, 'without the mediation of language'." Once this epistemological outlook—and the emphasis on epistemology itself—was abandoned, philosophical thinking was bound to undergo a profound revision whose general repercussions could only dimly be perceived at this point: "If the traditional 'spectatorial' account of knowledge is overthrown, the account of knowledge which replaces it will lead to reformulations everywhere else in philosophy, particularly in metaphilosophy."[20]

These last comments—afterthoughts in the context of the Introduction—obviously carried important implications for the status of language and the overall significance of the "linguistic turn." If what was actually happening in our age—behind the surface developments and events portrayed in the volume—was a major reversal in Western epistemology, then this change was prone to affect, and perhaps erode, the epistemological-methodological commitments of a linguistic philosophy tied to the legacy of logical empiricism. The same change, however, clearly did not jeopardize the philosophical import of language itself—thus presenting the "linguistic turn" in an entirely new light. Considerations of this kind are pursued and elaborated in Rorty's more recent book, *Philosophy and the*

Mirror of Nature. Going beyond the level of suggestive intuitions, the study offers a full-scale critique of the tradition of Western epistemology construed as a "spectatorial" theory of knowledge; it also develops in greater detail the notion of an "immaterial eye" (alternatively spelled "immaterial I"), now restyled as a synonym for "our glassy essence." Regarding philosophical approaches to language, Rorty distinguishes in the study between two kinds of treatment, a "pure" and an "impure" kind — the first concerned with language for its own sake, the second nurturing this concern for ulterior, epistemological motives. In the case of a "pure" philosophy of language, he writes, we have "a discipline which has no epistemological *parti pris,* nor, indeed, any relevance to most of the traditional concerns of modern philosophy." By contrast, the motivation of the second approach "is explicitly epistemological. The source of this 'impure' philosophy of language is the attempt to retain Kant's picture of philosophy as providing a permanent ahistorical framework for inquiry in the form of a theory of knowledge." The first type of treatment (exemplified, among others, by the later Wittgenstein), he adds, generates a "de-epistemologized conception of the philosophy of language"; on the other hand, spokesmen of the second camp have been led, "at various times and in various ways, to various forms of operationalism, verificationism, behaviorism, conventionalism, and reductionism" — perspectives revealing "a last nostalgic attempt to hook up a new kind of philosophical activity with an old problematic."[21]

Switching from the Anglo-American context to the Continental European setting, I want to draw attention briefly to the phenomenological "school" or movement. Within the confines of that movement, the shift toward language is evident in the works of a number of leading thinkers: in Heidegger's articulation of a "hermeneutical phenomenology" in *Being and Time* and his progressive disenchantment with epistemology (in Rorty's sense); in Gadamer's formulation of a "philosophical hermeneutics" in *Truth and Method;* and in Merleau-Ponty's move from the "primacy of perception" to a quasi-structural phenomenology of language.[22] For present purposes I intend to focus on Paul Ricoeur — mainly because he has provided a succinct account of his intellectual journey, in an essay of 1971 entitled "From Existentialism to the Philosophy of Language." Regarding intellectual parentage, Ricoeur took his point of departure from Husserlian phenomenology construed as a method of inquiry, while applying this method in a novel fashion to various "existentialist" themes. As will be shown more fully later, Husserl's approach concentrated basically on the "logos" of phenomena, that is, on their "essence" or invariant cognitive meaning as seen from the vantage point of a purified or "transcendental" consciousness. In an oversimplified manner one might say that, starting from Husserl's position, Ricoeur was progressively led to treat the "logos" as the language of phenomena rather than their epistemic core, a language in need of careful exegesis.

Several of his early writings concentrated on the issue of human will, probing such aspects as motivation, intention, and purpose; in a Husserlian vein, the aim was to grasp the "essence" or invariant structure of voluntary acts.[23] In large measure, this investigation could proceed by relying on direct phenomenological analysis and description, and also on the use of terms available in everyday language. The adopted mode of inquiry, Ricoeur's essay states, "did not yet raise any particular problem of language, for a direct language was thought to be available," namely, "ordinary language in which we find words like purpose, motive, and so on." However, in the further pursuit of the investigation, difficult problems and quandaries emerged — especially "experiences such as guilt, bondage, alienation, or, to speak in religious terms, sin." In an unforeseen manner, these quandaries injected into his research "new linguistic perplexities," by showing the inadequacy of a literal construal of language and the need for symbolic interpretation. "The fact is," Ricoeur writes, "that we have a direct language to say purpose, motive, and 'I can', but we speak of evil by means of metaphors such as estrangement, errance, burden, and bondage. Moreover, these primary symbols do not occur unless they are embedded within intricate narratives of myth which tell the story of how evil began." As a result of these and similar experiences, his path of inquiry was deflected from straightforward phenomenological description toward "a roundabout way, the detour of a hermeneutic of these symbols. I had to introduce a hermeneutical dimension within the structure of reflective thought itself."[24]

The discovery of hermeneutics, however, was only an initial phase in Ricoeur's intellectual journey; the significance of the discovery was still narrowly restricted, as he admits, to the "interpretation of symbolic language" or to the "art of deciphering indirect meanings." Roughly at this time, several events or developments occurred which compelled him to deepen his "linguistic turn" and to shift his philosophical interest to "the problem of language as such." Four major factors or developments are listed in the essay: first, his growing preoccupation with "the structure of psychoanalytic theory"; secondly, a pervasive and "important change in the philosophical scene, at least in France, where structuralism was beginning to replace existentialism and even phenomenology"; thirdly, issues emerging in religious-biblical exegesis, mainly due to "the so-called theologies of the Word in the post-Bultmannian school"; and lastly, the increasing influence of Anglo-American "ordinary language philosophy" in which he detected "a way both of renewing phenomenology and of replying to the excesses of structuralism." Each of the listed factors had a strong impact on Ricoeur's thought and his conception of language. According to the essay, his study of psychoanalysis revealed to him the existence of not one but two kinds of hermeneutics: namely, a "reductive" hermeneutics aiming at a "reductive explanation" of symbols, and a second type "tending toward a recollection or a retrieval" of their "original meaning." Even more decisive was the encounter with structuralism or the "structural model"—an outlook which, he notes, affirms mainly "that language, before being a process or an event, is a system, and that this system is not established at the level of the speaker's consciousness, but at a lower level, that of a kind of structural unconscious." As a result of this encounter, Ricoeur's initial subject-centered or "romanticist" view of hermeneutics was transformed into a more objective or "objectivist" version: "I tried to incorporate within hermeneutics as much as I could of this structural approach by means of a better connection between the stage of objective explanation and the stage of subjective appropriation." In the domain of post-Bultmannian theology, the same transformation entailed a deemphasis of the direct disclosure of the "Word" as "Kerygma" in favor of a closer attentiveness to the biblical text as narrative. The value of ordinary language analysis, finally, resided in its demonstration of the multifaceted or "polysemic" quality of words and in its insistence on the rich "descriptive power" of everyday expressions, "particularly in the realms of action and feelings."[25]

Conceptions of Language

Coming from opposite directions, Rorty's and Ricoeur's formulations contribute to bridging the gulf between Anglo-American and Continental thought; in both instances the connecting link is found in language. In this manner both accounts attest to the pervasiveness of the linguistic turn in our time; but they do not exhaust its scope. A similar turn can be detected in the context of the so-called "critical theory of society" developed by the Frankfurt School—as several writers have noted. Still within the Continental setting, one might also point to trends in French "post-structuralism," and especially to explorations of such themes as "discourse" (or "discursive practices") and "grammatology."[26] Clearly, despite a shared concern with language, the mentioned trends and formulations are by no means homogeneous. In fact, far from constituting a unified movement, the noted turn to language is fragmented into a plethora of perspectives whose premises and objectives appear not only diverse but entirely incompatible. The title of the present chapter is adapted from a book published by George Steiner in 1976, under the heading *After Babel: Aspects of Language and Translation*. In his study Steiner focused primarily on the difficulties of translation occasioned by

the profusion of vernacular languages and idioms and the absence of a
universal linguistic code.[27] As it seems, a similar profusion or confusion
prevails today with regard to conceptions of language or what are sometimes called "meta-linguistic" theories; differently put: we are facing a
Babel not only of tongues, but of "meta-tongues," that is, of construals
of what a tongue or language is all about. Is it possible to bring a semblance of order into these conflicting views or to cut a path through the
maze of approaches?

In order to make some headway along this road, I shall enlist the help
of several experienced guides or mentors. In a sense, the first guide has
been a silent partner in this inquiry from the beginning—his name being
implicitly invoked in the subtitle of the present study. As readers have no
doubt detected, the phrasing of the subtitle—"Why Does Language Matter to Political Philosophy?"—is actually a variation on the title of a book
by Ian Hacking devoted to a discussion of the language-philosophy relationship (and published in 1975). Hacking's study contains a great
number of insights and valuable observations on this theme—some of
which I can only mention here in passing. Thus, regarding the pervasiveness of the topic in our age he notes: "It is a manifest fact that immense
consciousness of language is at the present time characteristic of every
main stream in Western philosophy." Other intriguing comments have to
do with the overall significance of the linguistic turn. In some measure,
Hacking seems to share Rorty's intuition that what is happening underneath many surface changes or developments is a transformation of the
status of epistemology or the nature of knowledge; as he wryly points
out: "Knowledge is not what it used to be." Paralleling the distinction
between "pure" and "impure" approaches, the study indicates some relatively "unimportant" or "trifling" ways in which language may matter to
philosophy—among them the epistemological concerns of the logical-
empiricist movement, manifest both in the attempted construction of
"ideal languages" and in the descriptive analysis of ordinary usage. "On
the one hand," he writes, "language has been held to matter to philosophy because common speech leads into confusion"; on the other hand,
the "opposite opinion" is urged that "reflective use of common speech is
the very way to avoid confusion, and defining new terms will actually
augment confusion." One or the other of these "curiously contrary beliefs," he adds, "may nowadays be most often thought of as an answer
to the question Why does language matter to philosophy? Neither seems
to me enough."[28]

Though illuminating, statements of this kind are not directly at issue,
however; where I wish to draw on Hacking is in his distinction between
major conceptions or treatments of language. Subdivided into three sections, Hacking's study delineates three broad approaches to language

which correspond to successive historical phases of philosophical inquiry: namely, to the "Heydays" of "Ideas," of "Meanings," and of "Sentences" respectively. (Presumably, a chapter might have been added at the beginning on the era of "Substances," covering the period of classical antiquity.) In Hacking's presentation, the "Heyday of Ideas" extends roughly from the age of Descartes and Hobbes into the nineteenth century; the chief preoccupation of the phase, as far as language is concerned, was with the realm of internal "ideas" or—in Hobbesian vocabulary—with "mental discourse," as distinguished from intersubjective communication. "Hobbes' phrase 'mental discourse' is instructive," he writes. "There is something mental, enough like language to call it discourse, but which is logically prior to language. Seventeenth-century manuals very often recommend that we should strip our thought of as much language as possible, because public language, unlike mental discourse, is so prone to abuse." In contrast to this era of suspicion, the "Heyday of Meanings"—denoting the early part of our own century—heralded a decisive shift to language, but on a narrowly circumscribed plane: the plane of relatively stable or invariant units of meaning and linguistic structures. The term "meaning" in this context is borrowed from Gottlob Frege's writings, especially from his well-known differentiation between *Sinn* and *Bedeutung* or between conceptual-linguistic "meaning" and empirical "reference." The overall ambition of this phase was to stabilize "meaning" either in a logical-apodictic manner or else by tying it to discrete objects and sense-experiences (that is, to reference); differently phrased, the chief accent was on the development of a "logical syntax" and of a logical-empirical "semantics." Emerging in the postwar period, the "Heyday of Sentences" is said to usher in the dethronement of fixed, apodictic meanings and their absorption in the fabric of sentences, discourses, and "language games."[29]

Notwithstanding its virtues, I find Hacking's analysis limited in two main respects. First, the distinction between "meanings" and "sentences" remains somewhat hazy and in need of further elaboration. Secondly and more importantly: while recognizing the pervasive impact of language, his study restricts itself deliberately (with a few exceptions) to the portrayal of the Anglo-American philosophical tradition, especially the empiricist strand in that tradition. To correct these limitations I want to enlist as my second guide the German philosopher Karl-Otto Apel, whose works contain several important proposals relevant to our topic. One such proposal, advanced in *Towards a Transformation of Philosophy* (1973), concerns what one may call the basic design or architecture of language. Relying on the teachings of Peirce and Charles Morris, the study differentiates between three main "sign functions" or dimensions of language: namely, "syntax" or "syntactics," "semantics," and "pragmatics." In this scheme, syntactics deals with the internal "relationships between signs," semantics with the "relationship of signs to extra-linguistic objects or states of affairs represented by signs," and pragmatics with the "relationship between signs and their users, human beings." Reflecting the "logical structure of formalized languages," syntactics is said to be "the starting-point of modern, mathematical logic"; in its concern with external reference, on the other hand, semantics forms the focus of modern empiricism seen as continuation of traditional epistemology embodied in "Aristotle's correspondence theory of truth." The field of pragmatics, finally—which, the study insists, must not be identified with an empiricist analysis of linguistic behavior—marks the point of departure for "the Peirce-inspired semantics of American pragmatism, an outlook primarily interested in the functioning of language, knowledge and science in the context of human life-practice." The central point of Apel's portrayal of sign dimensions is the growing importance of the "pragmatic turn" in contemporary philosophy of language—particularly during the "heyday of sentences" (to borrow Hacking's vocabulary). "It is no secret," he writes, "that, in the course of the development of linguistic philosophy, the accent of scientific and theoretical interest has shifted successively from syntactics over semantics to pragmatics."[30]

A second, related proposal has to do with the broader historical evolution of approaches to language. Along these lines, the portrayal of sign functions suggests a subterranean linkage between linguistic pragmatics and the longstanding tradition of rhetoric or rhetorical "humanism." A more detailed discussion of historical background is contained in one of Apel's earlier studies, focusing on the "idea of language" in Renaissance and Baroque thought. Sketching a complex panorama of philosophical orientations, the study highlighted four basic linguistic perspectives as they could be found on the eve of the modern era: "empiricism," "rationalism," "humanism," and "logos-mysticism." Inspired by the nominalist stance championed by Occam in the late Middle Ages, empiricism was characterized by the juxtaposition of language and reality—that is, by the segregation of conceptual categories from empirical data—and by the focus on sense perception as the fountain of knowledge. While endorsing a similar segregation, rationalism (epitomized in the Cartesian *cogito* and the Leibnizian program of a *mathesis universalis*) insisted on the cognitive potency of mind or the autonomous role of internal mental faculties. In contrast to this dual epistemological tradition, Renaissance "humanism" cultivated the faculty of speech and commonsense argumentation; its parentage resided chiefly in the classical legacies of "practical philosophy" and rhetoric. Yet, left to its own devices, the humanist outlook was in constant danger of succumbing to a narrowly mundane pragmatism or to the flux of contingent speech patterns. To counteract this peril—the study noted—was the chief aim of "logos-mysticism," an orientation sympathetic to humanism but nurtured more deeply by Platonic and biblical impulses. Instead of serving as epistemological tool or being reduced to haphazard usage, language from this vantage point was the medium of a transcendental act of communication or a kerygmatic disclosure of meaning.[31]

Among the historical alternatives listed in the study the last category is surely the most elusive and unconventional (its chief representatives being Christian mystics and metaphysicians). In an effort to reduce the unfamiliarity or idiosyncracy of the category, Apel at various places casts "logos-mysticism" in a somewhat different light: by redescribing it either as a "transcendental" or transcendentally grounded hermeneutics or else as a mode of poetry or poetic thinking.[32] The latter version seems to me particularly deserving of attention. In order to buttress this version I enlist as my third and final guide Aristotle's corpus. In contrast to Plato's relative reticence on the topic, Aristotle, as is well known, devoted several works to questions of language: primarily the treatise *On Interpretation* and the books on *Rhetoric* and *Poetics*. In the first treatise, language in the sense of sounds and written symbols was depicted as a reflection of mental-cognitive categories or experiences which, in turn, represented or signified the invariant forms or essential features of nature; in this manner, the work furnished the take-off point for a long line of investigations, a line merging later into the empiricist and rationalist branches of modern epistemology. Deviating from these epistemological-metaphysical concerns, the books on *Rhetoric* and *Poetics* shifted the accent to human speech and communicative interaction—the first exploring a goal-directed and partially manipulative orientation, the latter a basically aimless or nondirective stance. In Ricoeur's words: "The duality of rhetoric and poetics reflects a duality in the use of speech as well as in the situations of speaking." While rhetoric "originally was oratorical technique" and its aim "to know how to persuade," poetry "is not oratory. Persuasion is not its aim; rather, it purges the feelings of pity and fear. Thus, poetry and oratory mark out two distinct universes of discourse."[33]

Suitably adapted and welded together, the mentioned conceptions and dimensions of language provide the parameters or theoretical guideposts for the following inquiry. My ambition here is not to offer an overview of historical trends through the ages—mainly because competent historical accounts are already available.[34] Rather, the focus of the inquiry will be almost exclusively on the present century: in Hacking's terms on the "heydays of meanings and sentences." The next two chapters will deal respectively with the empiricist and rationalist versions of modern epistemology, as they manifested themselves chiefly during the era of "meanings," that is, with efforts to develop a stable logical syntax and semantics. Under the rubric of empiricism, the emphasis will be on the logical-empiricist movement and also on Skinner's linguistic behaviorism, while the rationalist outlook will be exemplified by Husserlian phenomenology and Chomsky's structural linguistics. The fourth chapter probes the offshoot of rhetorical humanism in the period of "sentences": that is, the turn toward pragmatics intended either as a replacement or an amplification of syntactical and semantic analysis, and illustrated by existential phenomenology as well as ordinary-language and "speech-act" theory. Pursuing one of Apel's suggestions, the fifth chapter examines various attempts to stabilize pragmatics through attention to the "universal" matrix or "transcendental" conditions of possibility of speech. In the sixth chapter the central topic will be poetic and especially metaphorical language—in line with the preeminence accorded to the latter in Aristotle's *Poetics*.[35] Weaving together the various strands of the presentation, the concluding chapter will try to indicate interconnections and the broader relevance of the language-politics theme.

Implications: Reading and Writing

Before embarking on the sketched route, a final reminder may be in order. This inquiry does not pretend to yield a systematic "philosophy of language" nor even a full-fledged treatment of the language-politics issue; rather, as previously mentioned, the discussion is guided by more limited theoretical considerations. Thus, after outlining relevant linguistic conceptions or frameworks, each chapter will trace the repercussions of such frameworks within the confines of political philosophy. Even these confines, however, require additional specification. To render my task manageable, I have adopted a descriptive-phenomenological approach by concentrating on the manifest or concrete enterprise of political theorizing. Without wishing to shortchange the element of quiet reflection or meditation, I find this enterprise to encompass two main activities or endeavors: reading and writing (or else listening and speaking) —both of which are intimately tied to language. Differently phrased: whatever else their métier may demand, political theorists or philosophers typically are engaged both in absorbing ideas and studying transmitted texts—among them works of political philosophy—and in articulating their own views and frameworks, frequently by producing new theoretical texts. To be sure, the two types of activity—the receptive-interpretive and the active-productive modes— can be separated only for limited, pragmatic purposes; at a closer look, they appear intricately linked. While some theorists may slight receptivity in favor of radical innovation, their products still are liable to reflect a certain reading of texts—provided "texts" are seen to include not only written statements but the broader fabric of political experience.

Pursued in a sustained or professional manner, the two kinds of endeavor follow complex rules and yardsticks—which again are closely connected with alternative conceptions of language. To indicate what is involved on this level (and to anticipate some subsequent terminology), I wish to conclude with a few comments on reading and interpretation. Like writing, interpretation is not the exclusive province of political theorists, but an undertaking rooted in a long humanistic tradition and shared with such disciplines as jurisprudence, biblical hermeneutics, and literary criticism. For purposes of illustration and clarification, subsequent chapters will repeatedly explore affinities between political-theoretical and literary exegesis. A chief motive behind such explorations is the comparatively well-developed state of literary criticism, a condition reflected in its analytical vocabulary. Thus, a widely read and cited work in that field differentiates between at least four customary modes of literary inquiry: namely, the perspectives of "imitation," of "expression," of "effect," and of intrinsic essence or "structure." The first mode approaches a literary work from the viewpoint of its reference or subject matter, "seeing it as a way of reproducing or recreating the experiences of life in words." Sometimes this outlook is expanded to include attention to the work's historical or social-economic setting. In the second mode, the accent is placed on authorship, the literary text being regarded "as the product of the poet, dramatist, or novelist." Again, as in the case of "imitation," the notion of "expression" may vary in meaning, ranging from the purely mental intentionality of the author to his biographical and social-psychological motivations. In the third mode—sometimes called "pragmatic"—the focus is on "the effect that literature may have on its readers or, in the case of drama, on its spectators," a focus which also may extend to the reader's creative contributions in interpreting a text. In the last perspective, the aim of critics is to concentrate "on the work itself rather than its background, and to pass judgment on the essential nature of the work, not on the personality or intention of the writer, or the possible effect on the reader. This is the aim, in fact, of what John Crowe Ransom calls ontological criticism" (although formal or structural criticism would usually be more appropriate terms).[36]

Going beyond the level of general classification schemes, some writers have sketched a historical sequence of schools of thought in the domain of literary criticism; in the context of the present inquiry I shall adopt some of the categories developed by Hayden White (without necessarily embracing his broader frame of reference). In White's presentation, successive schools of interpretation in our century carry labels such as these:

"elementary," "reductive," "inflationary," "generalized," "existentialist," and "absurdist." The first approach sought to place texts into the stream of ideas or the "history of the culture" in a relatively "impressionistic" manner and with little critical self-awareness. By contrast, reductionism pursued a deliberate, quasi-scientific goal: the goal of unmasking "the ideological understructure of the text," thus revealing "the ways in which not only literature, but all forms of art, sublimated, obscured, or reinforced human impulses more or less 'physical' or more or less 'social' in nature." In opposition to both historicist and reductivist tendencies, the "inflationary" mode—championed by such movements as the "New Criticism" and aesthetic "formalism"—insisted on treating "the art-work as a thing-in-itself, a specifically aesthetic artifact" ultimately "governed by its own autotelic principles" and largely independent of "its historical context, its author, and its audience(s)." Broadly compatible with the latter emphasis, the "generalized" outlook—typified by structuralism—endeavors to ground texts in a "universal science of humanity, culture, or mind." As a reaction against formalist abstraction, a counter-trend developed in the postwar period which first took the form of existentialism intent on "closing the gap not only between literature and life, but also between art and work, thought and action, history and consciousness." However, due to a certain disenchantment with subjectivism (partly prompted by structuralism), existentialist criticism eventually gave way to an "absurdist" perspective—preferably called "hermeneutical" or "deconstructivist"—which "treats language itself as a problem" and probes "the surface of the text, in the contemplation of language's power to hide or diffuse meaning" and "to resist decoding or translation."[37]

Analytical rubrics of this kind are not entirely unfamiliar to students of political theory or philosophy; to some extent, works on political-theoretical exegesis parallel the schemes employed by literary critics. Thus, a popular, introductory book in this field differentiates between four major "approaches" to interpretation: an "environmental" approach emphasizing historical and sociological conditions; a mode of "close textual analysis" focusing on the intrinsic "consistency and inconsistency within and between sources"; a perspective stressing the author's "intent"; and an approach accentuating the "effect" of arguments on readers or listeners. As the study indicates, the third alternative can be amplified through attention to the author's biography and psychological motivations, just as the last mode may consider readers' practical and "ideological" commitments. A more elaborate list of categories—but couched in a more lively style—has been articulated by Andrew Hacker in several of his writings, including his *Political Theory: Philosophy, Ideology, Science.* In Hacker's treatment, the environmental mode is labeled "camera-eye" approach, since texts are assumed to mirror the conditions of a period or society. The author-centered focus carries such designations as "hero-worship" and "mind-reading"—depending on whether the accent is on biographical detail or on the author's hidden intention—while the emphasis on audience or readers is captured in phrases like "influencing the intelligentsia" and "influencing the masses." The mode of internal textual analysis, at least in one of its versions, is presented as "timeless questions" perspective, an outlook concentrating on the so-called "Great Books" or standard texts in the history of political thought. As Hacker observes, the goal of political theory or philosophy—in both its constructive and receptive-interpretive stances—is always "to enhance the understanding. And great knowledge rises out of those insights which only the engaged mind and the quickened concern are able to create."[38]

2

Empiricism and Behaviorism:
The Truncated Vocabulary of Politics

. . . vas pretiosum labia scientiae

Language and politics are not merely furtive chimeras; both are some-how related to what we loosely and intuitively call the "real" world. Traditionally, the investigation and corroboration of this intuition has been the province of epistemology, and particularly of its empiricist-realist variety. To be sure, construed as a theory of knowledge, empiricism is a broad label encompassing a number of diverse accents. If we follow Apel's suggestion, modern empiricist epistemology has been close-ly tied to the "nominalist" legacy, with its distinctive separation of logic and reality or of conceptual apparatus and sense data; however, more radical postures—tending toward a reductive materialism or naturalism —have not been lacking in modern times. In the present chapter, the primary emphasis will be placed on the nominalist strand of empiricism, mainly because of its prominence (and virtual predominance) during our century; more cursory treatment, by comparison, will be given to reduc-tive behaviorism. From the nominalist perspective, conceptual-linguistic categories are viewed as tools or instruments for empirical analysis, tools which are relatively independent of their subject matter. Differently phrased: cognitive-mental faculties are basically assigned a mirror func-tion—the task of reflecting empirical conditions as clearly as possible— without in turn being submerged in empirical psychological processes. Translated into a measure of professional competence, nominalism en-joins a division of labor between philosophers and scientists, with the former tending to logical-epistemological issues and the latter to em-pirical research. In reductive behaviorism, by contrast, this division tends to be revoked; like the rest of nature, logic and language fall squarely within the scientist's domain.

As presented by Apel, nominalism is a long-standing epistemological tradition; however, the full implications of the logic-science correlation only unfolded in our own century, particularly under the aegis of the "logical-empiricist" movement. Several circumstances contributed to this development. One factor was the unparalleled refinement of the logical tools of analysis—a refinement standing in marked contrast to fact-gathering approaches of the past, and attributable to a string of powerful logicians stretching from Frege over Tarski to Quine and Dummett. Another factor—especially important in the present context—was the growing identification of logic and language, that is, the tendency to treat cognition as a linguistic issue rather than an internal-mental process. In Hacking's terminology, the latter identification marks the threshold leading from the earlier era of "Ideas" to the "Heyday of Meanings," a period covering roughly the first half of the present century. As previously mentioned, the turn to language effected during that time was qualified and circumscribed by overarching epistemological ambitions; to serve these ambitions, language had to be pruned and molded into a pliant and univocal means of cognition—an aim ideally embodied in mathematics and a quasi-mathematical symbolic logic.[1] Throughout the period, empiricists differed on the proper manner of pruning language and of approximating it to the mathematical ideal: while some found the model naturally embedded in every language, underneath the surface of idiomatic ambiguities, others—defenders of "constructivism"—insisted on the need to fashion univocity through deliberate design. Whichever procedure was followed, however, the twin goals were commonly the formulation of a logically transparent "syntax" and an empirically grounded "semantics." As Apel observes, these twin goals "reflect the tendency of logical empiricism to arrange all meaningful problems of cognition under two rubrics: they either concern analytical truths in the sense of a tautological explication of sign rules within a linguistic system; or else they deal with synthetic (aposteriori) statements in which case they must be anchored in extra-linguistic states of affairs denoted by language."[2]

Sense Immediacy: Russell

One of the early pioneers of a logically refined empiricism in our century was Bertrand Russell. His *Principles of Mathematics* (1903) and especially his *Principia Mathematica,* co-authored with Whitehead on the eve of the first World War, provided crucial impulses for the development of quantitatively sharpened tools of analysis; the *Principia,* in particular, succeeded in demonstrating the possibility of translating pure mathematics into logic and, conversely, of transcribing logical reasoning into a mathematical or quasi-mathematical language or symbol system. At the same time, partly under the influence of Moore, his writings championed a radical version of empiricism or realism according to which all knowledge ultimately derives from direct sense experience; especially during his early phase (and to some extent throughout his life), Russell insisted on the primacy of sense perception for purposes of cognition, a primacy predicated on the direct or immediate "acquaintance" with reality accruing from such perception. Given the dual stress on logic and empiricism, the chief epistemological question for Russell was how sense experience could be adequately captured in language, that is, how words or statements could be properly "hooked up" with concrete sense data or "immediate objects" of sensation. The guiding yardstick in this operation was the dependence of conceptual and linguistic significance on direct experience—a yardstick revealing Russell's uncompromising attachment to an empirical semantics or to what some language theorists call a "referential theory of meaning."[3]

The actual implementation of this epistemological program varied somewhat over time; however, a relatively constant feature was the reliance on a kind of atomistic phenomenalism—the notion that real objects are essentially made up of discrete bits of sense experiences, including both actual and possible sensations. In order not to lose one's empiricist moorings, it was necessary in Russell's view to cling as closely as possible to "immediate objects" as they present themselves in a temporal and spatial setting. As he pointed out in an essay written during the interbellum period: "At any given moment, there are certain things of which a man is 'aware', certain things which are 'before his mind'. Now although it is very difficult to define 'awareness', it is not at all difficult to say that I am aware of such and such things. If I am asked I can reply that I am aware of this, and that, and the other, and so on through the heterogeneous collection of objects." The most expedient or straightforward manner of preserving the referential meaning of language was to use such terms as "this, that, and the other" as direct designations or what Russell termed "proper names" for the experienced phenomena, since ordinary descriptions were liable to exceed the bounds of acquaintance: "If I describe these objects, I may of course describe them wrongly; hence I cannot with certainty communicate to another what are the things of which I am aware. But if I speak to myself, and denote them by what may be called 'proper names', rather than by descriptive words, I cannot be in error." A major dilemma involved in this naming process was not only the peril of a linguistic solipsism but the relatively ephemeral or evanescent status of knowledge garnered through sense immediacy—a consequence shouldered by Russell without trepidation: "It is only when you use 'this' quite strictly, to stand for an actual object of sense, that it is really a proper name. And in that it has a very odd property for a proper name, namely, that it seldom means the same thing two moments running and does not mean the same thing to the speaker and to the hearer."[4]

In a more elaborate form Russell's epistemological outlook during this period is known as "logical atomism"—a phrase denoting a close correlation between logically pruned "atomic sentences" and distinct or atomic units of sense experience. Rigorously stated, the logical-atomist position involved not only a loose correlation or parallelism but rather an actual "isomorphism" of linguistic terms and statements, on the one hand, and the structure of reality (seen as a compound of sense data), on the other. As guidepost for the achievement of this isomorphism served the basic empiricist "principle of acquaintance"; as Russell stated in his lectures on "Logical Atomism" (1918): "In order to understand a proposition in which the name of a particular occurs, you must already be acquainted with that particular."[5] The same principle carried over into the character of atomic sentences and their constituent parts. In line with the requirement of sense immediacy, such sentences in Russell's presentation had to be simply structured, containing basically "names" for particular sense data together with terms designating their properties and various interrelations between data; usually, he held, basic or atomic statements would be composed of only one or a few names linked with a single predicate or relational term, and would assert merely that a named entity has a given property or stands in a specified relation with other entities. The central advantage of properly constructed atomic sentences was their amenability to empirical testing: given the sense correlates of their constituent parts such sentences could readily be verified or falsified by direct experience. Even more complex strings or compounds of sentences were in principle subject to the same empiricist yardstick—provided these compounds could be broken up or reassembled into a series of atomic units, each of which satisfied the requirement of immediate sense correlation.

As Russell realized, of course, ordinary linguistic practices were far from conforming to the canons of logical atomism; in many instances, the application of these canons required elaborate efforts of "logical redescription" aimed at transforming everyday expressions into the "logical form" or structure of atomic sentences. The difficulties encountered along this road were notorious in the case of counterfactual assertions; however, even seemingly factual statements could be frought with logical hazards. To illustrate these hazards Hacking uses such apparently descriptive phrases as "The golden mountain does not exist" and "The present King of France is bald." Both phrases are grammatically correct and superficially intelligible; yet both lack concrete referents and thus violate the empiricist yardstick of sense correlation. To correct this defect, Russell held, it was necessary to resort to logical redescription. The mentioned phrases in his view were deceptive because of their compliance with ordinary linguistic conventions: their manifest "grammatical form"

adhered closely to the standard subject-predicate relationship — although
the "subject" in these instances was nonexistent. Only through reliance
on the empiricist yardstick was it possible to discover the real "meaning"
of such statements, a meaning embedded in their logical-atomic structure
buried underneath grammatical conventions. In phrases where the osten-
sible or grammatical subject was devoid of reference — and which consequently could not be verified or falsified through appeal to sense experience — redescription as advocated by Russell yielded a new "logical subject" amenable to empirical testing. Thus, in the case of "The golden
mountain does not exist," Russell's procedure generates the logical-atomic
reformulation: "It is not the case that something is a golden mountain";
likewise, the statement "The present King of France is bald" is rephrased
with the help of a quantifier: "There is one and only one present King
of France, and every King of France is bald." Although the latter sentence
is obviously false, its advantage resides in the structural correlation of its
constituent parts with sense data. In Hacking's words, the expression
"the present King of France" may function as grammatical subject, "but
because it requires this analysis it cannot be what Russell calls a 'logical
subject'. That is, it is not the subject of the sentence given by logical
analysis."[6]

Logical Construction: Carnap

Although hedged in through various commonsense qualifications, the
implications of Russell's redescriptive method were potentially far-reaching:
if extended to cover all ordinary grammatical statements, the proposed
analysis was bound to issue ultimately in a fully transparent logical language which in every respect would mirror the empirical state of the
world.[7] At the time Russell was writing in this vein, several other empiricist thinkers were actually moving in this direction, with greater or
lesser success (depending on individual talent and persistence). In Russell's
own view, his endeavors were most closely paralleled in Ludwig Wittgenstein's *Tractatus Logico-Philosophicus* (1921) — although the latter hardly endorsed the postulated "atomism" of sense data or the belief in direct
or immediate "acquaintance." What rendered the work of the two philosophers compatible during this phase was not so much the detail of their
arguments as the broad aim of linking language and reality; in Wittgenstein's case, this aim was reflected in an intricate network of logically
pruned and interconnected propositions, a network designed to match
or correspond to the overall structure of empirical states of affairs and
their interrelations. In the present context, I do not intend to review the
Tractatus — mainly because of its staggering complexity (and also because
of its latent metaphysical dimensions). Instead, I want to draw attention

to another philosophical initiative of the interbellum period animated by similar ambitions: the writings of Rudolf Carnap, and especially his *Logical Structure of the World* (1928) and *Logical Syntax of Language* (1934).

Like Russell, Carnap was basically a logician committed to empiricist canons of epistemology. The first-mentioned study—frequently referred to by its German title, *Der logische Aufbau der Welt*—sought to correlate language and reality by means of an elaborate "constructional system" (*Konstitutionssystem*) in which concepts and sense data were intimately meshed. In Carnap's usage, a constructional system was "an epistemic-logical system of objects or concepts," where the term object stands "for anything about which a statement can be made" and where "to every concept there belongs one and only one object: 'its object'." In terms of empiricist epistemology, the starting point of the study was akin to Russell's phenomenalism: namely, the principle that knowledge had to be ultimately grounded in, or derived from, immediate sense experience. Accordingly, the foundation or "basis" of the constructional system was a set of "basic elements" termed "elementary experiences" which were not further analyzable; the goal of the inquiry was then to show how the entire empirical world could be grasped as a complex structure composed of, and ultimately reducible to, these experiences. Regarding analytical apparatus, the *Aufbau* appealed chiefly to the arsenal of symbolic logic, and particularly to the quasi-mathematical "theory of relations" as developed in *Principia Mathematica* and similar logical works. Matching the structure of sense data, the task of logical analysis was to pinpoint the formal linkages—such as "ascension forms," "transformation rules" and the like—between levels of reality. In Carnap's words, "an object (or concept) is said to be *reducible* to one or more other objects if all statements about it can be transformed into statements about these other objects." A full-fledged constructional system implied "a step-by-step ordering of objects in such a way that the objects of each level are con-structed from those of the lower levels." Due to "the transitivity of re-ducibility, all objects of the constructional system are thus indirectly con-structed from objects of the first level. These *basic objects* form the *basis* of the system."[8]

From the vantage point of the *Aufbau*, the world of sense data was composed of four main layers or levels: namely, the levels of individual-psychological or "autopsychological" objects, of physical objects, of "heteropsychological" objects, and of cultural objects. Mainly because of a presumed epistemological primacy of individual experience, "autopsy-chological" data were placed at the basis of the constructional pyramid, while physical objects were treated as intermediary and the remaining data as most remote or derivative in character. The basic conceptual

category used for ordering sense data was a distinct logical "relation" between elementary experiences termed "recollection of similarity" and
defined as the cognitive act in which one experience is remembered as being similar to another. With the help of this relational category, sense experiences were arranged into broader "similarity circles," which in turn
formed a platform for the construction of "sense classes" and "visual field
places" on the various levels of the system. As mentioned, the chief linguistic tool employed in the *Aufbau* was symbolic logic or the "symbolic
language of logistics" which, Carnap noted, "alone gives the proper and
precise expression for the constructions." In addition, the study enlisted
three alternative languages in support of the constructional effort: namely, ordinary or "word language"; the "realistic" or object language customary in the empirical sciences; and the "language of fictitious constructive operations" designed for testing purposes—a diversity mitigated by
the assumption that these "other three languages offer nothing but translations from the basic language of logistics." Amplified by empirical
research in various fields, the analytical scheme of the study was meant
to provide the framework for a comprehensive or "unified science" of
reality. While construction theory, the *Aufbau* concluded, furnished the
appropriate logical categories, the actual "formation of the constructional system as a whole is the task of unified science." Once objects and
object levels are placed in "one unified constructional system, the different 'sciences' are at the same time recognized as branches of the *one*
science and thus integrated into a system."[9]

At the time of publishing the *Aufbau*, Carnap was already a member
of the Vienna School or Circle, composed of prominent scientists,
mathematicians, and philosophers dedicated to the rigorous scrutiny and
reconceptualization of empirical inquiry. Partly under the influence of
this circle, partly as a result of his own further reflections, Carnap subsequently came to modify several tenets of his early study. One of these
features was the foundational role of individual psychology. As mentioned, the constructional system in the *Aufbau* was erected on a phenomenalist basis, in the sense that the elementary report or "protocol"
sentences were couched in terms of "autopsychological" experiences.
Swayed by the arguments of Otto Neurath, another member of the Vienna group, Carnap decided to abandon the phenomenalist approach in
favor of "physicalism"—the position that basic report sentences can and
should be stated in physicalist language, that is, in the form of quantitative descriptions referring to concrete space-time points. The chief advantage of such descriptions was seen in their reliance on (presumably)
inter-sensual or intersubjective data, a reliance bypassing at the outset
the quandary of a linguistic solipsism encountered by Russell. The mentioned change did not affect the principle of reduction or reducibility as

outlined in the *Aufbau*: on the various levels of sense data the propositions of all sciences—including biological, psychological, and human sciences—were assumed to be equivalent or reducible to sentences in the physicalist idiom. Another change or innovation concerned the status of the analytical framework. To some extent, the method of the *Aufbau* reflected Russell's beliefs regarding redescription: although hidden behind ordinary linguistic conventions, a logically "correct" and scientifically useful language was held to be retrievable through redefinition and immediate sense correlation. Difficulties besetting the constructional system—especially the linkage between logical and report sentences— prompted Carnap to move steadily in a "constructivist" direction, that is, toward the deliberate invention of "ideal" or formal-logical languages compatible with the requirements of scientific research.

The sketched trends were clearly evident in *Logical Syntax of Language*—probably his most well known and influential book. The central aim of the study was to design logically precise and univocal linguistic instruments which could serve as "metalanguages" for the analysis of the report or "object languages" employed by sciences in various sense-data domains. In Carnap's presentation, such metalanguages were logical-syntactical structures fashioned for strictly analytical or "philosophical" purposes, and made up of a number of "formation" and "transformation rules." As he pointed out, his objective was "to provide a system of concepts, a language, with the help of which the results of logical analysis will be exactly formulable." More provocatively phrased: *"Philosophy is to be replaced by the logic of science*—that is to say, by the logical analysis of the concepts and sentences of the sciences, for *the logic of science is nothing other than the logical syntax of the language of science."* In implementing this objective, the study delineated two linguistic models, termed "Language I" and "Language II," of which the first was more "simple in form" covering a "narrow field of concepts," while the second was "richer in modes of expression" so that "in it all the sentences both of classical mathematics and of classical physics can be formulated." The two models, however, were meant merely as illustrations of linguistic possibilities and by no means as barriers to further experimentation. In line with constructivist premises, Carnap actually asserted that "we have in every respect complete liberty with regard to the forms of language" and that "both the forms of construction of sentences and the rules of transformation may be chosen quite arbitrarily." This belief formed the core of the so-called "Principle of Tolerance" according to which *"it is not our business to set up prohibitions, but to arrive at conventions."* As he added: *"In logic, there are no morals.* Everyone is at liberty to build up his own logic, that is, his own form of language as he wishes."[10]

Although forcefully stated, Carnap's "principle of tolerance," one should note, was not unlimited: while applicable to logical-syntactical conventions, the maxim did not extend to many traditional modes of theorizing—such as metaphysics, ethics, and aesthetics—provided they were treated as philosophical enterprises. Rigorously defined, "philosophy" in his view coincided with logical-syntactical analysis—to which he later added a logically constructed semantics—as gateway to empirical-scientific inquiry. Drawing on skeptical sentiments voiced by Russell and Wittgenstein, Carnap from the beginning adopted a determined anti-metaphysical stance, a stance generally shared by members of the logical-empiricist movement. Contours of this posture were sketched in the conclusion of the *Aufbau* and in a simultaneously published monograph, entitled *Pseudoproblems in Philosophy,* where all statements except logical-syntactical and empirically grounded propositions were dismissed as senseless or devoid of cognitive "meaning." Some four years later this critical thrust was sharpened and expanded in an essay devoted to "The Elimination of Metaphysics Through Logical Analysis of Language." In line with logical-syntactical canons, the essay distinguished between two kinds of "pseudo-statements": those made up of words lacking empirical reference, and those whose constituent terms, though empirically relevant, are strung together in violation of syntax or "in a counter-syntactical way, so that they do not yield a meaningful statement." Noting that both varieties occur abundantly in traditional metaphysics, Carnap pointed with particular relish to sentences in Heidegger's *What is Metaphysics?*—portrayed as representative of "that metaphysical school which at present exerts the strongest influence in Germany." Relying on the advances in modern logic and epistemology, the essay affirmed that "in the domain of *metaphysics,* including all philosophy of value and normative theory, logical analysis yields the negative result that *the alleged statements in this domain are entirely meaningless.* Therewith a radical elemination of metaphysics is attained.[11]

Verificationism

Carnap's views on logic and its effects were not simply idiosyncratic preferences, but typical of widespread epistemological convictions. Erected into a general tenet, the restriction of philosophy to logical analysis in the service of scientific research is known as "verificationism" or the "verifiability principle"—easily the most distinctive trademark of the logical-empiricist movement. In its early and most ambitious formulation, the tenet postulated that, apart from strictly syntactical-analytical propositions, the "meaning" of any statement is determined by the conditions or methods of its verification, differently phrased: that a statement makes sense only if, and to the extent that, its empirical reference can be firmly corroborated. As can readily be seen, the principle established both an epistemological and a linguistic yardstick—by stipulating simultaneously what counts as knowledge and what counts as meaningful language, and by fixing the boundaries of one in terms of the other. To some extent, verificationism was implicit in Russell's notion of acquaintance, with its reliance on "immediately given" sense data, and also in the "picture theory" of reference outlined in Wittgenstein's *Tractatus;* however, specification of the principle's precise content was mainly a concern of the Vienna Circle.

In Carnap's writings, the criterion of "meaning" was adumbrated, though not fully developed in his *Aufbau* and in *Pseudoproblems in Philosophy.* An elaborate attempt to pinpoint the principle was undertaken in his essay on "The Elimination of Metaphysics." Following up the attack on metaphysical and other "pseudo-statements," the essay advocated as a general rule that "the meaning of a statement lies in the method of its verification" and that "a statement asserts only so much as is verifiable with respect to it." Actually, to accommodate logical-syntactical considerations, Carnap differentiated between two broad types of legitimate assertions: namely, on the one hand, "statements which are true solely by virtue of their form ('tautologies' according to Wittgenstein)" and also the "negations of such statements ('contradictions')," and, on the other hand, statements whose truth or falsehood is predicated on the "protocol sentences" and which are therefore "(true or false) empirical statements." The first category in this account said or reported "nothing about reality" and contained "the formulae of logic and mathematics," while the second group of sentences was content-laden and basically co-extensive with "the domain of empirical science." As presented in the essay, the bulk of meaningful statements tended to fall into the second rubric; accordingly, the question arose what was "left over for *philosophy,* if all statements whatever that assert something are of an empirical nature and belong to factual science?" Anticipating formulations in the *Logical Syntax of Language,* the essay identified philosophy basically with "method": namely, the "method of logical analysis" seen as yardstick for "inquiring into logical foundations," that is, for a properly " 'scientific philosophy' in contrast to metaphysics."[12]

Arguments of a similar kind were advanced roughly at the same time by Moritz Schlick, another founder and leading spokesman of the Vienna group. In a programmatic essay of 1930, Schlick invoked the "profound inner rules of logical syntax" as specifications of the boundaries of knowledge and meaningful language. Rigorously stated, every "meaningful problem" in his view indicated the road leading to its resolution—which was the road of verification. This process of verification, he wrote, "in which the path to the solution finally ends is always of the same sort: it is the occurrence of a definite fact that is confirmed by observation, by means of immediate experience. In this manner the truth (or falsity) of every statement, of daily life or science, is determined." According to the essay, there could be "no other testing and corroboration of truths except through observation and empirical science" and every science had to be seen as "a system of cognitions, that is, of true experiential statements" — whereas nonexperiential statements were merely "empty sounds" or "meaningless sequences of words." Together with Carnap, Schlick assigned to philosophy not a separate object domain but the task of logical analysis. The "great contemporary turning point" was located in the construal of philosophy as "that activity through which the meaning of statements is revealed or determined. By means of philosophy statements are explained, by means of science they are verified; the latter is concerned with the truth of statements, the former with what they actually mean." As he added, the "content, soul and spirit of science is lodged naturally in what in the last analysis its statements actually mean; the philosophical activity of giving meaning is therefore the Alpha and Omega of all scientific knowlege." A few years later the same idea was rephrased in another essay which affirmed: "We cannot by philosophical analysis decide whether anything is real, but only what it *means* to say that it is real; and whether this is then the case or not can be decided only by the usual methods of daily life and of science, that is, through *experience*."[13]

In the years following these programmatic announcements, verificationism encountered numerous formidable challenges and, as a result, underwent a series of transformations and modifications. I shall not give a detailed account here of these successive reformulations, mainly because the story has been told repeatedly by competent writers.[14] In its original inspiration, the empiricist meaning criterion tended to demand complete verification of nonanalytical statements through direct observation; given the interference of temporary obstructions or obstacles, however, the criterion was quickly relaxed to denote "verifiability in principle" through logically possible observation. Difficulties arising from the application of the yardstick to universal propositions or lawlike generalizations prompted Karl Popper to restate the criterion in terms of falsification or "falsifiability in principle." Faced with these and related quandaries Carnap himself was induced to veer increasingly toward "confirmation" or "confirmability," a standard according to which statements qualify as meaningful if they can be translated into "thing-language" or at least be linked with such a language through "reduction sentences." Elaborate efforts to salvage the meaning criterion were undertaken by Alfred Ayer in his *Language, Truth and Logic,* a book which, in Hacking's words, "presented the essence of the Vienna programme to

English readers." Relying like Carnap on some form of reducibility or deducibility, the first edition of the study (in 1936) specified as "the mark of a genuine factual proposition, not that it should be equivalent to an experiential proposition, or any finite number of experiential propositions, but simply that some experiential propositions can be deduced from it in conjunction with certain other premises without being deducible from these other premises alone." Subsequent editions further qualified the criterion by differentiating between direct and indirect modes of testing and by subjecting each mode to complex deduction rules; thus recast, empiricist corroboration required "of a literally meaningful statement, which is not analytic, that it should be either directly or indirectly verifiable, in the foregoing sense."[15]

Rejoinders

Taken as an epistemological and linguistic doctrine, logical empiricism has not weathered too well the test of time: over the years all or most of its tenets have succumbed to critical challenges or attacks—attacks frequently launched by empiricist philosophers. Verificationism is a case in point. By the end of the Second World War Friedrich Waismann, himself a member of the Vienna group, called into question not only specific wordings of the principle, but the very feasibility of verifying individual terms or isolated sentences. Noting the "open-textured" character of all content-laden language, Waismann stressed the impossibility of fixing univocal meaning—and thus satisfying the empiricist criterion—through a correlation of logical-conceptual analysis and observation predicates. The same linguistic porousness in his view carried ambivalence into empirical research: in the absence of broader delimiting frameworks the scientific investigation of object domains was inexhaustible due to the "essential incompleteness" of empirical descriptions. Matched against dilemmas of this kind, simple reformulations of the criterion were of little or no avail—even such ingenious rephrasings as found in the successive editions of Ayer's study. As Hacking wryly comments, referring to Ayer's efforts: "We owe him an immense debt for setting out the principles for scrutiny. Had he not done that, people might still believe that a statable verification principle lurked in the offing. We now know that there is none."[16]

The fate of verificationism has been shared by other distinctive features of empiricist epistemology. To illustrate the general thrust of rejoinders, I intend to rely mainly (though not exclusively) on the arguments of empiricist thinkers, especially advocates of a contextualized or "holistic" approach. Among pioneering empiricist formulations in our century, Russell's "logical atomism" has come in for a fair amount of criticism; his stress on atomistic sense data as basis of empirical knowledge, in particular, has been attacked by a host of writers, including Wilfrid Sellars, as part of a broader critique of the "myth of the given." Sellars' essay "Empiricism and the Philosophy of Mind" (1963) launched a full-scale assault on the notion of direct cognition, that is, of a knowledge gained through direct "acquaintance" or through contact with "immediately given" sense experiences (what some have called "raw feels"). A major theoretical weapon in this assault was the distinction between sensory experience or awareness, on the one hand, and judgmental awareness as locus of knowledge claims, on the other. "In characterizing an episode or a state as that of *knowing*," Sellars wrote, "we are not giving an empirical description of that episode or state; we are placing it in the logical space of reasons, of justifying and being able to justify what one says." While sensory experience, in this account, involved only reactive behavior and some modes of signaling shared with animals, judgmental awareness was restricted to human beings seen as creatures endowed with language and thus capable of using sentences for purposes of cognitive justification and validation; only the latter dimension was able to sustain the concept of "knowledge"in the sense of "justified true belief"— a belief vindicated before the tribunal of a language community. Regarding Russell's postulate of a "logical" or logically pruned language tailored to sense data, other writers have endeavored to show the circularity of the proposal, by pointing to the understanding of ordinary "grammatical form" as a requisite for the intelligibility of logical "redescriptions."[17]

Criticisms of a similar kind have been leveled against Carnap's constructivist perspective, especially against the juxtaposition of logical analysis and empirical research and against the postulated reduction of complex propositions to basic observation or "protocol sentences." Nowhere have the flaws of these features been more trenchantly exposed than in Willard Quine's justly celebrated essay on "Two Dogmas of Empiricism" (1953). In Quine's presentation, the two dogmas pervading logical empiricism as a whole and Carnap's perspective in particular were pinpointed as the "analytic-synthetic" dichotomy and the doctrine of "reducibility"—tenets which he defined in these terms: "One is a belief in some fundamental cleavage between truths which are *analytic*, or grounded in meanings independently of matters of fact, and truths which are *synthetic*, or grounded in fact. The other dogma is *reductionism*: the belief that each meaningful statement is equivalent to some logical construct upon terms which refer to immediate experience." The critique of the first tenet obviously dealt a blow to the logical-empiricist paradigm, by challenging its central "meaning" or verifiability criterion and also by eroding its axiomatic division of labor—the division between logical-linguistic scrutiny (as province of philosophy) and empirical inquiry (as the task of science). The first dogma was intimately linked with the second, since "meaning" implied the reducibility of synthetic statements to direct sense experiences. In the latter context, the essay addressed itself specifically to Carnap's position, as outlined chiefly in the *Aufbau*. Liberally or reasonably construed, Quine noted, the reductionist doctrine demands "that our statements as wholes be translatable into sense-datum language," without necessarily being "translatable term by term." It was this flexible version of the doctrine which permeated the work of Vienna theorists: "Radical reductionism, conceived now with statements as units, set itself the task of specifying a sense-datum language and showing how to translate the rest of significant discourse, statement by statement, into it. Carnap embarked on this project in the *Aufbau*." After retracing the main steps of the work, Quine judged the enterprise abortive, chiefly because of its disregard of the holistic character of scientific inquiry. "My countersuggestion, issuing essentially from Carnap's doctrine of the physical world in the *Aufbau*," he wrote, "is that our statements about the external world face the tribunal of sense experience not individually but only as a corporate body." Differently phrased: "The unit of empirical significance is the whole of science."[18]

In a sense, Quine's accent on the "whole of science" and the "corporate body" of statements implied (or at least intimated) an appeal to the corporate or professional community of scientists—and thus the replacement of a direct referential semantics by an intersubjective or "interpretative" semantics. In varying formulations, the same shift of accent surfaces in the writings of many contemporary empiricists and logicians—including even Michael Dummett (otherwise a strict epistemologist). In an essay on the "theory of meaning," Dummett differentiates between direct referential truth conditions and the grounds or reasons buttressing argumentatively raised truth claims. Acknowledging the frequent unavailability of apodictic methods of fixing truth conditions, he asserts that "an understanding of a statement consists in a capacity to recognize whatever is counted as verifying it, that is, as conclusively establishing it as true. It is not necessary that we should have any means of deciding the truth or falsity of the statement, only that we be capable of recognizing when its truth has been established." Instead of being anchored in inductive evidence or a deductive algorithm, a "plausible theory of meaning" in Dummett's view explicates the meaning of a sentence "in terms of the grounds on which it may be asserted"—distinguishing at this point "a speaker's actual grounds, which may not be conclusive or may be indirect" from "direct, conclusive grounds"; from this vantage point, a statement about a state of affairs involves basically a "commitment that a speaker undertakes in making that assertion," that is, "a kind of gamble that the speaker will not be proven wrong." As he adds, in some instances reliable criteria for grounding assertions may be entirely lacking due to the opacity of ordinary language: "The difficulty arises because natural language is full of sentences which are not effectively decideable, ones for which there exists no effective procedure for determining whether or not their truth conditions are fulfilled."[19]

The role of interpretation—hesitantly embraced today in some analytical writings—has been for some time, of course, a main bone of contention between Anglo-American and Continental thought. In several of his writings, Apel located the chief defect of twentieth-century empiricism in its "monological" character, a character owing to its exclusive concern with reference and logical deduction and its neglect of communicative understanding. The political (or political-theoretical) implications of interpretative frameworks have recently been highlighted by Michael Shapiro. Drawing strongly on Foucault's teachings regarding "discursive practices," Shapiro's *Language and Political Understanding* affirms that cognitive statements are "not appropriately thought of as being about objects or as representations of objects," but should be regarded "as complex, rule-governed utterances that rely on implicit norms or standards which organize an otherwise shapeless material reality. Moreover these norms or standards are constitutive of human action, rendering episodes of performance as belonging to social, political, and other relations." One of the central merits of Foucault's opus, according to the study, resides in its focus on the "political significance of the implicit rule structures that give rise to the identification of various objects and situations which receive attention by a particular discipline, profession, or administrative grouping." The distinctly political impact of discursive frameworks or practices emerges primarily in their specification of speaker roles, above and beyond the delimitation of object domains: "If we recognize that among the conventions which give statements meaning are those that determine who must make the statement for it to have a particular meaning, we are in a position to relate the meaning of statements to the distribution of power in a society."[20]

Behaviorism: Skinner

The discussed criticisms and rejoinders have the effect not of exorcising concern with empirical reality, but of rendering empiricist epistemology more flexible by reducing the rigidity of its initial claims. Seen in conjunction, the arguments of Sellars, Quine, and their successors cast doubt on the dualism of theoretical and observation sentences, of analytical and synthetic truths, and (more broadly) of language or linguistic analysis, on the one hand, and empirical inquiry, on the other—but without submerging the distinctions in one of the opposing elements. As previously indicated, however, our century has also seen the rise of a more radical empiricist variant — a version in which the analytic-synthetic dichotomy is cast aside, not through resort to a Quinean holism or to an "interpretative" semantics but for the sake of a further reduction: the reduction of thought and language to empirical psychological (or psycho-physiological) processes. The relationship between what I have called "nominalist" and "behaviorist" strands has been complex and ambivalent; but on the whole the two modes have tended to follow separate paths. Reacting to Watsonian behaviorism at the beginning of the century, Russell applauded its scientific ambitions but considered its exclusive reliance on physical processes and its denial of mental images "empirically indefensible." A similarly guarded attitude was adopted by Carnap; while sharing the behaviorists' attachment to reduction or reducibility, the *Aufbau* questioned the epistemological coherence of their position.[21]

My ambition here is not to review the behaviorist movement in its many ramifications; for present purposes I want to concentrate on one of its most ardent and uncompromising champions, B. F. Skinner, mainly because of his impact on contemporary social and political science. The issue of language or linguistic behavior moved only gradually into the foreground of Skinner's research program. As a professional psychologist, he initially gained prominence chiefly through his experimental research in the field of animal behavior — a research reflected, for example, in his book *Behavior of Organisms* (1938). As outlined in this study as well as in related subsequent publications, the basic goal of the research was to explain animal behavior in conformity with the "behaviorist" model of stimulus-response relations, although the model was reformulated and expanded in a novel manner. According to Skinner, animal responses could be divided into two main categories, called "respondents" and "operants" — the former being defined as reflexes elicited by direct sensory stimulation and the latter as behavioral responses of organisms in the absence of direct stimuli. The central concern of *Behavior of Organisms* was with operant behavior and especially with the question how animals can be "conditioned" to emit various operants without being subjected to immediate sensory influences. The experimental setting employed to explore this question consisted chiefly of a box (popularized as the "Skinner box") in which a bar was attached to one wall in such a fashion that when the bar was pressed, a food pellet dropped into a tray; a rat placed in the box was found soon to learn how to press the bar — an experience which in turn became a "reinforcing event" increasing the psychological strength of the bar-pressing operant. By introducing various changes in the experimental conditions under which responses were strengthened or reinforced in this sense, it was possible to investigate to what extent and how speedily animals adapted to environmental modifications, and thus to manipulate and predict relatively complex forms of behavior.[22]

What renders Skinner's work relevant at this point is his attempt to apply the sketched model to the explanation of human language acquisition and linguistic conduct; his book *Verbal Behavior* (1957) was specifically devoted to this task. The overriding ambition of the study was to provide a "functional analysis" of linguistic behavior, through identification of the key variables shaping or conditioning verbal interactions. In line with the findings regarding reinforcement of animal behavior, Skinner presented "verbal behavior" as an emitted response on the part of a human speaker, a response reinforced through the mediation of other persons or listeners who, in turn, have been conditioned to reinforce such conduct. In an effort to grasp the more subtle dimensions of verbal interactions, the study introduced a refined experimental setting reflected in a complex new vocabulary — including terms like "mands" (verbal operants reinforced by practical consequences), "tacts" (operants reinforced through "generalized" approval), "autoclitics" (responses evoked by covert or potential verbal acts), and similar expressions. Irrespective of terminological complexities, however, the central thesis of the book was relatively simple and straightforward: namely, that in explaining language acquisition and verbal conduct environmental factors and modes of reinforcement are of primary significance, and that behaviorist laboratory research holds the key to the analysis of human language. In the words of one popular text, the chief assumption of *Verbal Behavior* was "that the operant repertory for the speech of the child (the sounds it emits during its vocalizations) are the raw materials on which the contingencies of reinforcement provided by the child's verbal community (its immediate social environment) operate to mold and determine its verbal behavior" — more simply phrased: "that language is acquired as a result of the slow and careful shaping of verbal behavior through differential reinforcement."[23]

Skinner's linguistic behaviorism has been challenged and criticized from many quarters — most trenchantly in a review essay written by Noam Chomsky. Pointing to the central propositions of *Verbal Behavior*, Chomsky affirmed "that these astonishing claims are far from justified" and "that the insights that have been achieved in the laboratories of the reinforcement theorist, though quite genuine, can be applied to complex human behavior only in the most gross and superficial way." What particularly aroused the linguist's opposition was Skinner's stress on external conditioning and his almost complete neglect of a speaker's indigenous contributions. "It is simply not true," Chomsky countered, "that children can learn language only through 'meticulous care' on the part of adults who shape their verbal repertoire through careful differential reinforcement." According to Chomsky, the most important aspect ignored by the behaviorist account was the role of unconditioned or inborn (possibly genetically encoded) linguistic capacities in the acquisition of languages. "The child who has learned a language," Chomsky wrote, "has in some sense constructed a grammar for himself on the basis of his observations of sentences and nonsentences"; in so doing, the child "has succeeded in carrying out what from the formal point of view, at least, seems to be a remarkable type of theory construction. Furthermore this task is accomplished in an astonishing short time, to a large extent independently of intelligence, and in a comparable way by all children. Any theory of language must cope with these facts." On the whole, these anti-behaviorist arguments strike me as quite persuasive—provided "innate" endowments are not elevated into foundational "a priori" categories (with a concomitant rejuvenation of epistemological "analyticity"). The quarrel, from my view, is not so much with empirical psychology or psycholinguistics, as with Skinner's claim to explain *homo loquens* entirely in terms of operant conditioning.[24]

Empiricist and Historicist Interpretation

Turning to implications for political thought and, first of all, to issues of political-theoretical exegesis, an initial caveat is in order. As previously indicated, empiricist epistemology—in both its nominalist and behaviorist versions—was strongly bent on univocity and basically uncongenial to intersubjective or "interpretative" understanding; consequently, exegetic efforts inspired by this epistemology are bound to be restricted and restrictive in character. Using Hayden White's vocabulary (fashioned in the context of literary criticism), interpretation predicated on empiricist or behaviorist premises can be labeled "elementary" or "reductive"— where the first term denotes a vaguely historicist approach and the second a more ambitiously scientific or quasi-scientific type of analysis. As practiced in the early part of this century through the interbellum period, White notes, elementary exegesis was "inspired by philosophers as different as Arnold, Croce, Taine, or Dilthey," but their teachings "were entertained 'naively' insofar as they were assumed justifications for criticizing rather than treated as grounds for problematic consideration of the nature of criticism in general." Viewed in the elementary vein, texts were seen as part of a "literary realm" grounded "in the 'history' of the culture out of which it had originally arisen"—a realm to be recaptured by the interpreter through empathy or empathetic reconstruction. Championed by adherents of positivism, "scientific" Marxism, and "the various forms of the sociology of knowledge," reductivism on the other hand defined the task of exegesis as "the unmasking of the ideological understructure of the text" and as disclosure of the ways in which texts "sublimated, obscured, or reinforced human impulses more or less 'physical' or more or less 'social' in nature"; instead of focusing on historical-cultural settings or conditions, interpreters in this case probe the "more basic drives, needs, or desires" underlying literary expressions.[25]

In the domain of political-theoretical exegesis, the mentioned modes were never very neatly segregated; during the period under consideration, historicist assumptions tended to be blended with occasional reductive arguments. A case in point is George Sabine's *A History of Political Thought* (1937), one of the most widely used textbooks in mid-century America. According to Sabine's Preface, his book proceeded from "the hypothesis that theories of politics are themselves a part of politics" and "are produced as a normal part of the social *milieu* in which politics itself has its being." The social setting or *milieu* of theorizing, moreover, was identified with the particular historical context conditioning a given theoretical work: "It cannot be supposed that any political philosophy of the present time, more than those of the past, can step out of the relationships in which it stands to the problems, the valuations, the habits, or even the prejudices of its own time." Apart from adhering to historicist concerns, the Preface endorsed the basic tenets of logical-empiricist epistemology, particularly the distinction between logical (analytical) and factual (synthetic) statements and the further dichotomy between meaningful (that is, logical or factual) assertions and evaluations or political preferences. "Taken as a whole," Sabine affirmed, "a political theory can hardly be said to be true. It contains among its elements certain judgments of fact, or estimates of probability, which time proves perhaps to be objectively right or wrong. It involves also certain questions of logical compatibility respecting the elements which it tries to combine. Invariably, however, it includes valuations and predilections, personal or collective, which distort the preception of fact, the estimate of probability, and the weighing of compatibilities." Under these circumstances, the most that critical exegesis can do is "to keep these three factors as much as possible distinct: to prevent preferences from claiming the inevitableness of logic or the certainty of fact."[26]

Examples in this genre could readily be multiplied, but a review of literature would only yield differences of accent.[27] In his writings on political exegesis, Andrew Hacker has outlined handy, ideal-typical profiles of relevant approaches. In his presentation, a moderate empiricist outlook—focusing on social-historical conditions along realist-mimetic lines—is termed a "Camera-Eye" mode of interpretation, a mode whose adepts are likely to maintain "that Tocqueville gives us a good historical picture of pre-Revolutionary France, or that Aristotle informs us of the constitutions of Ancient Greece." Similar mimetic relationships can readily be traced between Hobbes and Stuart England, Locke and the Glorious Revolution, or Hegel and the Prussian state. A reductive-behaviorist reading of texts exemplifies the "Capital and Carbuncles" method of exegesis where "we are concerned to know how a particular book came to be written in a particular way. Thus, the fact that Marx had carbuncles made him vent all the more vitriol on the bourgeoisie in his *Capital*. Or we are told that Rousseau's constricted bladder made him all the less coherent at the time he wrote the *Social Contract.*" Apart from capturing (perhaps caricaturing) the thrust of empiricist and behaviorist approaches, Hacker is attentive to the logical-analytical ambitions of logical empiricism—by setting aside a special exegetic category called the "Logic-Book" treatment. In this mode, he notes, "we are bidden to take up a 'Great Book' in one hand and an elementary logic-book in the other. We then search for (and are bound to find) tautologies, excluded middles, inconsistencies, and non-sequiturs galore." As he wryly adds: "These are logic-book exercises, or (in some people's eyes) philosophy, but it is not a study of politics.[28]

Liberalism and Social Engineering

In the domain of productive theorizing or the active formulation of political views, empiricism and behaviorism have had diverse—although not entirely incompatible—repercussions. On the whole, the nominalist epistemological strand (as delineated in this chapter) has tended to encourage a flexible, experimental outlook broadly compatible with traditional "liberal" doctrines: by differentiating between thought or language and empirical reality and by segregating meaningful or verifiable from evaluative assertions, empiricists lent credence, implicitly or explicitly, to the distinction between general knowledge based on nonarbitrary canons, on the one hand, and freely chosen individual beliefs or preferences, on the other. By contrast, the cancellation of the thought-reality bifurcation on the part of behaviorists was prone to contract the range of individual discretion; once language and beliefs are seen as products of operant conditioning, political attitudes and institutions likewise become feasible targets for deliberate planning or efforts at "social engineering" undertaken by behavioral experts. What links the two discordant perspectives is their common scientific commitment: in the end, behaviorists can as little bypass the tentativeness of science as can empiricists the origin of preferences. In the present context, I want to illustrate briefly these general points through reference to some of the discussed thinkers.

Regarding behaviorist psychology, its broader implications have not been left to speculation or guess-work: in several popular writings—

including *Walden Two* (1948) and *Beyond Freedom and Dignity* (1971)
— Skinner has stressed the significance of conditioning for social and
political settings. The first mentioned book extolled the virtues of a
"behavioral and cultural technology" based on "positive reinforcement,"
a technology permitting achievement of "a sort of control under which
the controlled, though they are following a code much more scrupulously
than was ever the case under the old system, nevertheless *feel free*. They
are doing what they want to do, not what they are forced to do." Replac-
ing fictional narrative by straightforward exposition, the second book
radicalized this defense of behavioral control. "Almost all our major
problems involve human behavior," *Beyond Freedom and Dignity* stated,
"and they cannot be solved by physical and biological technology alone.
What is needed is a technology of behavior, but we have been slow to
develop the science from which such a technology might be drawn." According to Skinner, the main obstacles to proper social engineering have
been "traditional prescientific views" centered around the conception of
an unconditioned or "autonomous man"—a conception commonly derived from inner intuition or "mentalist" introspection. "Freedom and
dignity illustrate the difficulty," he continued. "They are the possessions
of the autonomous man of traditional theory, and they are essential to
practices in which a person is held responsible for his conduct and given
credit for his achievements. A scientific analysis shifts both the responsibility and the achievement to the environment."[29]

Generally speaking, the issue of freedom (and dignity) has tended to
be treated less nonchalantly by empiricist philosophers. As indicated,
Carnap's "Principle of Tolerance" granted to everyone "complete liberty
with regard to the forms of language," that is, liberty to construct "his
own form of language as he wishes." His tolerance was even more pronounced outside the range of logical analysis or empirical inquiry. The
concluding sections of the *Aufbau* differentiated clearly between scientific "knowledge," on the one hand, and the domain of speculative
thought and practical life-experience, on the other. "The proud thesis
that for science no (cognitive) question is in principle unsolvable," Carnap stated, "concurs quite well with the humble insight that even the
solution of all such questions still leaves untouched life's practical
demands." Seen in a strict philosophical light, scientific cognition was
"one specific, well-circumscribed, and important task in life," a task for
which common standards of analysis were either available or could in
principle be constructed; life's practical exigencies, by contrast, could be
met only through a battery of resources and diverse individual responses:
"We should readily admit to ourselves, who are engaged in scientific
work, that the mastery of life requires the investment of the most diverse
capacities, and should be wary of the shortsighted belief that life's

demands can be fulfilled through conceptual cognition alone." Although emphasizing the distinction between scientific knowledge and life-experience, Carnap in the end detected a linkage between the two domains in the category of freedom manifest in unhampered inquiry and unrestricted personal choice—that is, in "an orientation which, while recognizing the opacity of life's fabric, insists everywhere on clarity" and which, "though acknowledging the bonds that tie men together, also strives for free development of the individual. Our work is carried by the faith that this attitude will win the future.[30]

Carnap's comments on practical and political life were sporadic by comparison with some of his empiricist colleagues, of whom none was more outspoken and eloquent than Bertrand Russell. Actually, apart from being a leading epistemologist, Russell also can be classified as a major political thinker of our age, a status buttressed by a string of publications including *Political Ideals* (1917), *Roads to Freedom* (1918), *Freedom and Organization* (1934), and *New Hopes for a Changing World* (1951). Paralleling Carnap's arguments, Russell differentiated not only between logical-scientific language and ordinary or everyday modes of communication but also, and more importantly, between his own roles as philosopher and as a citizen. In his capacity as philosopher dedicated to the advancement of knowledge, he felt bound by the empiricist "meaning" criterion governing logical and inductive statements; the same constraint was not operative, however, in the domain of citizenship comprising the articulation of practical-moral goals and political preferences. The distinction between the two roles was discussed in several of his writings; it occupied center stage in his essay on "Philosophy and Politics" (1947). In traditional thought, the essay noted, the two domains were frequently fused, yielding a hybrid blend of cognition and practice: "Philosophy, in this historically usual sense, has resulted from the attempt to produce a synthesis of science and religion, or, perhaps more exactly, to combine a doctrine as to the nature of the universe and man's place in it with a practical ethic inculcating what was considered the best way of life." In more recent times, however, especially "in the universities of the Western democratic world," this fusion or confusion has increasingly been challenged. "Many teachers of philosophy," Russell continued, "would repudiate, not only the intention to influence their pupils' politics, but also the view that philosophy should inculcate virtue." Rigorous "knowledge, they would say, should be the sole purpose of university teaching; virtue should be left to parents, schoolmasters, and Churches. But this view of philosophy, with which I have much sympathy, is very modern, and even in the modern world exceptional."

Having opposed an indiscriminate merger, Russell did not rest his case with a dichotomy; searching, like Carnap, for a viable linkage he located it in the experimental, undogmatic posture characteristic of both empirical science and liberal-democratic politics. In his view, this posture was the strongest asset in Locke's epistemological and political legacy: "The only philosophy that affords a theoretical justification of democracy, and that accords with democracy in its temper of mind, is empiricism. Locke, who may be regarded, so far as the modern world is concerned, as the founder of empiricism, makes it clear how closely this is connected with his views on liberty and toleration." The advantages of Locke's position persisted into our scientific age, undergirding the affinity between experimental inquiry and the liberal practice of "live-and-let-live." "The essence of the Liberal outlook lies not in *what* opinions are held," the essay stated, "but in *how* they are held: instead of being held dogmatically, they are held tentatively, and with a consciousness that new evidence may at any moment lead to their abandonment. This is the way in which opinions are held in science." Actually, according to Russell, the two pursuits were not only vaguely compatible but necessarily connected in the sense that science demanded a liberal-political setting and vice versa: "Science is empirical, tentative, and undogmatic; all immutable dogma is unscientific. The scientific outlook, accordingly, is the intellectual counterpart of what is, in the practical sphere, the outlook of Liberalism." Succinctly put: "Order without authority, this might be taken as the motto of both science and of Liberalism."[31]

The Truncated Vocabulary of Politics

Despite the obvious benefits of tolerance, Russell's position is not free of quandaries or drawbacks—drawbacks endemic to the entire empiricist and logical-empiricist perspective. While precariously linking knowledge and practice, his argument tends to reduce philosophy to science (or a handmaiden of science) and politics to the display of personal whims. To underscore this point I want to draw attention, by way of conclusion, to a professional political theorist whose intellectual roots are in "linguistic analysis" in the broad sense of that term: I am referring to T. D. Weldon whose study *The Vocabulary of Politics*, published in 1953, has been acclaimed by some as the "classical book in analytical political philosophy" (and which, incidentally, furnished the subtitle for the present chapter). As it seems to me, Weldon's writings document the persistent influence of empiricist epistemology during the early phase of the "ordinary language" approach—an influence evident in the neat differentiation between neutral-descriptive analysis and personal preference, and also between the respective roles of the philosopher and the citizen. For brevity's sake I shall focus here on one of his shorter essays—entitled "Political Principles"—which succinctly summarizes his views. The essay strongly emphasized the purely logical-analytical character of philosophy—its status as a "second order" enterprise by comparison with empirical, mundane, and practical pursuits. "Philosophical problems are entirely second order problems," we read. "They are problems, that is, which are generated by the language in which facts are described and explained." Drawing his inspiration from Gilbert Ryle and other linguistic analysts, Weldon insisted on the "advantages derived from the division of labor" between first and second order pursuits in our age of increasing specialization. Cautioning against a careless mixing of domains, he defined the task of philosophy—including political philosophy—as the effort "to expose and elucidate linguistic muddles; it has done its job when it has revealed the confusions which have occurred and are likely to recur in inquiries into matters of fact because the structure and use of language are what they are."

Vindicating the mentioned division of labor, Weldon recognized, meant going against the grain of much traditional theorizing; in fact, the sketched analytical approach had "been widely criticized, both on the ground that the aim which it proposes is trivial and on the ground that it is subversive." The accusation of triviality was brushed aside as "itself rather a trivial affair." The charge of subversiveness, in turn, was said to be "no better founded," since the philosopher's aim was "not to establish or to demolish physical, economic, political or any other principles" but merely "to clarify their meaning, or to examine their logical force." Statements to this effect did not prevent Weldon from endorsing the expression of political preferences or first-order commitments, provided no philosophical warrant was invoked. Given that the philosopher's job was "to reveal the confusions and misunderstandings which may follow from the careless or uncriticized use of language as it is," there was "nothing logically disreputable about my own or anyone else's political intuitions, revelations, value judgments or whatever else you prefer to call them. Any particular set of them may be (and should be) criticized on non-philosophical grounds." Buttressing this argument was again the division of labor, now phrased as a functional distinction of roles: "If this point is agreed, I see no reason why a philosopher or a clergyman or a communist should not advocate his own views. And there is in particular no reason why anyone who is engaged in second order talk about politics should not use his own first order principles as examples." As he added: "Certainly in choosing these as examples he is not performing as a philosopher, but he is not acting as a crook either."[32]

The reason I consider Weldon's vocabulary of politics "truncated" is that—like much of logical empiricism—it tends to restrict language or discourse to the two options of rigorous logical analyses and whimsical "first-order" talk. In addition, his argument exhibits at least one of the "dogmas of empiricism" which Quine had criticized in the writings of the Vienna Circle: in large measure the distinction between logical-philosophical and first-order language can be seen as a variant of the earlier creed of "analyticity." The possibility or impossibility of segregating neutral description from evaluative preferences and assessments has been widely discussed in post-positivist literature; some of the main dilemmas have been cogently exposed by Joseph Margolis, in a review of Weldon's book. Focusing on the different levels or "orders" of language, Margolis finds Weldon's analysis of political terms opaque and troublesome. In carrying out this analysis, he observes, Weldon proposes to define terms by giving "instances of sentences in which the relevant word is used and thereby clear up its logical function." This procedure seems relatively simple and straightforward; yet, "we soon discover that Weldon means not merely to *elucidate,* in the sense of 'give the ordinary use of . . .', but also to *rule* on the admissibility or meaningfulness of the ordinary uses of words." In doing so, his study by a sleight of hand expands the role of philosophy beyond the strictly descriptive-analytical domain. Seen in this light, the review concludes, the descriptive "study of ordinary usage may well be a pre-condition for philosophical analysis; it is not a substitute for it."[33]

3

Rationalism Old and New:
The Voice of Logos

Although powerful and widely influential, empiricism has not held undisputed sway in twentieth-century epistemology; sometimes obliquely
and sometimes more directly or frontally, its predominance has been
challenged by another posture—or rather a string of related postures—
which can broadly be labeled "rationalism." As an epistemological
category, the latter term does not merely denote the application of reason
or rationality to cognitive inquiry or the pursuit of knowledge. As shown
in the preceding chapter, empiricism in our century has been marked by
the intensive cultivation of logical and mathematical modes of
reasoning—a cultivation leading sometimes to the identification of
"philosophy" with logical analysis. What is at issue at this juncture is not
merely the instrumental utility but the very character and potency of
rational-mental endowments: instead of being ancillary to empirical
research, "mind" from a rationalist vantage point is an arsenal or source
of substantive knowledge—of a knowledge, moreover, which in contrast
to purely contingent sense impressions can claim in some sense apodictic,
"a priori," or "universal" status. It is mainly because of these connotations that the label was uniformly rejected by leaders of the logical-
empiricist movement. Thus, Carnap's *Aufbau* made it plain that the
commitment to rational inquiry was not synonymous with a rationalist
epistemology. The position presented in his study, he observed, "namely,
that (rational) science not only can deal with any subject matter but never
encounters a limit or a basically insoluble problem, is sometimes termed
'rationalism'—but wrongly." Since "every scientific statement from a
constructivist angle is at bottom a statement about relations between
elementary experiences, it follows that each substantive (not purely formal) insight derives from experience—for which reason 'empiricism' is
the more appropriate designation."[1]

On an epistemological plane, the distinction between empiricism and
rationalism is not of recent origin. To some extent, the rationalist variant
of cognition can be traced to Plato's dialogues, especially to some
arguments in *Meno* and the notion of an intellectual intuition of "forms."
In the modern context, the same variant tends to be tied more explicitly
to human cognitive faculties—faculties summarized variously under such
labels as "thinking substance" (*res cogitans*), "consciousness," and even

"transcendental consciousness"; in this sense, the modern rationalist camp comprises the thought of Descartes, Spinoza, Leibniz, and Christian Wolff—in part also Kantian philosophy and aspects of German idealism. During the Baroque and Enlightenment periods, the contrast between epistemologies was sometimes portrayed in graphic terms: the conception of mind as a "blank slate," "table of wax," or *tabula rasa* was opposed to the imagery of a "block of marble" or a tablet imprinted with "innate ideas." In his *New Essays Concerning Human Understanding* (1703), Leibniz formulated the contrast in a vivid manner. "Our differences are on subjects of some importance," he wrote. "The question is to know whether, following Aristotle and Locke, the soul in itself is entirely empty, like a tablet on which nothing has yet been written (*tabula rasa*), and whether all that is traced thereon comes solely from the senses and from experience; or whether as I, with Plato, believe, the soul contains originally the principles of several notions and doctrines which external objects merely awaken on occasions."[2] Leibniz went on to elaborate on his own thesis of a "block of marble," a thesis picturing the infant as grained, like marble, in a distinct fashion so that only some shapes can be hewn from it by experience. Without denying the role of sense experience, the *New Essays* also stressed the importance of insights garnered from reason alone (*vérités de raison*)—as a supplement to, and even presupposition of, the more commonly recognized modes of empirical information (*vérités de fait*).

My ambition here is not to trace the development of modern rationalism; for present purposes, I shall concentrate on manifestations in our own century—a period marked by the ascendancy of language in rationalist epistemology or, in Hacking's terms, by the shift from "ideas" to "meanings." Despite the contrast between epistemological approaches, both variants were linked, at least during the "Heyday of Meanings," by a common linguistic commitment: the search for univocity or a stable set of significations. While empiricists stabilized meanings through recourse to a formal-logical idiom whose terms were expected somehow to match sense data, rationalists pursued a similar aim by focusing on language itself and—assuming a connection between language and thought—on the inherent structure and capacities of "mind." Instead of using external "reference" as a stabilizing loadstone or anchor, the moorings of language in the second case were found in pure syntax, grammar, and other "internal" factors. To be sure, rationalists in our age (as in preceding times) have not formed a completely unified phalanx; as in the empiricist camp, it is possible to discern a number of distinct accents and orientations—accents revolving around the degree of epistemological "reflexivity" or refinement. Without jeopardizing the autonomy of reason, language and mind can be viewed either under quasi-empiricist (or quasi-naturalist) auspices or else in a more philosophically reflective vein. In the following presentation, I intend to proceed along a spectrum corresponding to a progressive distantiation from empiricism: starting from structural linguistics and anthropology—marked by quasi-empiricist premises—I shall move on to a more dynamic or "generative" model of linguistics and finally to a philosophically refined version of rationalism, a version treating language as product of the "constitutive" functions of mind or of a purified "transcendental consciousness."

Structural Linguistics and Anthropology

As employed in contemporary social science and philosophy, "structuralism" is easily one of the most vacillating and many-faceted terms; especially after being appropriated by an intellectual "movement," the term quickly acquired connotations of an amorphous trend or cause. In the present context, I consider it imperative to pare down the range of application. According to a recent study on the topic, structuralism carries at least three main senses corresponding to three distinct enterprises: namely, first, a pure method of analysis (initially developed in mathematics); secondly, the same method as applied to the examination of language or "sign" systems and, subsidiarily, to various social sciences and humanities; and thirdly, a broader "philosophical orientation." My own focus here will be basically on the second dimension, that is, on structuralism seen as a methodology and epistemology of linguistics and adjacent disciplines; by contrast, I shall bypass the domain of structuralist philosophy—mainly because of its ambivalent character, its tendency to shade over into "post-structuralism," and (as noted in the cited study) its actual "indifference to structures."[3] Construed as a method and epistemology, structuralism denotes a mode of inquiry which is neither purely "a priori" or deductive nor empiricist or inductive—a mode which rather concentrates on deep-seated cognitive and linguistic "structures" which, though not devoid of a certain natural-real status, underlie and are presupposed by contingent-empirical phenomena. "Structure," in this frame of reference, stands for a system of interrelated elements displaying the internal consistency of a quasi-logical code. In the words of Jean Piaget, the "idea of structure" suggests first of all "an ideal of intrinsic intelligibility supported by the postulate that structures are self-sufficient and that, to grasp them, we do not have to make reference to all sorts of extraneous elements," and secondly "certain insights" such as the view "that structures in general have, despite their diversity, certain common and perhaps necessary properties."[4]

Seen as an applied type of inquiry—in contrast to a purely algebraic-logical formula—the structural method first made its appearance in the investigation of language; in large measure this emergence was due to the work of Ferdinand de Saussure who for this reason is frequently described as the "father of modern linguistics" or at least as the "founder" of structural linguistics. His chief study (actually a series of lectures) entitled *Course in General Linguistics* was first published in 1916 and immediately exerted a profound impact. Deviating from the descriptive and historicist treatments of natural idioms prevalent at the turn of the century, Saussure's book shifted attention to the implicit and largely invariant architecture of language itself—to what he called the "system" and what later came to be known as the "structure" of language. Not being able to give a detailed review of the *Course*, let me indicate some highlights. Basically, Saussurean linguistics was marked by several important accents, especially by three interrelated sets of priorities: namely, the priorities of language (*langue*) over speech (*langage* and *parole*), of "synchrony" over "diachrony," and of an unconscious mental code, attributed to a social collectivity, over reflective awareness. Epistemologically, his approach steered a curious course between empiricism and mentalism, ending up with the endorsement of a kind of "formal" analysis or theory of linguistic forms. Apart from these intrinsic features of his presentation, the *Course* had a seminal influence beyond linguistics narrowly defined: by treating language as a sign system and the study of signs as the paradigm for all social and human sciences, the book laid the foundation for a unification of disciplines along structuralist lines. "A science that studies the life of signs within society is conceivable," Saussure wrote; "it would be a part of social psychology and consequently of general psychology; I shall call it *semiology*." From this broader vantage point, linguistics was "only a part of the general science of semiology; the laws discovered by semiology will be applicable to linguistics, and the latter will circumscribe a well-defined area within the mass of anthropological facts."[5]

Among the mentioned priorities the distinction between language and speech is probably the most well-known. Language or *langue*, in Saussure's portrayal, designated a rule-governed system of signs amenable to rigorous structural analysis; by contrast, speech referred either to the domain of speech phenomena or processes in general (*langage*) or else to concrete speech performance by individual speakers (*parole*). As a scientific discipline, linguistics was essentially concerned with language rather than speech. "Taken as a whole," the *Course* noted, "speech is many-sided and heterogeneous; straddling several areas simultaneously—physical, physiological, and psychological—it belongs both to the individual and to society; we cannot put it into any category of human facts, for we cannot discover its unity. Language, on the contrary, is a self-contained whole and a principle of classification." Given the disparate character of speech, linguists had to "give language first place" in order to "introduce a natural order" into the mass of phenomena: "From the very outset we must put both feet on the ground of language and use language as the norm of all other manifestations of speech." According to Saussure, however, the focus on language was justified not only by its internal coherence but also by its foundational status in relation to speech. The faculty of "articulating words," he stated, "is exercised only with the help of the instrument created by a collectivity and provided for its use; therefore, it is not arbitrary bias to claim that language gives unity to speech." The more basic status of language was evident also in regard to individual speech performances or "speaking": "In separating language from speaking we are at the same time separating (1) what is social from what is individual, and (2) what is essential from what is accessory and more or less accidental."[6]

Treated as a system of signs, language in Saussure's view was a set of interdependent elements, with each element gaining its significance through its relationship with the others. Just as the game of chess resides entirely in the "combination of different chesspieces," he observed, language has the character of "a system based entirely on the opposition of its concrete elements." As a self-contained set or system, moreover, language was not tied to the Fregean distinction between sense (*Sinn*) and external reference (*Bedeutung*), but only to the sign-internal distinction between "sound-image" and concept or meaning—or between what Saussure called the "signifier" and the "signified." Sound-image in this context denoted not merely a physical process but "the psychological imprint of the sound, the impression it makes on our senses," in contrast to the "generally more abstract" character of the concept. Linguistics as a science of signs had to deal with the chain of sound-images as well as the chain of concepts and their reciprocal connections; its subject matter was a "homogeneous field in which the only essential thing is the union of meanings and sound-images, and in which both parts of the sign are psychological." As portrayed in the *Course*, what was crucial in linguistic analysis were not the signs considered singly or individually, but rather the systematic variations, contrasts, or "differences" between signs, that is, the contrasts among sound-images and concepts and the relations of one set of components to the other. At one point, the *Course* even dropped the notion of elements in favor of correlations: "What the preceding adds up to is the conclusion that in language there are only differences. More important still: a difference normally presupposes positive elements or terms between which it obtains; but in language there are only differences without positive terms."[7]

The second priority defended in the *Course* was that of "synchrony" over "diachrony" or of "static" over "evolutionary" lingustics. In Saussure's presentation, the synchronic approach "deals with logical and psychological relations obtaining between coexisting terms of a given system," whereas diachrony refers to "relations obtaining between successive elements"; more succinctly put: the former concentrates on a "linguistic state" or condition, the latter on evolutionary "events." Although elaborating on both types of questions, the *Course* left little doubt as to their respective significance: as a scientific discipline linguistics had to focus first of all on synchronic states and their internal correlations, while diachronic changes were subordinate to systemic analysis. The two approaches, we read, "are not equally important. For, clearly, the synchronic perspective takes precedence over the other, since it is the true and only reality for the community of speakers. The same holds true for the linguist: from the angle of diachrony he is no longer able to perceive language itself but only a series of events that modify it." The chief rationale for the preeminence of synchrony, in Saussure's description, was the greater scientific intelligibility of self-contained stable states in comparison with the randomness of "exogenous" changes happening to a system; stable states were rule-governed systems or sets of regularities as distinct from exceptional events: "All diachronic phenomena are thus particular; the transformation of a system is brought about by events which are not only external to it but which are isolated and not coordinated into a system." The major source of systemic changes or innovations identified in the *Course* was individual speech performance: "Everything diachronic in language is diachronic only by virtue of speaking. For speaking contains the seeds of all changes."[8]

The third priority is of a more implicit than explicit character and has to do with levels or layers of the mind: the subordination of individual consciousness to a quasi-unconscious code or rule system. According to Saussure, language was always tied to or embedded in a speech community (as distinguished from individual speakers). In his presentation, language was a "social bond" — more specifically "a storehouse sedimented through speech in the members of a given community, a grammatical system existing potentially in each brain and actually in the brains of a group of individuals. For, language is not complete in any speaker, but exists fully only in a collectivity." Considered independently of a social matrix, linguistic phenomena remained abstract and chimerical, since "a speech community is needed to give reality to language." As a system of regularities, language possessed a quasi-rational or quasi-logical character — without being the outgrowth of reason or a purely "rational will" (as these terms had been used in the rationalist tradition): "Doubtless, group psychology does not operate on a purely logical basis; one also needs to consider everything that deflects reason in actual interpersonal contacts." While not coinciding with rationality, language in Saussure's view also was not synonymous with nonrational or irrational impulses—and certainly not with the Freudian "unconscious"; rather, seen as a Durkheimian "social fact," its rules were lodged in a collective depth consciousness. The distinction from Freudian teachings has been aptly emphasized by Ricoeur, who comments that Saussure's depth layer "is not the Freudian unconscious of instinctual, erotic drives and its power of symbolization; it is more a Kantian than a Freudian unconscious, a categorial, combinative unconscious." As he adds, it may be called "a Kantian unconscious, but only as regards its organization, since we are concerned with a categorial system without reference to a thinking subject."[9]

The status of language between reason and unreason had a parallel in Saussure's epistemology and its ambition to clear a path between positivist empiricism and mentalism (or idealism). On the one hand, the *Course* insisted strongly on the possibility of a scientific, quasi-empiricist analysis. "Language no less than speaking," we read, "is a concrete object—which is favorable to scientific inquiry. Although basically psychological, linguistic signs are not abstractions; as associations bearing the stamp of collective approval (and jointly constituting language), they are realities whose seat is in the brain. Besides, such signs are tangible: it is possible to reduce them to conventional written symbols." On the other hand, Saussure was determined to distinguish the inner core from the contingent-empirical hulk of language or "internal" from "external linguistics." Relying again on the game of chess to exemplify the distinction he wrote: "In chess, what is external can be separated relatively easily from what is internal: the fact that the game passed from Persia to Europe is external; by contrast, everything having to do with its system and rules is internal. Whether I use ivory or wooden chesspieces has no effect on the system; but if I decrease or increase the number of pieces, this change has a profound effect on the 'grammar' of the game." The same ambivalence pervaded the theory of signs and their character: on the one hand, sound-images and concepts were presented as concrete psychological elements coalescing into a system seen as a "social fact"; on the other hand, as mentioned, language was described as a correlation devoid of "positive" elements or terms. In the end, the *Course* opted in favor of a formalist (or quasi-formalist) approach, by denying the "substantive" character of the linguist's domain: "Linguistics then works in the borderland where the elements of sound and thought combine; their combination produces a form, not a substance." More pointedly put: *"Language is a form and not a substance."*[10]

In the period following the publication of the *Course*, linguistics (as

envisaged by Saussure) developed into a complex academic discipline—
especially due to the efforts of such professional groups as the "schools"
of Prague and Copenhagen. During the interbellum period, theoretical
works in the field frequently underscored the static and formalist
qualities of the discipline, sometimes going beyond Saussure's scheme of
relative priorities; a case in point are the *Prolegomena to a Theory of
Language* by the Danish linguist Louis Hjelmslev. According to
Hjelmslev, the task of "true linguistics" was to grasp language, not as "a
conglomerate" of nonlinguistic phenomena, but "as a self-sufficient
totality, a structure *sui generis*." In the pursuit of this task—in which induction had to be subordinated to logical-deductive procedures—formal
properties necessarily took precedence over substantive ingredients and
stable states over change processes. "A linguistic theory," he wrote,
"which searches for the specific structure of language through an exclusively formal system of premises must, while continually taking account of the fluctuations and changes of speech, necessarily refuse to
grant exclusive significance to these changes; it must seek a *constancy*,
which is not anchored in some 'reality' outside language—a constancy
that makes a language a language, whatever language it may be, and that
makes a particular language identical with itself in all its various
manifestations." A central thesis advanced in the *Prolegomena* was "that
for every *process* there is a corresponding *system*, by which the process
can be analyzed and described by means of a limited number of premises"
and "a limited number of elements recurring in various combinations."
Together with Saussure, Hjelmslev saw language as a set of correlations
and differences or as a "self-sufficient" entity of internal "dependences"—
dependences obtaining both between signs and, inside the sign function,
between "signifier" and "signified" or (in his words) between "expression" and "content." The same structural principle applied even to relationships between languages: "Both the similarity and the differences between
languages rest on what, following Saussure, we have called the form, not
on the substance that is formed."[11]

Simultaneously with the emergence of a far-flung professional
discipline of linguistics, the structuralist approach also began to put its
stamp on adjacent fields—a development anticipated by Saussure's vision
of a general "semiology" comprising the various social and human
sciences. Among the latter sciences, the impact has no doubt been most
profound in anthropology—sometimes described as the basic, architectonic or "synoptic" social science—and this due chiefly to the pioneering
efforts of Claude Lévi-Strauss. The linkage between structuralism or
structural linguistics and anthropological inquiry has been profiled by
Lévi-Strauss in numerous publications, and probably most succinctly in

his early programmatic work (actually a collection of essays dating from the immediate postwar period) entitled *Structural Anthropology*. "Structural linguistics," he observed there, "will certainly play the same renovating role with regard to the social sciences that nuclear physics, for example, has played for the physical sciences. In what does this revolution consist?" Appealing to the teachings of the main founder of structural phonology, Trubetzkoy, the book identified the structural method with four basic principles or operations: "First, structural linguistics shifts from the study of *conscious* linguistic phenomena to the study of their *unconscious* infrastructure; second, it does not treat *terms* as independent entities, taking instead as its basis of analysis the *relations* between terms; third, it introduces the concept of *system*" or structure; and lastly, it aims "at discovering general laws" preferably through "logical deduction, which would give them an absolute character." As a corollary of these central emphases, *Structural Anthropology* accorded a relative precedence to transtemporal invariance over historical change. Although structures were said to exist "both synchronically and diachronically," structural analysis was bound to push beyond "historical contingency" and conscious intent: "Anthropology cannot remain indifferent to historical processes and to the most highly conscious expressions of social phenomena. But if the anthropologist brings to them the same scrupulous attention as the historian, it is in order to eliminate, by a kind of backward course, all that they owe to the historical process and to conscious thought. His goal is to grasp, beyond the conscious and always shifting images which men hold, the complete range of unconscious possibilities."[12]

The main example used in *Structural Anthropology* to illustrate the affinity with linguistics was kinship. According to Lévi-Strauss, kinship satisfied the requirements of the structural model in being anchored in the unconscious infrastructure of social life and in operating not on the level of isolated terms or entities but on that of correlations—and especially of oppositional pairs (like father-son, husband-wife, maternal uncle and his sister's son); moreover, correlations of this kind were relatively invariant by comparison with diachronic changes. Actually, in Lévi-Strauss's view, there was not merely a loose affinity between kinship and language, but a close analogy and even homology. Like sign systems, he noted, kinship "is an arbitrary system of representations, not the spontaneous development of a real situation"; both types of systems were based on an underlying set of rules or a quasi-logical "code": the first on linguistic rules, the second on marriage rules. If the accent is placed on these rules, *Structural Anthropology* asserted, kinship can be said to form "a kind of language, a set of processes permitting the establishment, between individuals and groups, of a certain type of communication. That the mediating factor, in this case, should be the *women of the group*, who are *circulated* between clans, lineages, or families, in place of the *words of the group*, which are *circulated* between individuals, does not at all change the fact that the essential aspect of the phenomenon is identical in both cases." Subsequent portions of the study proceeded to the explanation of more complex and ambitious analogies, comprising myth, art, and social organization. "The question must be raised," Lévi-Strauss stated, "whether the different aspects of social life (including even art and religion) cannot only be studied by the methods of, and with the help of concepts similar to those employed in linguistics, but also whether they do not constitute phenomena whose inmost nature is the same as that of language." In order to test this hypothesis, it was necessary to sharpen the analysis of different social domains "so that a deep enough level can be reached to make it possible to cross from one to the other; or to express the specific structure of each in terms of a sort of general language, valid for each system separately and for all of them taken together." The same kind of cross-cutting analysis was employed later in *The Savage Mind* (1962), devoted to the investigation of the broad spectrum of primitive culture or "savage" thought ranging from kinship over art to mythology.[13]

Instead of reviewing successive publications, however, I want to flesh out briefly their Saussurean features, by dwelling mainly on the notion of structure, the deemphasis of history, the search for an "unconscious" anchorage, and related epistemological issues. The connotations of "structure," understood as a set of correlations, were spelled out repeatedly in *Structural Anthropology*. Approached from a rigorously "theoretical point of view," we read there, "language can be said to be a condition of culture because the material out of which language is built is of the same type as the material out of which the whole culture is built: logical relations, oppositions, correlations, and the like." Seen in this light, language could be regarded as a sort of "structure of structures" or "order of orders," as "laying a kind of foundation for the more complex structures which correspond to the different aspects of culture." Elaborating in greater detail on definitional problems, a later passage asserted that the term "social structure" has "nothing to do with empirical reality but with models which are built up after it," that it "exhibits the characteristics of a system" and is "made up of several elements, none of which can undergo a change without effecting changes in all the other elements." The formal-logical and partially mathematical quality of structures was further highlighted in *Totemism* (1962). "The ideas of opposition and correlation, and that of pairs of opposites, have a long history," the study observed, "but it is structural linguistics and subsequently structural anthropology which rehabilitated them in the vocabulary of the human sciences." According to Lévi-Strauss, ideas of this type could be used to salvage and repair traditional associational psychology: "Associationism had the great merit of sketching the contours of this elementary logic, which is like the least common denominator of all thought, and its only failure was not to recognize that it was an original logic, a direct expression of the structure of the mind (and behind the mind, probably, of the brain), and not an inert product of the action of the environment on an amorphous consciousness." Contrary to associationist tenets, it was "this logic of oppositions and correlations, exclusions and inclusions, compatibilities and incompatibilities, which explains the laws of association, not the reverse. A renovated associationism would have to be based on a system of operations which would not be without similarity to Boolean algebra."[14]

In pointing to the "structure of the mind" *Totemism* was not, or not primarily, referring to conscious human awareness but rather to a depth layer or dimension—which Lévi-Strauss frequently described as "unconsciousness." Accentuating the contrast to traditional humanities, *Structural Anthropology* asserted that "history organizes its data in relation to conscious expressions, while anthropology proceeds by examining its unconscious foundations." Concurring with the anthropologist Franz Boas, the study emphasized that "the structure of a language remains unknown to the speaker until the introduction of a scientific grammar. Even then the language continues to mold discourse beyond the consciousness of the individual, imposing on his thought conceptual schemes which are taken as objective categories." In Lévi-Strauss's presentation, the depth layer of mind was basically coterminous with a universal and invariant categorial scheme underlying cultural and historical variations. "If, as we believe to be the case, the unconscious activity of the mind consists in imposing forms upon content," he wrote, "and if these forms are fundamentally the same for all minds—ancient and modern, primitive and civilized (as the study of symbolic function, expressed in language, so strikingly indicates)—it is necessary and sufficient to grasp the unconscious structure underlying each institution and each custom, in order to obtain a principle of interpretation valid for other institutions and other customs, provided of course that the analysis is carried far enough." To uncover the deeper and unconscious dimension it was commonly imperative to penetrate through the screen of conscious conceptions or beliefs and their frequently dissimulating effect: "When the structure of a certain type of phenomena does not lie at a great depth, it is more likely that some kind of model, standing as a screen to hide it, will exist in the collective consciousness. For conscious models, which are usually known as 'norms', are by definition very poor ones, since they are not intended to explain the phenomena but to perpetuate them."[15]

By piercing through conscious models, anthropological inquiry also moved beyond contingent historical processes or beyond the "always shifting images which men hold." To be sure, as a social scientist survey-ing a broad range of cultures, Lévi-Strauss could not simply ignore history; rather, what structural analysis dictated in his case was the quest for both synchronic and diachronic structures or what has been called an "invariant diachronics." As he explained in *The Savage Mind*: "History does not therefore escape the common obligation of all knowledge, to employ a code to analyse its object, even (and especially) if a continuous reality is attributed to that object. The distinctive features of historical knowledge are due not to the absence of a code, which is illusory, but to its particular nature: the code consists in a chronology." Actually, in Lévi-Strauss's view, history did not have a distinct object comparable to the subject matter of other disciplines—particularly not the object of social progress or human self-realization. Once the focus on subject mat-ter was abandoned, it became plain that history "consists wholly in its method, which experience proves to be indispensable for cataloguing the elements of any structure whatever, human or non-human, in their en-tirety." Thus, he continued, it is "far from being the case that the search for intelligibility comes to an end in history as though it were its ter-minus. Rather, it is history that serves as the point of departure in any quest for intelligibility. As we say of certain careers, history may lead to anything, provided you get out of it."[16]

In terms of epistemology, structural anthropology on the whole pur-sued a Saussurean course between positivist empiricism and idealist men-talism. In *The Savage Mind*, this approach was described as an intellec-tual "bricolage," characterized by recourse to a "heterogeneous reper-toire"—especially the combination of sensual images and concepts and their mediation through signs. Referring to Marxist terminology, a later passage in the same study noted: "Without questioning the undoubted primacy of infrastructures, I believe that there is always a mediator be-tween *praxis* and practices, namely the conceptual scheme by the opera-tion of which matter and form, neither with an independent existence, are realized as structures, that is as entities which are both empirical and intelligible." The same intermediary position was defended in the famous "Overture" to *The Raw and the Cooked* (1964). In anthropological in-quiry, Lévi-Strauss stated, we are "seeking to transcend the opposition of the perceptible and the intelligible by straight-away placing ourselves on the level of signs. Through signs the one is conveyed by means of the other. Yet, even when restricted in number, they lend themselves to rigorously grouped combinations which can translate, in their most discrete nuances, the whole diversity of sense experience. Our hope is to attain a level where logical properties will be manifested as attributes of things quite as directly as flavors and perfumes." The "Overture" also contained an approving nod toward Ricoeur and his conception of a "Kantian unconscious": "What we are attempting to do is well described in Paul Ricoeur's qualification of our effort as 'Kantianism without a transcendental subject'. We see no indication of a lacuna in this restriction." Rather, "by pursuing conditions where systems of truth become mutually convertible and can therefore be simultaneously admissible for several subjects, the ensemble of these conditions acquires the character of an object endowed by a reality proper to itself and independent of any subject."[17]

Generative Grammar: Chomsky

In several respects, especially in groping for a structural or invariant diachronics, structural anthropology was straining against the confines of Saussurean linguistics. In the meantime, these boundaries have been breached on many fronts—mainly as a result of the rise of transformational anaylsis (and also of genetic psychology and epistemology). In the domain of linguistics, the most important innovations during recent decades are clearly associated with the name of Noam Chomsky and center around his conception of a "generative" or "transformational grammar"—a phrase which deliberately joins together the notions of genesis and grammatical structure, thus transgressing the antinomies of structure and event or synchrony and diachrony. In bridging these dualisms, the same conception also narrows in some measure the gulf between language (*langue*) and speech (*parole*), by making larger room in linguistic theory for the creative role of the speaker (and hearer)—although a speaker understood not merely in a psychological or sociological sense, but construed as a generalized, quasi-universal agent. As Chomsky states in *Current Issues in Linguistic Theory* (1964): "The central fact to which any significant linguistic theory must address itself is this: a mature speaker can produce a new sentence of his language on the appropriate occasion, and other speakers can understand it immediately, though it is equally new to them." Seen in this light, "normal mastery of a language involves not only the ability to understand immediately an indefinite number of entirely new sentences, but also the ability to identify deviant sentences and, on occasion, to impose an interpretation on them." In a similar vein, pointing to the "creative aspect of language use, that is, its unboundedness and freedom from stimulus control," he observes in another context: "The speaker-hearer whose normal use of language is 'creative' in this sense must have internalized a system of rules that determines the semantic interpretations of an unbounded set of sentences; he must, in other words, be in control of what is now often called a *generative grammar* of his language."[18]

As presented by Chomsky, language use is not simply a contingent everyday activity but the outgrowth of a deep-seated categorial capacity which he terms "linguistic competence," a competence seen as basically unlearned and unconditioned. It is primarily at this point that he departs from Saussurean linguistics—which is accused of being static and narrowly preoccupied with surface phenomena. In Saussure's model, he writes in *Language and Mind* (1968), "processes of sentence formation do not belong to the system of language at all," with the result that "the mechanisms of sentence formation are otherwise free from any constraint imposed by linguistic structure as such"; thus, sentence formation "is not strictly a matter of *langue*, but is rather assigned to what he called *parole*, and thus placed outside the scope of linguistics proper." Against the defects of Saussurean descriptivism as well as against any form of behaviorist reductionism, Chomsky pits the notion of a generative cognitive and linguistic endowment undergirding creative speech. "It has, I believe, become quite clear," he affirms, "that if we are ever to understand how language is used or acquired, then we must abstract for separate and independent study a cognitive system, a system of knowledge and belief, that develops in early childhood and that interacts with many other factors to determine the kinds of behavior that we observe; to introduce a technical term, we must isolate and study the system of *linguistic competence* that underlies behavior but that is not realized in any direct or simple way in behavior. And this system of linguistic competence is qualitatively different from anything that can be described in terms of the taxonomic methods of structural linguistics, the concepts of stimulus-response psychology, or the notions developed within the mathematical theory of communication or the theory of simple automata." The latter approaches—and particularly the domain of "behavioral science" —have "no concept corresponding to 'competence', in the sense in which competence is characterized by a generative grammar."[19]

The stress on a deep-seated cognitive system or endowment links transformational linguistics more tightly with rationalist premises than was the case in earlier structuralism. On repeated occasions, including *Language and Mind* and *Cartesian Linguistics* (1966), Chomsky has paid tribute to Descartes' philosophy, to Port-Royal grammarians, and even to the romantic idealism of Humboldt for whom language was never merely a neutral code but the result of a continuous production or generation—though a production nourished by universal principles. The rationalist or Cartesian position, he observes at one point, is "that in its normal use, language is free from stimulus control and does not serve a merely communicative function, but is rather an instrument for the free expression of thought and for appropriate response to new situations." In this view, language and speech are tied to the faculty of "human reason as 'a universal instrument which can serve for all contingencies' and which therefore provides for unbounded diversity of free thought and action." The same outlook was preserved in the "philosophical grammar" of Port-Royal and by thinkers of the romantic period like Herder and Humboldt. The latter, in particular, located the "fundamental property of a language" in its capacity "to use its finitely specifiable mechanisms for an unbounded and unpredictable set of contingencies"; accordingly, he developed "the notion of 'form of language' as a generative principle, fixed and unchanging, determining the scope and providing the means for the unbounded set of individual 'creative' acts that constitute normal language use." Chomsky's attachment to the rationalist legacy, one should note, does not simply amount to an endorsement of speculative metaphysics: despite its important merits, he finds the legacy marred by its "mentalist" and insufficiently scientific orientation. On the whole, the postulated generative capacity in his view is not so much a conscious and deliberate human skill as rather a subconscious (though quasi-logical) attribute of the human race; relying on recent biological and neurophysiological findings, he tends to treat linguistic competence as a "species specific" constituent of the human organism — a treatment prompting Piaget to speak of "the fascinating mix of geneticism and Cartesianism characteristic of Chomsky."[20]

Notwithstanding scientific reservations, generative grammar presents itself explicitly as a continuation and refinement of earlier precedents; this is particularly true of the distinction between "deep" and "surface structure" — a distinction anticipated by Port-Royal grammarians and by Humboldt's juxtaposition of "form of language" and normal usage. "Following the Port-Royal theory to its logical conclusion," Chomsky states, "the grammar of a language must contain a system of rules that characterizes deep and surface structures and the transformational relation between them, and — if it is to accommodate the creative aspect of language use — that does so over an infinite domain of paired deep and surface structures." In this terminology, deep structure denotes an "inner mental aspect" or the "underlying abstract structure that determines its semantic interpretation," while surface structure refers to an "outer aspect" or the "superficial organization of units which determines the phonetic interpretation and which relates to the physical form of the actual utterance, to its perceived or intended form." Translating these terms into two systems of syntactical rules, Chomsky also speaks of "a *base system* that generates deep structures" and "a *transformational system* that maps these into surface structures": "The base system consists of rules that generate the underlying grammatical relations with an abstract order (the rewriting rules of a phrase-structure grammar); the transformational system consists of rules of deletion, rearrangement, adjunction, and so on." In this theoretical scheme, similar surface structures may require different depth-grammatical interpretations, just as divergent surface structures may converge in their syntactical or "logical form" on the level of deep structure. Despite the "creativity" of human speech, the model assumes a restricted and hierarchically ordered set of recursive rules accounting for the range of new sentences on the surface level. "The central idea of transformational grammar," we read in *Aspects of the Theory of Syntax* (1965), is not only that surface and deep structures are distinct but that "surface structure is determined by repeated application of certain formal operations called 'grammatical transformations' to objects of a more elementary sort."[21]

The notion of a deep linguistic structure restricts the import of cultural variations, vindicating the rationalist maxim of universalism against a contingent-empiricist particularism. According to Chomsky, linguistic competence as rooted in the "base system" has a universal character transcending natural languages—although it is somehow instantiated in each of them. While surface structures and transformational rules may differ among natural idioms, the "base rules" of the deep structure have the status of formal "language universals" common to all languages; setting limits to cultural-linguistic diversity, they are "the universal conditions that prescribe the form of any human language." As portrayed in *Aspects*, "all languages are cut to the same pattern"—which does not mean "that there is any point-by-point correspondence between particular languages"; the important point entailed by the stipulation of "universal categories" as "formal properties of the base" is that "much of the base is common to all languages." Tracing out the implications of the Port-Royal theories, *Language and Mind* speaks of a "universal grammar" whose study reveals the general "nature of human intellectual capacities": "It tries to formulate the necessary and sufficient conditions that a system must meet to qualify as a potential human language, conditions that are not accidentally true of the existing human languages, but that are rather rooted in the human 'language capacity', and thus constitute the innate organization that determines what counts as linguistic experience and what knowledge of language arises on the basis of this experience." Using the essentialist vocabulary of the Cartesian legacy, another passage of the same study describes the "innate schema that characterizes the class of potential languages" as "the 'essence' of human language."[22]

The thesis of an "innate" and universally shared linguistic schema is probably the most distinctive (and most rationalist) trait of generative grammar—a trait with important epistemological and methodological consequences. "The central doctrine of Cartesian linguistics," Chomsky asserts, elaborating on this thesis, "is that the general features of grammatical structure are common to all languages and reflect certain fundamental properties of the mind." Such general or universal features, he adds, "are not learned, rather, they provide the organizing principles that make language learning possible, that must exist if data is to lead to knowledge. By attributing such principles to the mind, as an innate property, it becomes possible to account for the quite obvious fact that the speaker of a language knows a great deal that he has not learned." In line with Cartesian teachings, generative grammar holds "that the principles of language and natural logic are known unconsciously and that they are in large measure a precondition for language acquisition rather than a matter of 'institution' or 'training' "; differently put: "Language aquisition is a matter of growth and maturation of relatively fixed capacities, under appropriate external conditions. The form of the language that is acquired is largely determined by internal factors." Given the internal or unacquired character of basic linguistic competence, its analysis cannot follow the path of empirical or "inductive procedures of any known sort"; in particular, the native speaker's "internalized grammar" cannot be uncovered through "inductive generalization" from surface data. In Chomsky's words: "It seems plain that language acquisition is based on the child's discovery of what from a formal point of view is a deep and abstract theory—a generative grammar of his language—many of the concepts and principles of which are only remotely related to experience by long and intricate chains of unconscious quasi-inferential steps." Thus, "it may well be that the general features of language structure reflect, not so much the course of one's experience, but rather the general character of one's capacity to acquire knowledge."[23]

Transcendental Phenomenology: Husserl

The preceding recapitulation of Chomsky's outlook, though admittedly condensed, should have conveyed his main innovations in linguistic theory, innovations centering around the notion of transformational analysis linking deep and surface structures. Yet, despite these new departures, one can hardly fail to notice also the continuity between his model and structural linguistics: although moving beyond earlier antimonies and correlating more closely language and speech, generative grammar still exhibits the primacy of general competence over ordinary usage or performance, of invariant structure over contingent event, and of "base rules"—operating on a subconscious or pre-intentional level—over conscious intent. With some modifications, the same priorities also pervade the philosophically most reflective rationalist perspective I wish to consider in this context: Edmund Husserl's transcendental phenomenology (I shall bypass here his later turn to the "life-world"). Philosophical reflectiveness in this case means primarily a resolute break with all types of objectivism—including the lingering "psychologism" of structural linguistics and the biological-genetic connotations of transformational grammar. While paying tribute—like Chomsky—to the Cartesian legacy, Husserl's philosophy can be seen as culmination of a long line of efforts to reformulate the character of the *cogito*, a line leading from the conception of a "thinking substance," over Kantian apriorism, to the assumption of a purified "transcendental consciousness" seen as foundation and condition of possibility of thought. Once this reflective move is taken into account, affinities with structuralism are still readily apparent especially with regard to the critique of contingency and the abandonment of surface explanation in favor of deep-seated categories. In one of his programmatic writings, entitled *Philosophy as Rigorous Science* (1910), Husserl sharply demarcated his position from two contemporary postures: namely, "naturalism" identified with a naive-positivist empiricism, and "historicism" viewed as a denial of invariant forms.[24]

Husserlian phenomenology is sometimes equated exclusively with the search for "essences" or the elucidation of pure intentional meanings or "noemata." Although this is clearly a centerpiece of his work, one should note that investigation of meanings in his case was closely connected with the analysis of basic grammatical and syntactical rules. Apart from (and prior to) being a phenomenologist, Husserl was also an eminent logician, and it was chiefly in this capacity that he addressed himself to questions of grammar and syntax—in a manner which in many ways was akin to, or an anticipation of, transformational analysis. The similarities and differences between Husserl's and Chomsky's approach have been ably profiled by James Edie, in his study on the phenomenology of language. "Edmund Husserl's project of a 'pure logical grammar'—which is probably the most recent full-scale proposal in this area from the side of philosophy," he observes, "has fallen upon deaf ears. But now, within the past decades, Noam Chomsky has begun to propose, from the side of linguistics itself, a program for the study of grammar which, if it were to succeed, might seem to justify the earlier intuitions of rationalistic philosophy and to give a new grounding to its ancient quest." Edie also highlights some of the main contrasts or divergences. "Like Plato and Descartes," he writes, "Chomsky seems to feel that from the very fact that it is possible to locate and describe certain apriori (and therefore universal) features of language, these aprioris must be treated as 'innate' ideas or even as 'biological' constituents of the human organism. Husserl would certainly never draw such a conclusion, because it would involve him in the kind of 'psychologism' which he spent the first half of his philosophical life learning to avoid." As he adds: "What divides Husserl and Chomsky, then, is whether the universals of grammar are to be understood in a genetically biological (and thus necessarily psychologistic) sense or whether they are to be understood in terms of the logical transcendentalism of Kantian and Husserlian phenomenology."[25]

Husserl's thoughts on grammar and syntax are developed in several of his writings, especially in *Logical Investigations* (1900) and *Formal and Transcendental Logic* (1929). Both works also contain important contributions to a general semantics construed as a formal theory of "intended meanings"—a theory said to be firmly anchored, however, in prior grammatical norms (I shall follow here this logical sequence). To illustrate the importance of language for philosophy, *Formal and Transcendental Logic* appealed to the Greek term "logos." Setting forth the term's connotations, the study argued that "logos" referred simultaneously to speaking and thinking, that is, both to the articulation of meaning in speech and to the process of thinking and ultimately the (linguistic) structure of thought itself—in Saussure's vocabulary, to *parole* as well as *langue*. Viewed against this background, speech conforming to "logos" presupposed that meanings be grammatically well contructed and exhibit an internal coherence traceable to the formal laws of phonology, morphology, and syntax. Husserl's own efforts in this domain were concentrated on the formulation of what he called a "pure apriori (or logical) grammar" or a "pure morphology of significations," a grammar outlining the rules governing the constitution of meanings or thought objects in general. Reflection on the premises of thought and language, in his view, revealed that all natural idioms manifest basic "apriori laws" or an "ideal" and stable framework undergirding cultural and empirical diversities. As he affirmed in *Logical Investigations:* "Language has not only physiological, psychological and cultural-historical, but also apriori foundations. These last concern the essential meaning-forms and the apriori laws of their combinations and modifications, and no language is conceivable which would not be essentially determined by this apriori. Every linguist, whether or not he is clearly aware of the fact, operates with concepts stemming from this domain." Recognizing that, among his contemporaries, the sense or appreciation of the apriori had "threatened almost to atrophy," Husserl exhorted philosophers and linguists alike to again "learn by heart" that "it is of the greatest importance sharply to separate the apriori from the empirical" and merely contingent.[26]

The details of this Husserlian depth grammar are spelled out in the celebrated fourth investigation in the same study. "Modern grammar," the preamble to this section noted, "thinks it should build exclusively on psychology and other empirical sciences. As against this, the old idea of a universal or even *apriori grammar* gains an unquestionable foundation and a definite sphere of validity once we demonstrate that there are apriori laws which determine the possible forms of meaning." The central aim of the investigation was to show that general semantics is grammatically structured, differently put: "that meanings are subject to apriori laws regulating their combination into new meanings" and that, in fact, "there are obviously apriori laws of essence governing all meaning combinations." Through a study of such basic rules, the section asserted, "we rise to the insight that all possible meanings are subject to a fixed schema of categorial structures built, in apriori fashion, into the general idea of meaning, that apriori laws govern the realm of meaning, whereby all possible concrete meaning-patterns systematically depend on a small number of primitive forms, fixed by laws of existence, out of which they flow by pure construction." Together with Chomsky, Husserl was led by this insight to "take up the cudgels for the old doctrine of a *grammaire générale et raisonnée*, a philosophical grammar." Once attention was focused on the source of meaning-combinations, he noted, "we recognize the undoubted soundness of the idea of a *universal grammar* conceived by the rationalists of the seventeenth and eighteenth century"—and especially by those "older grammarians" who recognized that "even in the sphere of grammar there are fixed standards, apriori norms that may not be transgressed." In a quasi-Chomskyan vein, Husserl also viewed depth grammar as a universal core underlying and linking natural idioms. Investigation of the source of meaning-constitution, we read, will "lay bare an ideal framework which each actual language will fill up and clothe differently, in conformity both with general human characteristics and with empirical motivations that vary at random. To whatever extent the actual content and grammatical forms of historical languages are thus empirically determined, each is bound to this ideal framework"—which is an "absolutely fixed" framework "more or less perfectly revealed in empirical disguises."[27]

Seen in the context of a general semantics or a formal logic of meanings, apriori grammar constituted for Husserl the primary and most basic level of analysis. Access to this level required a deliberate "epoché" or a phenomenological "bracketing": namely, a turn from ordinary mundane experience or the "natural attitude" to the realm of purely formal premises and thought structures. As presented in the fourth investigation, the main tasks or steps of grammatical analysis were the identification of "simple" versus "complex" and of "independent" versus "dependent" meanings; the specification of the rules governing the combination of partial meanings into well-formed composite units; and the construction of general syntactical norms regulating the generation of sentences. Within a broader theory of signs or a "formal study of signification," pure grammar was a fundamental echelon which was presupposed by the higher logical levels—those of the logic of noncontradiction and the logic of truth. As portrayed by Husserl, grammatical analysis established the rules necessary for rendering a statement meaningful at all—rules which preceded questions of consistency and formal validity raised on the higher levels. In his words, grammatical rules "which govern the sphere of complex meanings and whose role it is to divide sense from nonsense, are not yet the so-called laws of logic in the fuller sense of that term": by providing logic with "possible meaning forms" they merely "guard against senselessness (*Unsinn*)," whereas the latter protect "against formal-analytic nonsense (*Widersinn*) or formal absurdity." In the case of statements contravening logic, "certain partial meanings fail to coalesce into a unity of meaning as far as the objectivity or truth of the total meaning is concerned." In the case of ungrammatical statements, on the other hand, "the notion of unitary meaning excludes the possible coexistence of certain meanings in itself"; in this instance we "perceive that no object can ever correspond to such an idea, that is, that a meaning of the intended sort cannot exist."[28]

In the domain of semantics in the broader sense, Husserlian phenomenology treated "intentionality" as the cornerstone in the constitution or generation of meaning contents. The chief accent of his semantics was on intended meanings or "intentional objects" (*noemata*) and particularly on the identity of such objects—that is, on their "sameness" in thought over time and their emergence through a synthesis of diverse intentional acts. Two crucial distinctions were involved in this focus: first, between concrete psychological acts and their intended meanings; and secondly, between meaning content and the "real" object or state of affairs—with the latter distinction corresponding roughly to the Fregean juxtaposition of sense and reference (but recast in somewhat different vocabulary). Husserl's main concern was with intended meanings or meaning contents rather than with "real" objects and concrete psychological acts. As he repeatedly insisted, only meaning contents could be re-thought time and again from different angles, thus yielding identity or invariance of meaning—while invariance could never characterize real processes or states of affairs, either empirical objects or intentional acts seen as psychic occurrences. The significance of language, in this context, resided primarily in its ability to stabilize or fix intentions; construed as the voice of thinking or "logos," language embodied the potential for transcending real or mundane affairs in the direction of a realm of "ideal" concepts or the "ideality" of meanings. To be sure, in ascending to this realm it was necessary to differentiate not only between mundane processes and intentions in general, but also between meaning contents and the actual (spoken or written) words and sentences in which meanings are conveyed; in Husserl's portrayal, only conceptual contents—designated as "terms" or "propositions"—rather than concrete words or sentences were carriers of meaning invariance. If these semantic arguments are combined with the previously sketched grammatical considerations, Husserlian phenomenology attributes to language a twofold rationality, manifest in the dual "ideality" of meanings and of an underlying depth structure.[29]

Rejoinders

Before proceeding to implications for political thought, I want to review briefly some critical comments. Like its empiricist counterpart, rationalist epistemology has been charged with numerous failings; the most widespread reproach, however, again as in the empiricist case, has been the neglect of the interpretative dimension—a reproach attributable to the common epistemological focus on univocity and meaning invariance. With regard to (pre-Chomskyan) linguistics and anthropology, Ricoeur in *The Conflict of Interpretations* has weighed attentively the strengths and weaknesses of the structural approach. Referring specifically to *The Savage Mind*, he chided its author for truncating the range of reflectiveness and semantic richness, or at least for downplaying exegesis in favor of formal-semantic analysis. "Intelligibility," he wrote, "is attributed to the code of transformations which assure correspondence and homology between arrangements belonging to different levels of social reality (clan organization, nomenclatures and classifications of animals and plants, myths and arts, and the like). I will characterize the method in one word: it is the choice of syntax over semantics." This choice, he added, ultimately "lacks reflection on its conditions of validity, on the price to be paid for this type of comprehension, in short, a reflection on limits." Adopting an existentialist-hermeneutical stance, Ricoeur at another point delineated more broadly the general "costs" of the "structural point of view": "The act of speaking is excluded not only as exterior execution, as individual performance, but as free combination, as producing new utterances. Now this is the essential aspect of language—properly speaking, its goal. At the same time, history is excluded, and not simply the change from one state of system to another but the production of culture and of man in the production of his language." Most importantly, the structural perspective bypasses the primary "function" of language, "which is to say something about something"—a function which "constitutes its openness or opening" toward the polysemic or multivocal character of meanings.[30]

Objections of this kind have been advanced not only by philosophers, but also by social scientists. In his *The Interpretation of Cultures*, Clifford Geertz accused structural anthropology of shortchanging cultural-semantic diversity in favor of abstract-rationalist schemata. Lévi-Strauss's works, in his view, were basically "variant expressions of the same deep underlying structure: the universal rationalism of the French Enlightenment." As in the case of earlier rationalists, he noted, "Lévi-Strauss' search is not after all for men, whom he doesn't much care for, but for Man, with whom he is enthralled"; accordingly, "the 'unshakable basis of human society' is not really social at all but psychological—a rational, universal, eternal, and thus (in the great tradition of French moralism) virtuous mind." Addressing himself particularly to *The Savage Mind*, Geertz charged his fellow-anthropologist with constructing an "infernal culture machine": "It annuls history, reduces sentiment to a shadow of the intellect, and replaces the particular minds of particular savages in particular jungles with the Savage Mind immanent in us all." From this reductive perspective, despite differences between primitive and modern cultures, "the mind of man is, at bottom, everywhere the same: so that what could not be accomplished by a drawing near, by an attempt to enter bodily into the world of particular savage tribes, can be accomplished instead by a standing back, by the development of a general, closed, abstract, formalistic science of thought, a universal grammar of the intellect." In lieu of such formalism, Geertz's study advocated an "interpretive anthropology" dedicated to a "thick description" of cultures, that is, a description hovering close to the level of concrete diversities: "Only short flights of ratiocination tend to be effective in anthropology; longer ones tend to drift off into logical dreams, academic bemusements with formal symmetry." The central point of an interpretive approach "is to aid us in gaining access to the conceptual world in which our subjects live so that we can, in some extended sense of the term, converse with them."[31]

Chomsky's model has been taken to task by a diverse set of writers, including philosophers, social scientists, and literary critics—not to mention empirical linguists. Although endorsing the model's universalist thrust, Jürgen Habermas at one point castigated the individualistic (if not solipsistic) character of linguistic competence and the rigid bifurcation of competence and pragmatic performance—in addition to challenging three basic assumptions or "theses" operative in generative grammar: the theses of "monologism," "apriorism," and "elementarism" (denoting the reduction of complex meanings to a finite set of fixed units).[32] A more sweeping indictment of the model has been formulated by George Steiner in a collection of essays on "literature and the language revolution." Without questioning the model's technical virtues, Steiner challenged Chomsky's narrow rationalist predilections. "I am persuaded," he wrote, "that the phenomenon of language is such that a rigorously idealized and nearly mathematical account of the deep structures and generation of human speech is bound to be incomplete and, very possibly, distorting." Appealing to the contributions of hermeneutics and Wittgensteinian philosophy, Steiner deplored the scientistic overtones of transformational analysis: "Cut off from these philosophic traditions, contemptuous of the uncertainties and transcendental intimations which they enact, the new linguistics, with its declared meta-mathematical ideals, runs the risk of a powerful triviality." The same unreflective posture also was liable to thwart "any real access to language when it is in a condition of maximal concentration, when, as Heidegger says, language is total being, that is, to literature." In Steiner's view a philosophical approach could not treat linguistic diversity as purely contingent or incidental: "A comprehensive theory of language — which will also be a theory of man's singular humanity — cannot dismiss the question as pertaining merely to surface features. It is not in transformational grammars, but in hermeneutics, in the *Sprachphilosophie* of Walter Benjamin, with its unashamed roots in kabbalistic thought, that the implications of Babel are grasped."[33]

Regarding Husserl's perspective, its quandaries have been exposed not only by non-phenomenologists but also by later members of the phenomenological movement. Little probing is required to see that his separation of ideal meanings from actual usage, or of apriori structures from empirical processes, resembles the analytical-synthetic distinction criticized by Quine. From a phenomenological vantage point, mild reservations concerning Husserl's early thought were expressed by Maurice Merleau-Ponty in 1951 (in an essay reprinted in *Signs*). "In the fourth of the *Logical Investigations*," Merleau-Ponty noted at the time, "Husserl sets forth the concept of an eidetic of language and a universal grammar which would establish the forms of signification indispensable to every language if it is to be a language, and which would allow us to think with complete clarity about empirical languages as 'confused' realizations of the essential language. This project assumes that language is one of the objects supremely constituted by consciousness, and that actual languages are very special cases of a possible language which consciousness holds the key to" — an assumption preventing language from playing "any other role in respect to thought than that of an accompaniment, substitute, memorandum, or secondary means of communication." In somewhat more pointed terms, a similar criticism was voiced by Ricoeur (in his previously mentioned study). From the angle of a hermeneutics concerned with multivocal meanings, he observed, "the early Husserl, the Husserl who goes from the *Logical Investigations* to the *Cartesian Meditations*, is held in grave suspicion"—at least to the extent that he "only reconstructed a new idealism, close to the neo-Kantianism he fought: the reduction of the thesis of the world is actually a reduction of the question of being to the question of the sense of being." Accordingly, the development of an interpretive semantics required a break with univocal apriorism: "It is thus finally against the early Husserl, against the alternately Platonizing and idealizing tendencies of his theory of meaning and intentionality, that the theory of understanding has been erected."[34]

New Criticism and Neo-Classicism

As the preceding comments and criticisms indicate, the status of exegesis in the rationalist paradigm (broadly construed) was bound to be limited; to the extent that it was cultivated, exegesis was prone to be circumscribed by the concern with meaning invariance, an invariance manifest in meaning contents, literary forms, or underlying structures. This assumption or expectation tends to be borne out in the domains both of literary criticism and political-theoretical interpretation. Within the former domain, Hayden White speaks of an "Inflationary" mode of reading, prevalent largely during the interbellum and early postwar period. A focus on the timeless meaning or form of texts, he notes, intimated "that the literary world was self-contained and self-generating, hovered above other departments of culture and bore little responsibility to them, and finally existed for itself alone—like a Platonic idea or an Aristotelian autotelic form. Criticism in this mode may thus be called *Inflationary*, differing as it did from the Elementary mode by virtue of its theoretical self-consciousness, and from the Reductivist mode by its desire to save the sphere of art from a theoretical grounding in 'mere' life." The chief ambition of "Inflationary" critics, according to White, was "to defend 'literature' against reductivism in all its forms" and to rescue the timeless, "objective" quality of texts: "Instead of the impressionistic methods that had prevailed in the Elementary mode and the pseudoscientific methods used in the Reductivist mode, the methods of the Inflationary critics were to be 'objective'. To be objective, however, meant to treat the artwork as a thing-in-itself, a specifically aesthetic artifact, linked in a number of different ways to its various historical contexts but ultimately governed by its own autotelic principles." He also points to a certain bent to literary "fetishism" and esoteric elitism inherent in this mode: "Their tendency to locate literature within a realm of cultural being which hovered above and gave meaning to 'ordinary human existence' but which was governed by its own autotelic principles did tend to make of literature a mystery which could be unraveled only by the most sensitive initiate into the 'tradition' that provided its context."[35]

In White's portrayal, the sketched exegetic approach was a sprawling movement, comprising such groups as the "New Critics," "transcendental moralists," and "formalists" — all united by the common endeavor "to keep the artwork at a distance from the critic (and the reader)." Among these groups the first mentioned was by all odds the most articulate and influential. Reflected in such works as T. S. Eliot's *The Sacred Wood* (1920) and Cleanth Brooke's *The Well Wrought Urn* (1947), the New Criticism concentrated on texts as self-contained units, sharply segregating their intrinsic literary qualities from extrinsic (social or historical) factors. "The extreme manifestation of the Inflationary attitude," White states, "was that which took shape in the New Critics' efforts to defend their claims of autotelism for the artwork. They progressively sheared away, as interpretatively trivial, the relations which the literary artifact bore to its historical context, its author, and its audience(s)." While New Critics championed aesthetic features, other groups extolled the moral and epistemological dimensions of literature. Thus, practical moralists viewed "the critic's task as that of 'bearing personal testimony' to the aesthetic and moral values contained in the works being studied, but these values were worthy of 'testimony' only insofar as they represented a transcendence of, or alternative to, the values of ordinary human existence"; on the whole, adherents of this outlook "tended toward the identification of 'significant art' with the 'Great Tradition' of Western European literary practice." More concerned with epistemological and technical questions, formalist critics urged their colleagues "to undertake the redescription of the artwork in such a way as to show its generic similarities to other artworks within a given tradition" or genre, insisting that "all literature was either about other literature or about the religious myths that historically preceded and informed every discernible literary tradition." In its attention to underlying (mythical) patterns, formalism was broadly akin to the structuralist or "Generalized" mode of criticism, characterized by "the search for a universal science of humanity, culture, or mind."[36]

Among the groups comprised in the discussed movement White does not specifically include transcendental phenomenology — although elsewhere he alludes to phenomenology's "tendency to elevate human consciousness into the fundamental category of Being-in-general" and "to construe literature as a special case of that 'language' which is consciousness's privileged instrument for conferring meaning on a world that inherently lacks it." Actually, a quasi-Husserlian approach to criticism has emerged in recent decades, marked by a dual emphasis on texts as "ideal" meanings and on the constitutive role of "intentionality"—an intentionality equated not with contingent-empirical motivations but with a deep-seated intent (rooted in a transempirical consciousness). The most prominent spokesman of this approach has been Eric Hirsch, author of such works as *Validity in Interpretation* and *The Aims of Interpretation*. In his writings, Hirsch distinguishes sharply between the mundane "significance" of a text as seen from varying social-historical perspectives and the intrinsic "meaning" of the same text discovered through a quasi-epistemic act of cognition or "re-cognition." Although discussions of concrete relevance and of social-historical contexts may be useful for some purposes, erection of "significance" into an interpretive yardstick is bound to entail skepticism and relativism; only by "bracketing" such mundane considerations, Hirsch holds, is it possible to arrive at an objectively "valid" interpretation, that is, to discover the text's intrinsic "meaning"—a meaning which is in principle "accessible," "determinate," and "unchanging": "To understand an utterance it is, in fact, not just desirable but absolutely unavoidable that we understand it in its own terms. We could not possibly recast a text's meanings in different terms unless we had already understood the text in its own." While thus stressing the text's autonomy, Hirsch departs from New Critics and formalists by treating meaning as "intended" meaning—namely, intended by the author. Relying in part on Husserlian teachings, he construes intention not simply as psychological process but as a faculty of consciousness through which "different intentional acts (on different occasions) 'intend' an *identical* intentional object." In his words, if an interpreter's "claim to validity is to hold, he must be willing to measure his interpretation against a genuinely discriminating norm, and the only compelling normative principle that has ever been brought forward is the old-fashioned ideal of rightly understanding what the author meant."[37]

The sketched exegetic modes have distinct echoes or parallels in the field of political philosophy. In the American context, such parallels—and affinities with the rationalist paradigm in general—are particularly evident in the works of Leo Strauss and in the school of thought associated with his name. Regarding broader affinities a few illustrative comments must suffice here. Despite a deliberate distance from contemporary social-scientific approaches, Strauss's perspective displayed some of the main accents or priorities characterizing structural linguistics and anthropology: above all the preference for timeless patterns (synchrony) over historical events (diachrony), and the rejection of a superficial empiricism in favor of "depth" explication and hidden criteria. With generative grammar his outlook shared the bent toward "innatism"—especially in its derivation from Platonic sources. According to his own admission, however, the most direct inspiration of his thought (among twentieth-century philosophical postures) derived from transcendental phenomenology. Borrowing directly from Husserl's *Philosophy as Rigorous Science*, Strauss launched a vigorous and sustained attack on two main trends of the age—(naturalist) positivism and historicism—mainly because of their enmity to transempirical "essences' and transtemporal insights. Jointly with Husserl and Hirsch (and most structuralists) his arguments strongly emphasized cognitive-epistemic goals. As he wrote in one of his programmatic and most well-known essays: "Philosophy, as quest for wisdom, is quest for universal knowledge, for knowledge of the whole"; and since "of philosophy thus understood, political philosophy is a branch," the latter's chief task was "to replace opinion about the nature of political things by knowledge of the nature of political things." Knowledge of "nature," in this case, signified knowledge of invariant essences or ideal "forms" (as differentiated from matter). By "political regime," he noted in the same essay, we mean accordingly "the order, the form, which gives society its character"—that is, a society's "style of life, its moral taste, form of society, form of government, spirit of laws."[38]

In terms of textual exegesis, the parallels with White's account are equally obvious. In line with axioms of the New Critics, Straussian interpretation stressed the "autotelism" of political-philosophical texts, that is, their autonomy from social-historical contexts. Together with practical moralists, his writings championed perennial values and the timelessness of the "Great Tradition" of theorizing—particularly of the central texts of classical political thought which "viewed man in the light of the unchangeable ideas, that is, of the fundamental and permanent problems." In accord with Hirsch's arguments regarding "validity" in interpretation, Strauss's approach pointedly separated the varying social-historical relevance of texts from their intrinsic and invariant meaning—a meaning accessible through epistemic cognition. "Political philosophy is not a historical discipline," he observed at one point; for, "the question of the nature of political things and the answer to it cannot possibly be mistaken for the question of how this or that philosopher or all philosophers have approached, discussed or answered the philosophic question mentioned." While not devoid of interest for some purposes, awareness of the "variety of political institutions and convictions in different countries and at different times" could by no means serve as a substitute for essential insight: "However important historical knowledge may be for political philosophy, it is only preliminary and auxiliary to political philosophy; it does not form an integral part of it." A correct grasp of textual meaning was independent not only of information about social-historical conditions, but also of the interpreter's varying concerns; especially in the case of classical philosophy, the text had definite primacy or preeminence over the reader's exegetic contributions—a primacy encouraging, by and large, a canonical-receptive (over a critically reconstructive) mode of interpretation.[39]

While stressing the autonomy of textual meanings, however, Strauss refused to sever text and author—provided the latter was viewed not merely in a mundane-biographical sense. Again in agreement with Hirsch, he actually treated authorial intent as the ultimate exegetical yardstick: "An adequate interpretation is such an interpretation as understands the thought of a philosopher exactly as he understood it himself"; for, "if we abandon this goal, we abandon the only practicable criterion of 'objectivity' in the history of thought." Yet, in Strauss's presentation, authorial intent was by no means synonymous with surface meanings discernible at a first glance; rather, to uncover the author's point it was regularly necessary to penetrate surface features in the direction of a deep-seated and more hidden intent. Particularly in troubled times or under repressive regimes, he argued, political texts were likely to exhibit hidden or esoteric modes of communication. As he stated in another context: "Persecution, then, gives rise to a peculiar technique of writing, and therewith to a peculiar type of literature, in which the truth about all crucial things is presented exclusively between the lines. That literature is addressed, not to all readers, but to trustworthy and intelligent readers only." To some extent, this accent on a hidden authorial intent—accessible only to the particularly astute or initiated—has become a hallmark of Straussian exegesis; its quandaries have not gone unnoticed. While undoubtedly legitimate in repressive circumstances, an indiscriminate reliance on concealed meanings may foster whimsical and (in principle) nonrefutable claims—as critics have pointed out.[40] Independently of authorial intent, the notion of perennial meanings embodied in canonical texts itself invites critical scrutiny. Thus, pointing to possible doctrinaire overtones, John Gunnell recently observed that, as defended by neoclassicists and other political theorists in mid-century, "the idea of the tradition has been articulated, elaborated, and finally transformed into what must be termed the myth of the tradition."[41]

Conservatism and Radicalism

Regarding the formulation and active sponsorship of political ideas, the discussed epistemological framework has engendered divergent (if not antithetical) perspectives. Approached straightforwardly, the focus on timeless texts and invariant structures or meanings seems to foster an aversion to historical flux and a predilection for political stability. To the extent that the modern era is marked by an ever-accelerating process of change and innovation, one might even expect among theorists wedded to the framework a pronounced anti-modernism or backward-looking conservatism. Within certain (narrow) confines, this expectation is not entirely misplaced. Thus, although disavowing direct political preferences, Strauss in several of his writings was a severe critic of the "modern project"; also, in commenting favorably on the "classical solution" to politics, he noted that "the classics rejected democracy because they thought that the aim of human life, and hence social life, is not freedom but virtue" and that "the order most conducive to virtue is the aristocratic republic, or else the mixed regime."[42] Similarly, a primary accent on meaning invariance has doubtless encouraged conservative leanings among some Husserlian (or post-Husserlian) phenomenologists. Yet, the expectation of symmetry can also be misleading; a case in point is the founder of the phenomenological movement himself. Although devoting a lifetime to the study of essences, Husserl considered himself basically a "radical" thinker in continuity with Enlightenment and Kantian ideas; rigorously performed, he believed, the phenomenological *epoché* (or method of "bracketing") was bound to erode conventional opinions and prejudices. Some of his followers later broadened his philosophical radicalism, extending it to the sphere of social and economic conditions—an extension exemplified in the thought of Enzo Paci whose *Function of the Sciences and the Meaning of Man* invoked Husserlian premises for the goal of broad-scale social reconstruction.[43]

A similar ambivalence prevails in the field of linguistics and structural anthropology. Given the concentration on permanent depth patterns, structuralism may seem naturally akin to a static political outlook; in fact, notions like "structure" and "code" have occasionally been invoked by political thinkers as stabilizing factors or as roadblocks to social and political experimentation. This, however, is not the complete picture. As is well known, Lévi-Strauss has expressed broad (though qualified) sympathies for Marxism—sympathies which blossomed into a full-fledged structuralist Marxism in the writings of Louis Althusser. More generally, at least in the French setting, structuralist analyses have tended to be associated with a left-leaning radicalism in politics.[44] Instead of surveying the structuralist panorama, however, I would like to limit myself here to one prominent American example: the work of Noam Chomsky. Apart from being a leading linguist, Chomsky also has published extensively on domestic and international political questions—as witnessed in books like *American Power and the New Mandarins, At War with Asia,* and *For Reasons of State.* On the whole, his political outlook can be described as a radical liberalism or progressivism, mixed with a dose of democratic socialism and intermittent traces of syndicalism and even anarchism. As he expressed his vision at one point: "The laws of our nature will achieve their fullest expression in a society of free and creative producers, linked by social bonds in a system of voluntary association." The socialist and anarchist ingredients in this vision are highlighted in *For Reasons of State*, where we read that the consistent anarchist would be "a socialist, but a socialist of a particular sort. He will not only oppose alienated and specialized labor and look forward to the appropriation of capital by the whole body of workers, but he will also insist that this appropriation be direct, not exercised by some elite force acting in the name of the proletariat." The same study quotes approvingly Bakunin's comment: "I am a fanatic lover of liberty," a liberty "that consists in the full development of all of the material, intellectual and moral powers that are latent in each person" and "recognizes no restrictions other than those determined by the laws of our own individual nature."[45]

As captured in these and similar statements, Chomsky's political views obviously are quite close to Bertrand Russell's — notwithstanding their pronounced epistemological differences. Chomsky in fact has paid tribute to the British philosopher in his "Russell Lectures" delivered in Cambridge in 1971. "While Russell's intellectual achievements remain a delight to the inquiring mind," he said in opening his lectures, "it is what Erich Fromm perceptively calls his renewal of the 'Promethean function in his own life' that will continue to inspire those who hope to be citizens of a free community." He also expressed his appreciation and gratitude for Russell's political initiatives, an appreciation that "can be shared by all those who value reason, liberty, and justice, who are captivated by Russell's vision of 'the world that we must seek', a world in which the creative spirit is alive, in which life is an adventure full of joy and hope, based rather upon the impulse to construct than upon the desire to retain what we possess or to seize what is possessed by others." In the course of his lectures Chomsky even had praise for aspects of Russell's empiricist epistemology — but he also voiced strong reservations. Connecting cognitive and political dimensions, he actually intimated that Russell's political views might more consistently have been based on rationalist or innatist premises than on an empiricist "blank tablet." "The image of a mind, initially unconstrained, striking out freely in arbitrary directions," he observed, "suggests at first glance a richer and more hopeful view of human freedom and creativity, but I think that this conclusion is mistaken." What empiricism neglected was that "the principles of mind provide the scope as well as the limits of human creativity. Without such principles, scientific understanding and creative acts would not be possible." As he added: "It is the intrinsic principles of mind that should be the object of our awe and, if possible, our inquiry. In investigating some of the most familiar achievements of human intelligence — the ordinary use of language, for example — we are struck at once by their creative character, by the character of free creation within a system of rules." Thus, "I think it is fair to say that it is the humanistic conception of man that is advanced and given substance as we discover the rich systems of invariant structures and principles that underlie the most ordinary and humblest of human accomplishments."[46]

Chomsky's political views have been challenged from many quarters; the most forceful attack can be found in a recent book by Geoffrey Sampson entitled *Liberty and Language*. As a fellow-linguist, Sampson largely endorses Chomsky's technical-linguistic premises or theses, especially as they relate to transformational grammar; what he criticizes, however, is the derivation of Chomskyan politics from these premises and, more importantly, the restrictiveness of his conception of both language and politics. "In his professional work," he writes, "Chomsky considers only one narrow aspect of human language (namely, syntax)—a strategy of research which, from the academic point of view, is perfectly proper and sensible." Yet, a consideration of "the semantic side of language," that is, "of the ways in which utterances convey meaning," leads to "a view of human nature which is sharply at variance with Chomsky's, and which suggests that political ideals very different from Chomsky's are the appropriate ones. Chomsky claims that syntax refutes liberalism, but the claim fails; Chomsky ignores semantics, and semantics strongly supports liberalism." A terminological reminder is in order here: "liberalism" in Sampson's usage is not a synonym for social-economic progressivism but rather for the doctrine of "free enterprise" (as championed, for example, by Friedrich Hayek). Laissez-faire economics, in his view, fosters and supports a multitude of individual initiatives, just as "semantics" deals with a variety of meanings or meanings contents. Turning against a purely syntactical approach, the study notes the paradoxical, and possibly conservative, implications of the thesis of a fixed human nature. "The essence of Chomsky's particular brand of rationalist politics," we read, "is that human behavior should not be controlled by governments because human nature is fixed rather than adaptable." So, if people are by nature "moderately selfish," then "we must on Chomsky's premises conclude (as many of us would conclude independently of Chomsky) that people will go on being moderately selfish and caring more for their family than for others in any future society." On the other hand, if (as Chomsky prefers to think) people are naturally unselfish and responsible, then why the need for politics—and why the fear that "the prospect of his political ideal being realized is a remote one?"[47]

To be sure, Sampson is not the first to notice the difficulties involved in linking politics with a determinate "human nature." Hannah Arendt has made the same point repeatedly in her writings; but it probably deserves restating. I do not wish to support in any manner the doctrinaire laissez-faire outlook espoused in Sampson's book; however, I find sensible his arguments regarding the nondeductive character of politics. The fact that human thought is syntactically circumscribed, he affirms, "despite its great interest for the psychologist and logician, is of no relevance for the political liberal; syntax provides merely the framework on which to hang any idea, novel or well-known, useful or pointless." A similar view was expressed more eloquently by George Steiner. "Chomsky," he wrote (in my view correctly), "is an exhilarating thinker, possessed as was Spinoza before him, by a passionate appetite for unity, for complete logic and explanation. There is a common bond of monism in Chomsky's desire to get to the root of things, be they political or linguistic. But it might be, to advance a cautionary platitude, that neither politics nor language is quite like that. Unreason and the obstinate disorder of local fact may prove resistant to the claims of either political justice or formal logic. It is part of the stature of Chomsky's work that the issues of disagreement raised by it are basic."[48]

4

Ordinary Language and Existentialism: Verbal Praxis

Favus mellis composita verba . . .

Compared with its former preeminence, epistemology today is no longer the undisputed linchpin of philosophical inquiry; both in its empiricist and its rationalist versions, its status has been challenged and eroded during the past several decades by a host of other philosophical concerns. Some of these challenges I have outlined in preceding chapters. Thus, in the empiricist domain, Sellar's attack on the "myth of the given" and defense of theoretical holism signaled a radical disenchantment with the elementaristic premises of logical atomism; similarly, Quine's critique of the analytic-synthetic bifurcation unsettled central tenets of the logical-positivist paradigm. In the rationalist camp, reference has been made to Geertz's and Steiner's rejoinders to structuralism and transformational grammar, and also to the growing disaffection with Husserlian idealism among spokesmen of the phenomenological movement. With regard to language, the chief preoccupation of epistemology was (as indicated) with "meanings," and more specifically with the univocal fixation of meanings—a fixation accomplished either by tying meanings to empirical referents or else by rooting them in syntactical structures or universal mental capacities. If we adopt the tripartition of "sign functions" associated with the names of Peirce and Morris—and recently revived by Karl-Otto Apel—the focus of epistemologists was primarily on syntactics and a narrowly construed (logical or referential) semantics, to the virtual exclusion of "pragmatics" or the role of natural speakers. Against this background the dethronement of epistemology involves essentially a reversal or at least rearrangement of the hierarchy of sign functions, a hierarchy variously reflected in the discussed priorities of *langue* over *parole*, of competence over performance, of ideal *noema* over *noesis*, and (more generally) of cognition over practice. In Hacking's terminology, this rearrangement is at the core of the shift from meanings to the "Heyday of Sentences," a period marked by attentiveness to human discourse, dialogue, and speech.

Although dramatic in the context of our century, the turn to speech is not entirely an innovation of our time, but can invoke time-honored

86

philosophical precedents. In his study of the "idea of language" in Renaissance and Baroque thought, Apel discusses at some length the perspective of "rhetorical humanism," a perspective drawing its inspiration both from Aristotelian "practical philosophy" and from Greek and Roman rhetorical traditions. The term "rhetoric" in Apel's usage refers not simply (or not exclusively) to techniques of verbal persuasion, but more broadly to ordinary speech and commonsense argumentation; instead of denoting a specialized tool of cognition, language from this vantage point serves as medium of everyday interaction and communication in a given life-world. Seen as a commonsense medium, rhetorical language has always been held in suspicion by epistemologists and professional philosophers. Thus, equating rhetoric with the "skill of public speaking," Leo Strauss asserts that "classical political philosophy rejected the identification of political science with rhetoric; it held that rhetoric, at its best, was only an instrument of political science." Buttressing the contrast by appealing to the distinction between *doxa* and *episteme*, he adds that ordinary political thought or discourse "is, as such, indifferent to the distinction between opinion and knowledge" while "political philosophy is the conscious, coherent and relentless effort to replace opinions about the political fundamentals by knowledge about them." Following in the footsteps of rhetorical humanism, the contemporary turn to speech and "sentences" is bound to mollify or cast doubt on this dichotomy. Among others, Hannah Arendt has referred to the "intramural warfare" between philosophy and common sense, a strife bridged by the imperative of linguistic communication. "In contrast to cognitive activities that may use thinking as one of their instruments," she wrote, philosophical reflection "needs speech not only to sound out and become manifest" but "to be activated at all. And since speech is enacted in sequences of sentences," reflection cannot consist in "some piece of self-evidence beheld in speechless contemplation."[1]

Attentiveness to speech and communication, to be sure, does not dictate a uniform theoretical mold, but permits a range of diverse accents — of which I can present here only a selective sample. In line with the modern heritage of philosophical subjectivity, contemporary theories of speech and rhetoric place a relatively strong emphasis on individual speakers seen as agents in communicative exchanges. This general focus, in turn, allows for divergent construals or assessments, depending on the concrete significance assigned to speech performance and agency. On the one hand, speakers may be viewed — in a straightforward or "commonsensical" fashion — as mundane-empirical actors operating in empirical social settings or contexts; on the other hand, approached from a more reflective (or "humanistic") vantage point, speech performance may be regarded as a properly "constitutive" or creative activity and even as a mode of self-enactment. By and large, and making due allowance for crossovers and reciprocal influences, the two options characterize respectively the dominant Anglo-American and Continental perspectives in this domain—perspectives customarily designated by the summary labels of "ordinary language analysis" and "existentialism." In terms of the genesis of linguistic meaning, the latter framework tends to stress individual intentionality and a purposive-individual "pragmatics," while the former accentuates contextual rules and meaning patterns. As Michael Shapiro observes, in his *Language and Political Understanding*, the assumption of linguistic analysts is not "that any given speaker arbitrarily employs rules to suit his or her purposes and thereby moves about in a world of personally constituted objects and events"; rather, their view is "that the language used by a society or culture contains rules which provide boundaries around phenomena and thereby produce the objects and events that are the referents of our speech."[2] In the following I shall sketch briefly some of the main arguments advanced by spokesmen of the two frameworks; in doing so I intend to move—as in the preceding chapter—along a spectrum leading from relatively empiricist to more reflective-humanist formulations.

How To Do Things With Words: Austin

In Anglo-American thought, the initial shift to speech and ordinary discourse is connected primarily with the names of Wittgenstein and John Austin, the founders respectively of the Cambridge and Oxford "schools" of linguistic analysis. In the case of Wittgenstein, the paradigm shift was particularly striking and noticeable—mainly because his earlier works (foremost among them the *Tractatus* of 1921) had espoused a brand of positivism or logical empiricism tied to the axiom of a logically purified language. His lectures and seminars offered in Cambridge during the interbellum and early postwar years signaled a progressive distantiation from positivist premises, a rift which finally culminated in 1953 in the publication of *Philosophical Investigations*. The latter study has been generally acclaimed (rightly I think) as a landmark in twentieth-century philosophy—but its teachings are exceedingly complex, multifaceted, and elusive. In terms of linguistic approach, two tenets of the study are customarily singled out as original Wittgensteinian contributions: namely, first, that the meaning of words and sentences is determined by their "use"; and secondly, that the proper use of words and sentences is in turn dependent on linguistic context or the relevant "language game." Viewed as broad guideposts or direction signals, the two tenets encapsulate unquestionably the most distinctive characteristics of "ordinary language analysis"; but closer inspection quickly reveals quandaries and complications—involving, for instance, the relation between meaning and use and the concept of games as "rule-governed" practices. For present purposes, the main lesson to be derived from the dual emphasis on usage and linguistic context is its corrosive effect on "verificationism" or the positivist meaning criterion. In Shapiro's words, the crucial significance of Wittgenstein's later linguistic theory resides not only "in its capacity to illuminate and account for the various functions for which language is employed in statements other than descriptions, but also [in] its account of simple descriptions in which we are shown that the word-object relationship is based upon tacit presuppositions rather than on simple correspondence."[3]

In comparison with the complexity of Wittgenstein's arguments, Austin's approach to language is more methodical and also more straightforwardly "pragmatic"—for which reason I shall concentrate on his work. Among Austin's writings none has exerted a stronger and more pervasive impact than his posthumously published study *How To Do Things With Words* (containing a set of lectures presented at Harvard in 1955). In large measure, the title of the study already announced its program or distinctive outlook, in the sense that the accent was placed on the pragmatics of language, that is, on language use as a mode of action, and more specifically as a linguistic act or "speech act." The same accent implied a break with logical-empiricist epistemology and its preponderant focus on the description and explanation of factual conditions. "For too long," Austin wrote, it was "the assumption of philosophers that the business of a 'statement' can only be to 'describe' some state of affairs, or to 'state some fact', which it must do either truly or falsely." Although grammarians frequently "pointed out that not all 'sentences' are (used in making) 'statements'," such views were usually downplayed or sidestepped by philosophers. "But now in recent years," he added, "many things which would once have been accepted without question as 'statements' by both philosophers and grammarians have been scrutinized with new care"—a scrutiny which entailed a direct challenge to the empiricist "view, not always formulated without unfortunate dogmatism, that a statement (of fact) ought to be 'verifiable'," and that other statements are "only what may be called pseudo-statements." As a result of this scrutiny, "it has come to be seen that many specially perplexing words embedded in apparently descriptive statements do not serve to indicate some specially odd additional feature in the reality reported, but to indicate (not to report) the circumstances in which the statement is made"—a realization implying "that the occasion of an utterance matters seriously, and that the words used are to some extent to be 'explained' by the 'context' in which they are designed to be or have actually been spoken in a linguistic exchange." However inchoate or ill-defined such notions may be, the study stated, "it cannot be doubted that they are producing a revolution in philosophy"; and "if anyone wishes to call it the greatest and most salutary in its history, this is not, if you come to think of it, a large claim."[4]

Moving beyond the confines of the empiricist paradigm, Austin initially introduced the distinction between two basic types of sentences or utterances, termed respectively "constative" and "performative" utterances —of which the former was said to report a given state of affairs, while the latter was more directly tied to conduct. The term "performative," he elaborated, "is derived, of course, from 'perform', the usual verb with the noun 'action': it indicates that the issuing of the utterance is the performing of an action—it is not normally thought of as just saying something." At least in their explicit form (and making due allowances for unusual circumstances), performative utterances were expressions of concrete individual agents; in grammatical terms, they typically were couched in the "first person singular present indicative active." In the words of the study: "Actions can only be performed by persons, and obviously in our cases the utterer must be the performer: hence our justifiable feeling in favor of the 'first person', who must come in, being mentioned or referred to; moreover, if the utterer is acting, he must be doing something—hence our perhaps ill-expressed favoring of the grammatical present and grammatical active of the verb. There is something which is *at the moment of uttering being done by the person uttering*." Apart from the linkage of "performatives" with conduct, the main difference between the two types of utterances resided in their respective standard of success or adequacy—which in one instance coincided with the "true-false" criterion and in the other with the propriety, adeptness, or "felicity" of the utterance, that is, with the proper meshing of speech and context. "Besides the uttering of the words of the so-called performative," we read, "a good many other things have as a general rule to be right or to go right if we are to be said to have happily brought off our action. What these are we may hope to discover by looking at the classifying types of cases in which something *goes wrong*." When this happens and linguistic conduct fails to reach its aim, "the utterance is then, we may say, not indeed false but in general *unhappy*. And for this reason we call the doctrine of *the things that can be and go wrong* on the occasion of such utterances, the doctrine of the *Infelicities*."[5]

Although plausible at a first glance, the initial bifurcation of utterances soon turned out to be unsatisfactory for a number of reasons. While ostensibly registering states of affairs, Austin noted, constative sentences were also regulary linked with conduct, namely, the conduct of reporting, stating, or asserting. The bifurcation was further blurred if attention was shifted from explicit utterances or formulations to the level of

more "primitive" or "primary" modes of speech—the level on which ordinary or everyday discourse is normally conducted and where language
use "is not precise" and "also not, in our sense, explicit." On this level
it could readily be seen that utterances overlap and that "very commonly
the *same* sentence is used on different occasions of utterance in *both*
ways, performative and constative." The blurring of boundaries also affected the relevant standards of success; for, "if we think of the alleged
contrast, according to which performatives are happy or unhappy and
statements true or false," we readily find "that statements *are* liable to
every kind of infelicity to which performatives are liable." In light of
these and similar difficulties the study opted in favor of the broader
category of "speech acts," a category comprising distinct elements or
components—chiefly the components of "locution" and "illocution"—
whose differentiation was one of situational or pragmatic emphasis. In
this parlance, locutions or "locutionary acts" involved the "performance
of an act *of* saying something," while illocutions or "illocutionary
acts"—stressing the pragmatic mode of speech—consisted in the "performance of an act *in* saying something." The chief point was the intimate
connection of the two components in ordinary discourse or communication: "To perform a locutionary act is in general, we may say, also and
eo ipso to perform an illocutionary act"; at a closer look, "the locutionary act as much as the illocutionary is an abstraction only: every genuine speech act is both." Instead of being radically segregated, Austin
suggested, the initially stipulated types of utterances simply accentuated
different facets of speech acts: "With the constative utterance, we
abstract from the illocutionary aspects of the speech act, and we concentrate on the locutionary," whereas in performative utterances we
highlight the illocutionary component, abstracting "from the dimension
of correspondence with facts."[6]

According to Austin, attention to the components of speech acts required a modification or amplification of the empiricist meaning criterion, tied to the Fregean notions of "sense" and "reference"—by making
room for the pragmatic "force" of utterances or the manner in which an
utterance is "to be taken." As he wrote: "I want to distinguish *force* and
meaning in the sense in which meaning is equivalent to sense and reference, just as it has become essential to distinguish sense and reference
within meaning." By heeding the pragmatic function of speech acts, he
added, it became feasible to differentiate or classify discursive modes in
terms of the particular "*illocutionary forces* of an utterance." The classification or typology proposed in the study included mainly five broad
rubrics: namely, "verdictives" involving the "giving of a verdict" such as
"an estimate, reckoning, or appraisal"; "exercitives" implying the exercise of certain "powers, rights, or influence"; "commissives" embracing

acts of promising, announcements of intentions, espousals, and the like; "behabitives" having to do with "attitudes and social behavior" such as commending, condoling, and challenging; and lastly "expositives" or expository phrases "making plain how our utterances fit into the course of an argument or conversation." As Austin made clear, the preceding list was exceedingly tentative and by no means to be taken as a rigorous or exhaustive typology of speech acts ("I am far from equally happy about all of them" and "am not putting any of this forward as in the very least definitive"). What was particularly important to remember, for purposes of a pragmatics of speech, was that all the proposed types—though in different ways—exhibited a close interconnection of force and meaning and also of the "true-false" and "happy-unhappy" standards of discourse. "It is essential to realize," the study concluded, "that 'true' and 'false', like 'free' and 'unfree', do not stand for anything simple at all; but only for a general dimension of being a right or proper thing to say as opposed to a wrong thing, in these circumstances, to this audience, for these purposes and with these intentions."[7]

Speech-Act Theory: Searle

Since the first publication of Austin's lectures, ordinary language analysis has been cultivated by a large number of philosophers, including both the members of his original Oxford circle and other Anglo-American thinkers exposed to his teachings; easily the most innovative and influential representative of the latter group is John Searle. On the whole, Searle shares Austin's pragmatic inclinations and his reservations regarding earlier empiricist epistemology—although in some respects he has modified (and occasionally moderated) his teacher's pragmatic approach. Broadly speaking, a chief difference between the two thinkers resides in the relatively more systematic and comprehensive character of Searle's work: his ambition not only to offer an analysis and taxonomy of selective utterances but to delineate a general philosophy of language. This ambition is clearly evident in a publication of 1970—probably his most well-known book—entitled *Speech Acts: An Essay in the Philosophy of Language*. As the author emphasized at the very outset, his study was not simply an exercise in "linguistic philosophy," construed as "the attempt to solve particular philosophical problems by attending to the ordinary use of particular words or other elements in a particular language"; rather, it was meant as a contribution to the "philosophy of language" seen as the effort "to give philosophically illuminating descriptions of certain general features of language, such as reference, truth, meaning, and necessity." The basic thesis or hypothesis animating the study was that language is essentially a "rule-governed intentional" activity and that, in particular, "speaking a language is engaging in a (highly complex) rule-governed form of behavior"; the specific shape this hypothesis took in the book was that "speaking a language is performing speech acts" and that "these acts are in general made possible by and are performed in accordance with certain rules for the use of linguistic elements." Countering assumptions prevalent among some linguists and semanticists, Searle asserted firmly that "the unit of linguistic communication is not, as has generally been supposed, the symbol, word or sentence, or even the token of the symbol, word or sentence, but rather the production or issuance of the symbol or word or sentence in the performance of the speech act. To take the token as a message is to take it as a produced or issued token." Highlighting the pragmatic thrust of this formulation he added: "If my conception of language is correct, a theory of language is part of a theory of action."[8]

I do not propose to review here in detail the arguments of *Speech Acts* (mainly because of the diversity of topics covered in the study); I merely wish to pick out a few main points or ingredients. Building on Austin's very tentative taxonomy, Searle at the time differentiated between four types of linguistic acts (or speech components); namely, "utterance acts" involving simply the uttering of words; "propositional acts" referring to or predicating a state of affairs; "illocutionary acts" consisting in the use of performative verbs; and "perlocutionary acts" concerned with the effects of speech on hearers. Austin's comments on standards of success served as backdrop and inspiration for a more elaborate specification of criteria or conditions for gauging the illocutionary "force" and successful execution of purposive utterances. Central among these criteria were "preparatory rules" referring generally to speech situations and speaker-hearer relations; "propositional content rules" linking speech to given states of affairs; "sincerity rules" pertaining to the intention and commitment of speakers; and "essential rules" indicating what kind of utterance counts as a particular speech act. Austin's teachings—though bent into a more epistemological and empiricist direction—are present also in broader theoretical facets of the study; this is particularly true of the interconnection between "force" and "meaning" and between speech and linguistic or semantic rules. Notwithstanding the stress on pragmatics and action theory, *Speech Acts* did not simply invert the linguistic priority scheme by substituting *parole* for *langue*: "I am arguing that an adequate study of speech acts is a study of *langue*." This contention was intimately related to the status of "meanings" in the Fregean sense. Opposing the bifurcation between pragmatic function and semantic meaning, Searle affirmed that "a study of the meaning of sentences is not in principle distinct from a study of speech acts. Properly construed they are the same study." This thesis in turn was backed up by the so-called "principle of expressibility"—specifically devised by Searle—which holds that "whatever can be meant can be said" and which, to a degree, revived or recaptured the epistemological concern with literalness and univocity of meanings.[9]

The relationship of meaning and function and its relevance for the status of speech acts has been further elaborated by Searle in subsequent writings, particularly in his *Expression and Meaning: Studies in the Theory of Speech Acts* (1979). To some extent, the book signaled a departure or relative assertion of autonomy from the original founders of ordinary language analysis—a departure manifest both in various specific criticisms and also in the larger philosophical ambition of the work. The criticisms had to do mainly with the issue of taxonomy or classification, one of the focal preoccupations of *Expression and Meaning*. Countering Wittgenstein's doubts regarding the enumeration of "how many kinds of sentence" there are, Searle found in such skepticism grounds "to arouse our suspicion"; for "why should language be more taxonomically recalcitrant than any other aspect of human social life?" Turning to *How To Do Things With Words*, Searle identified a number of "weaknesses" in Austin's typology of speech acts, and primarily the following: that "there is a persistent confusion between verbs and acts" (not all verbs being illocutionary verbs); that "there is too much overlap of the categories"; and most importantly, that "there is no consistent principle of classification." The larger philosophical ambition was reflected in the aim—only adumbrated in *Expression and Meaning*—to develop a "general theory of meaning," a theory demonstrating the moorings of language philosophy in the "philosophy of mind" and in particular the grounding of "certain features of speech acts" in the "intentionality of the mind." This reliance on intentionality—a grounding probably more solid and specific than envisaged in earlier linguistic analysis—was not designed to rupture the linkage between function and meaning or "intention" and "convention," that is, the general dependence of purposive speech on semantic background rules. As the study noted, even literal meaning "is dependent on context in the same way that other non-conventional forms of intentionality are dependent on context, and there is no way to eliminate the dependence in the case of literal meaning which would not break the connections with other forms of intentionality and hence would eliminate the intentionality of literal meaning altogether."[10]

The taxonomy of speech acts presented in the study in large part reflected the notion of contextually circumscribed intentions. In searching for a consistent principle (or set of principles) of classification, Searle initially reviewed a large number of scales or criteria in terms of which utterances could be differentiated — but ended up by concentrating on three or four. One of these criteria related to "differences in the point or purpose" of speech acts or the intent animating their performance; covered by the term "essential rules (or conditions)" in the earlier study, this aspect was now termed "illocutionary point." A second criterion resided in "differences in the direction of fit between words and the world" — where "direction of fit" referred to two types of "matching": "Some illocutions have as a part of their illocutionary point to get the words (more strictly, their propositional content) to match the world, others to get the world to match the words." A third dimension involved "differences in expressed psychological states," that is, in speaker's attitudes and commitments — an aspect earlier designated as "sincerity rule (or condition)." Although Searle proposed to "build most of my taxonomy" around these three features, at least one further criterion deserves mention: one referring to differences in speech situations and speaker-hearer relations (earlier called "preparatory conditions"). Relying on the mentioned yardsticks, the study delineated five main types of illocutionary acts, labelled respectively "assertives," "directives," "commissives," "expressives," and "declaratives." According to Searle, the illocutionary point of the first type is to "assert" a given state of affairs in line with traditional "true-false" standards; animated psychologically by "belief," the performance of such acts seeks to match "words to the world." In the second type, the speaker basically attempts "to get the hearer to do something," an attempt motivated psychologically by want or desire and aiming at a "world-to-words" fit. The point of the third type is "to commit the speaker to some future course of action," a course guided by a deliberate "intention" and again by the aim to match "world-to-words." In "expressives" the speaker simply manifests his prevailing "psychological state," without trying either "to get the world to match the words" or "the words to match the world." The last category finally embraces cases where changes in a given state of affairs are brought about solely by the performance of speech acts and where "word-world" matchings occur simultaneously in both directions "because of the peculiar character of declarations."[11]

Radical Existentialism: Sartre

In its stress on speaker's intention or "intentionality" and also on linguistic "expressiveness," *Expression and Meaning* carried at least subdued overtones of a reflective-humanist posture — a posture which has been the hallmark of Continental existentialism and existential phenomenology. In the context of the phenomenological "movement," the rise of existentialism involved primarily a distantiation from Husserl's transcendental epistemology, that is, an attempt to recover the living and acting human being behind or beyond purely cognitive operations. To this extent, existentialism—like ordinary language analysis—heralded a "pragmatic turn" designed as a correction to the syntactical and logical-semantic preoccupations of the earlier phase of "meanings."[12] Notwithstanding this mutual affinity, however, Continental thought differs from linguistic philosophy by virtue of the less empiricist (and also less methodical and academic) character of its arguments: instead of focusing on mundane-psychological motivations, these arguments typically accentuate a broadly experiential and "existential" dimension—where "existence" denotes not so much an empirical condition as a categorial and ontological structure of experience. As in the case of ordinary language theory, the existentalist departure from epistemology was initially very tentative and halting, gathering momentum only gradually in the course of several decades. This philosophical continuity is particularly evident in Jean-Paul Sartre's early writings (and I shall limit myself here entirely to his early work): although bent on a pragmatic-existential reformulation of phenomenology, Sartre at the time retained as a central premise Husserl's category of "transcendental consciousness"—a category now construed as a synonym for human "freedom" and as the ultimate source of human actions and intentional "projects." This emphasis on transcendental freedom also had implications for the status of language. Instead of denoting a preestablished arsenal of rules and symbolic meanings, language—or purposive language use—was seen as a mode of human action, and more specifically as a means of creative self-expression through speech.

The connection between language use and creativity is eloquently portrayed in the chapter on "Freedom" in Sartre's *Being and Nothingness: An Essay on Phenomenological Ontology* (1943). As the chapter noted, lingusitic philosophy and research tend to concentrate on pregiven rules or symbols, but the approach is misleading: "Statistics bring to light constants, phonetic or semantic changes of a given type; they allow us to reconstruct the evolution of a phoneme or a morpheme in a given period so that it appears that the *word* or the *syntactical rule* is an individual reality with its own meaning and history." What renders this appearance misleading is the abstract character of isolated linguistic elements. Actually, the chapter continued, psychologists have for some time "observed that the *word* is not the concrete element of speech" and that "the elementary structure of speech is the *sentence*. It is within the sentence, in fact, that the word can receive a real function as a designation." Thus, the individual word "has only a purely *virtual* existence outside of complex and active organizations which integrate it; it cannot exist 'in' a consciousness or an unconscious *before* the use which is made of it." According to Sartre, however, these considerations apply not only to words but to sentences as well. Sentences in turn, we read, "are mere commonplaces if they are looked at from the outside by a reader who recomposes the paragraph by passing from one sentence to the next, but they lose their banal and conventional character if they are placed within the point of view of the author who saw *the thing* (or point) *to be expressed* and who attended to the most pressing things first by producing an act of designation or re-creation without slowing down to consider the very elements of this act. If this is true, then neither the words nor the syntax nor the 'ready-made sentences' pre-exist the use which is made of them." Against this background, language use emerges as an exercise of freedom, more precisely, as the outgrowth of a "transcendental consciousness" manifesting itself in a free "project" or intentionality: "Since the verbal unit is the meaningful sentence, the latter is a constructive act which is purely conceived by a transcendence surpassing and nihilating the given toward an end."[13]

As presented in *Being and Nothingness*, language thus is governed and animated by purposive speech, the latter seen as an act of meaning-constitution and, more importantly, an act of the speaker's self-constitution and self-disclosure. "If the sentence pre-exists the word," the study affirmed, "then we are referred to the *speaker* as the concrete foundation of his speech." Viewed from the speaker's side, language is not simply a conglomeration of factual elements but a means of transgressing factual constellations in the direction of an uncharted future: "The sentence is a project which can be interpreted only in terms of the nihilation of a given state of affairs (the state one wishes to *designate*) in light of a posited end (its *designation* which itself supposes other ends in relation to which it is only a means)." If, however, a given condition "cannot determine the sentence any more than a word can," if on the contrary the sentence is required "to illuminate the given and to make the word understandable," then the sentence (or speech performance) is "a moment of the free choice of myself, and it is as such that it is understood by my companion." Intersubjective discourse, from this vantage point, emerges as an intersection of free projects or as an encounter (and empathetic reconstruction) of transcendental acts: "To understand a sentence spoken by my companion is, in fact, to understand what he 'means'—that is, to espouse his movement of transcendence, to throw myself with him toward possibles, toward ends, and to return again to the ensemble of organized means so as to understand them by their function and their end." Accordingly, for both speakers and hearers discursive exchanges involve simultaneously acts of creative self-disclosure and the reenactment of creative intentions—a reenactment particularly important in the case of ordinary idiomatic expressions: "If language is realized in speech, and if dialect or natural idiom constitutes the concreteness of language, then concrete idiomatic speech is the *free act* of designation by which I choose myself as designating agent; and this free act cannot be an *assembling* of words."[14]

In focusing on creative speech, *Being and Nothingness* does not entirely shunt aside the role of situational contexts or of syntactical and semantic rules. As Sartre explicitly recognizes, spoken language "is always interpreted in terms of the situation" and hearers "must understand *in terms of the world*." The accentuation of self-disclosure, he acknowledges, may seem to endorse a worldless intentionality; but actually "we do not thereby suppress the necessary *technical* connections nor the connections *in fact* which are articulated in the sentence." What the study opposes at this point is not so much the notion of contextual or linguistic rules as the view, sponsored by some linguists and epistemologists, that there is a self-contained language or *langue* representing the "impersonal life of the logos." The fault or flaw in this view, we read, is that it tries to "take speech which is dead (that is, already spoken) and infuse it with an impersonal life and force" which actually has been "borrowed from the personal freedom of the 'for-itself' which spoke; thus people have made of speech a *language which speaks all by itself*." From Sartre's perspective, by contrast, contextual and linguistic rules can indeed be detected and analyzed—but only retroactively and from the "outside," that is, from a third person's (rather than the speaker's) angle. The so-called "laws of language," he writes, really exist "not for the one who speaks but for the one who listens"; accordingly, speech "which is a free project *for me*, has specific laws *for others*." Even such externally construed laws or rules, however, could not exist or operate without the creative-synthetic activity of the speaker. Although a "regressive analysis" may bring to light "certain more general and simple structures which resemble legal schemata," such schemata remain "in themselves abstract": "Far from presiding over the constitution of the sentence and providing the mould into which it flows, they exist only in and through the sentence" which "appears as a free invention of its own laws." Therefore, even the "necessary" linguistic connections are not entirely self-sustaining; rather, "we *found* this necessity." Actually, in order for words or linguistic elements "to enter into relations with one another" and "to latch onto or repulse one another," it is necessary that "they be united in a synthesis which does not come from them: suppress this synthetic unity and the block called 'speech' disintegrates." Thus, "it is within the free project of the sentence that the laws of speech are organized; it is by speaking that I make grammar. Freedom is the only possible foundation of the laws of language."[15]

Speaking: Gusdorf

Sartre's equation of speech and creative freedom reverberates in the writings of many existentialists and existential phenomenologists—though rarely with the same radical and uncompromising fervor. A good measure of Sartre's élan and commitment to self-enactment and self-disclosure can be found in the work of Georges Gusdorf, particularly in his study entitled *Speaking* (*La Parole*) of 1953. In Gusdorf's portrayal, speech or speaking was the "threshold of the human world," that is, the gateway leading "from animality to humanity." Reviewing various conventional formulas defining "man," the study considered most appropriate the notion of *homo loquens*: "Man is the speaking animal: this definition, after so many others, is perhaps the decisive one. It overlaps and absorbs such traditional definitions of man as the animal who laughs, or the social animal." For, "human laughter testifies to an interior language within oneself, and between oneself and others," just as the concept of a "political animal" implies "that human relations are founded upon language"—where speech serves not merely "to facilitate those relations but constitutes them." Regarding the threshold between animality and humanity, speech or language use, in Gusdorf's view, signaled the emergence of human autonomy and eventually of human mastery over nature: "The advent of the word manifests the sovereignty of man. Man interposes a network of words between the world and himself and thereby becomes the master of the world." Whereas the animal "does not understand *sign*, but only *signal*," human speech "intervenes like an abstract" or conceptual synopsis, liberating man from the constraints of prevailing states of affairs; in this manner, an "ideational reality" is fashioned "beyond the instinctive and momentary reality" offered to sensations. This fashioning of a properly human dimension, he added, is never finished, but a continuous task or challenge: "Each individual who comes into the world resumes for himself that labor of the human species, essential to it from its inception: to come into the world is *to begin speaking* (*prendre la parole*), to transfigure experience into a universe of discourse." Speech, from this perspective, is not merely a means of communication but a mode of meaning-constitution—and ultimately a mode of transcendental self-enactment. In his words, speech "implies a projection of the world, a world in project." Through speaking, consciousness "bursts forth" into life, "revealing the world to man and disclosing man to the world"; thus, "language is the being of man carried to self-awareness—the overture to transcendence."[16]

Although ranging broadly over various linguistic functions, the focus of the study was clearly on "living language" or on speech seen as medium of existential self-expression. Together with Sartre, Gusdorf objected to the treatment of language as a "dead" object or "impersonal" mechanism. Properly construed, he asserted, "language does not constitute an exemplary reality, detached from speaking men," a "closed and perfect system" constraining "personal lives by its ontological force"; human speech "is not content merely to reflect an antecedent reality"—which would "take away from it all intrinsic efficacy." Consequently, it was important to "consider speech not as an objective system, in the third person, but as an individual enterprise," with linguistic structures offering "only an outline for the full development of verbal activity." Replicating Sartre's argument, Gusdorf appealed to the findings of some linguists demonstrating "that the basic unit of living speech is not in the form of nouns, verbs, or adjectives, all isolated from one another like so many grains in a sack. The unit of speech is a complex whole, given vitality by the intended meaning of the speaker: it is the *verbal image* that is expressed in more or less complex sentences, sometimes reduced to a single word, but always corresponding to the expression of a meaning." In light of these findings, living language was seen to be animated by an inner purpose or intention reflecting the dictates of self-enactment. Linguistic communication had a point only "insofar as it reveals that personal reality within the person who is himself speaking: to communicate, man *ex-presses* himself, that is, he actualizes himself, creating from his own substance." In a sense, expression could be said to encapsulate the core or essential "humanity" of existence: "Just as a face devoid of all expression would no longer be a human face, so too the whole person appears to us as an expressive being—in other words, as the origin of intentions that are appropriate to him and that permit him to transform the environment." The aspect of environmental transformation added further contours to human freedom and sovereignty, construed as meaning-giving endowments: "We are world centers: our behavior and moods bestow meaning, at any given moment, on the environment of beings and things. That which is called the personality of a man or woman is reflected in the decor of life, a decor which is the sedimentation of behavior, the inscription of an existence on the world."[17]

In *Speaking*, the stress on expression was not meant to deny the presence of a pregiven communicative medium governed by linguistic and contextual rules—what Gusdorf called a "tongue" (*langue*). "Before speech," he admitted, "there has always been a tongue, before the language-subject a language-object," that is, a "determinate reality, constituted by others, and the learning of which is imposed on the child by others." As a medium of ordinary discourse, a tongue furnished "the common stuff of every exchange of speech"; its task, basically, was to provide a "hyphen" between speakers and listeners—for language "is all the more intelligible the more it is a common denominator." From the angle of human self-enactment, the presence of a tongue was bound to appear as a counterpoint or negative constraint: "To say that language is other people is tantamount to saying that we are from childhood on reduced to captivity by our forced submission to the ready-made formulas of the established tongue. By a kind of paradoxical inversion, the individual finds himself deprived of the benefit of that magnificent invention of speech." In Gusdorf's account, this contrast brought into view what he called a "fundamental antinomy of human speech," namely, the antinomy between "the self-affirmation of the subject" and "the search for others," or between self-expression and ordinary communication. "On the one hand," he stated, "we have the expressive function of language: I speak in order to make myself understood, in order to emerge into reality and to add myself to nature. On the other hand, we have the communicative function: I speak in order to reach out to others, and I can join myself to them all the more insofar as I set aside what is mine alone. This polarity of expression and communication," he added, "corresponds to the opposition between the first person and the third, between individual subjectivity and the objectivity of meaning held in common." Pushed to an extreme, the polarity yields the alternatives of a completely unintelligible expression and a pointless or meaningless communication (at least one devoid of personal meaning): "If I want to be understood by all, I ought to use the language of everyone else, and therefore renounce in me whatever makes me different from everybody"; by contrast, "if I use an entirely personal language, one completely fabricated by me," it is clear "that I shall succeed thereby in expressing radically original formulas, but that no one will understand me."[18]

What relieved and, in a sense, reconciled the mentioned antinomy in Gusdorf's eyes was the fact that a common tongue cannot truly persist without the expressive function and that communication ultimately reflects an intersection of intentions and reciprocal acts of self-disclosure. Echoing again Sartre, the study insisted that "the established language must not be understood as a closed system" and that "a living tongue appears to be animated by a mysterious movement, as if the collective agreement sustaining it were in a state of constant renewal." Consequently, although it may be "true to say that the tongue furnishes the framework for the exercise of speech," one needed to recognize simultaneously that "the tongue only exists within the act of speaking which assumes and fosters it." Against this background, a common tongue emerges as "a field of comprehension," and communication as "the relation of two subjects situated in this field, a field that furnishes them a common domain of reference, a background against which their momentary relation stands out as a figure." Seen as a field or an intersection of purposive linguistic acts, communication could not radically be pitted against the expressive function; actually, communicative interaction "without expression is senseless, because my language could never be absolutely expropriated: it would not exist unless a personal intention had initially brought it into being." Once this was admitted, the initially stipulated polarity had to be replaced by the notion of an "intimate union between communication and expression"—a union most perfectly realized on the level of "authentic communication." Rather than denoting "the exchange of devalued words in which no one is involved," genuine communication according to *Speaking* implies "the revelation of a unity, that is, a piece of common labor: It is the unity of each with the other, but at the same time the unifying of each with himself, the rearrangement of personal life in the encounter with others." On this level, Gusdorf affirms, communication manifests creative freedom just as freedom intimates a genuine community: the "purest expression" is bound to found a "new communion," while "perfect communication liberates in us possibilities of expression that until then lay dormant."[19]

Gesture and Speech: Merleau-Ponty

In large measure, the antinomy of expression and communication is endemic to the existential-phenomenological perspective, but some spokesmen nonetheless have managed to fashion a somewhat closer blending of elements than is found in *Speaking*. An instructive example is Merleau-Ponty's early work (and, as in Sartre's case, I shall restrict myself here to his early phase). Like other existentialists, Merleau-Ponty at the time was strongly preoccupied with human intentionality and creativity; however, instead of denoting non- or extra-worldly endowments, intentionality and "consciousness" in his portrayal were from the beginning enmeshed in concrete worldly configurations and especially in a bodily dimension. One of the central themes of his early writings was (what he called) the "primacy of perception"—where "perception" stands neither for an empiricist or behaviorist process nor for an intellectual-rationalist intuition, but rather for an intimate interconnection between the human agent seen as a living organism and the world. With regard to the articulation of meaning, this focus entailed that language had to be seen neither as a purely natural faculty nor as a cognitive tool, but instead as a mode of human existence, that is, as a medium of man's ongoing self-discovery and self-disclosure as an embodied or incarnate creature. Merleau-Ponty's thoughts along these lines were spelled out in detail in his *Phenomenology of Perception* (1945), particularly in the chapter on "The Body as Expression and Speech." Apart from explicit linguistic types of symbolization, the study argued, man expresses and articulates his existence (or the meaning or point of his existence) through perceptual engagement, gestures, bodily movements, and chant; in this sense, words and linguistic symbols are continuous with, or elaborations of, the primordial acts of meaning-disclosure accomplished by the human body in its active-affective involvement in the world. Moreover, bodily expressions and words are not merely connected in a temporal sequence (with gestures antedating speech): they interpenetrate and mutually sustain each other. As he wrote: "The spoken word is a genuine gesture, and it contains its meaning in the same way as the gesture contains its." Viewed as a "phonetic gesture," speech "brings about, both for the speaking subject and for his hearers, a certain structural co-ordination of experience, a certain modulation of existence, exactly as a pattern of my bodily behavior endows the objects around me with a certain significance both for me and for others."[20]

A main reason of the linkage of gesture and speech, in *Phenomenology of Perception*, was the concrete-sensual character of the latter, its status as part of the pragmatics of "being-in-the-world." In turning to concrete language use, the study deliberately sought to move beyond traditional epistemology in both its empiricist and its rationalist versions. In Merleau-Ponty's view, empiricism and rationalism were equally guilty of truncating the expressiveness of speech: "In the first case, we are on this side of the word as meaningful; in the second we are beyond it. In the first there is nobody to speak; in the second, there is certainly a subject, but a thinking, not a speaking one." Consequently, "we refute both intellectualism and empiricism by simply saying that *the word has a meaning*" or conveys a point. From the vantage of rationalism or intellectualism, speech is merely an external garment clothing a prior idea or cognitive insight, a garment devoid of any intrinsic significance of its own — a view which reduces speech to an incidental pastime without properly doing justice to thought. For, "if talking were primarily a matter of meeting the object through a cognitive intention or a representation, we could not understand why thought tends towards expression as towards its completion, why the most familiar thing appears indeterminate as long as we have not recalled its name, why the thinking subject himself is in a kind of ignorance of his thoughts so long as he has not formulated them for himself, or even spoken and written them." According to the study, thought and speech are not two steps in an epistemological scheme but inseparable moments in a concrete learning process: "The denomination of objects does not follow upon recognition; it is itself recognition." More broadly phrased, "speech, in the speaker, does not translate ready-made thought, but accomplishes it" — a maxim which is particularly evident in communicative encounters or speaker-hearer relations. What we find in such encounters, Merleau-Ponty stated, is "a taking up of others' thought through speech, a reflection in others, an ability to think *according to others* which enriches our own thought.

Here the meaning of words must be finally induced by the words themselves or, more exactly, their conceptual meaning must be formed by a kind of deduction from a *gestural meaning*, which is immanent in speech." Speaking and listening (just as reading and writing) thus testify to "a *thought in speech* whose existence is unsuspected by intellectualism."[21]

Considerations of this kind, according to *Phenomenology of Perception*, were prone to restore to speaking "its true physiognomy"—by showing that speech is not merely "the 'sign' of thought, if by this we understand a phenomenon which heralds another as smoke betrays fire." Speech and thought could stand in this external relation only "if they were both thematically given, whereas in fact they are intertwined, the sense being held within the word, and the word being the manifest existence of the sense." Consequently, rather than being cognitive signs or labels, words and speech emerge as "the presence of thought in the phenomenal world and, moreover, not its clothing but its token or its body." Implicitly, the study's arguments on this point contained a critique of meaning invariance as expounded both by transcendental idealists (including Husserl) and structural linguists. Allusions to the former can hardly be overlooked in the comment that "thought is no 'internal' thing and does not exist independently of the world and of words. What misleads us in this connection, and causes us to believe in a thought which exists for itself prior to expression, is thought already constituted and expressed, which we can silently recall to ourselves, and through which we acquire the illusion of an inner life; but in reality this supposed silence is alive with words, this inner life is an inner language." Regarding the assumption of a universal syntax or linguistic code cherished by some linguists, the study did not so much reject "universalism" as cast it in a new light—by stripping it of its cognitive pretensions. "The predominance of vowels in one language or of consonants in another, and various structural and syntactical systems," we read, "do not represent so many arbitrary conventions for the expression of one and the same idea, but several ways for the human body to sing the world's praises and in the last resort to live it. Hence the *full* meaning of a language is never translatable into another." To the extent that languages are compatible, this is due to their oblique mutual inherence rather than to universal concepts: "If there is such a thing as universal thought, it is achieved by taking up the effort towards expression and communication in *one* single language, and accepting all its ambiguities, all the suggestions and overtones of meaning of which a linguistic tradition is made up and which is the exact measure of its power of expression."[22]

The insistence on the worldly or gestural character of speech was not intended as a bow to empiricism or to the reduction of meaning to behavioral or physical processes. As employed in "being-in-the-world," the study noted, the term "world" is not merely "a manner of speaking: it implies that the 'mental' or cultural life borrows its structures from natural life and that the thinking subject must have its basis in the subject incarnate"—which is not equivalent to saying that gestural meaning resembles or reflects "some physical or physiological phenomenon." Actually, meaning is "not contained in the word as a sound," and the human body is not simply an organism but "defined in terms of its faculty of appropriating, in an indefinite series of discontinuous acts, significations which transcend and transfigure its natural powers." Adumbrated in mute gestures, this faculty was fully developed in language use or speech. In Merleau-Ponty's words: "A contraction of the throat, a sibilant emission of air between the tongue and teeth, a certain way of bringing the body into play suddenly allows itself to be invested with a *figurative significance* which is conveyed outside us. This is neither more nor less miraculous than the emergence of love from desire, or that of gesture from the unco-ordinated movements of infancy." For this transformation to occur, he recognized, signification had to rely on pre-given or already constituted elements: thus, phonetic expression "must use an alphabet of already acquired meanings, the word-gesture must be performed in a certain setting common to the speakers, just as the comprehension of other gestures presupposes a perceived world common to all." Like other existentialists, however, Merleau-Ponty found these elements "not sufficient" for meaning-constitution; for, "speech puts up a new sense, if it is authentic speech, just as gesture endows the object for the first time with human significance, if it is an initiating gesture." Even settled or traditional meanings "must necessarily have been new once." Therefore, he concluded, we must "recognize as an ultimate fact this open and indefinite power of giving significance—that is, of both apprehending and conveying meaning—by which man transcends himself towards a new form of behavior, or towards other people, or towards his own thought, through his body and his speech."[23]

Merleau-Ponty's views on language and speech were modified and reconceptualized in several subsequent writings—revisions which never affected his original anti-epistemological posture. For present purposes I want to cast a rapid glance at his thoughts on language learning or acquisition, also formulated during his early period. While serving as professor of child psychology in the post-war period, Merleau-Ponty offered a lecture course at the Sorbonne on "Consciousness and the Acquisition of Language" which later was published in book form. Reviewing in detail some of the main approaches in learning theory, the lectures rejected as misleading both intellectualist and behaviorist perspectives, perspectives which reduce language acquisition either to a form of "operant conditioning" in Skinner's vein or else to the simple unfolding or application of a quasi-logical internal endowment in concrete settings. As the lectures tried to show, a child learns to speak a language in the same way as he learns to use his body, that is, without fully grasping the rules or underlying code governing his performance; by the same token, language use is not due to the efforts of parents or teachers to inculcate words or sentences—a finding which does not deny the importance of concrete experience. For Merleau-Ponty, language learning involved a combination of a "holistic" intuition and scattered experiences, that is, the gradual and piecemeal induction into the general "style" of a language. Learning to speak, the lectures asserted, is "to coexist more and more with the environment," in such a manner that language acquisition "no longer resembles the decoding of a text for which one possesses the code and key; rather, it is a deciphering (where the decipherer does not know the key to the code)." Instead of being an "intellectual act," such learning constitutes a "vital operation" through which the child embraces the "style of a language" which "possesses not a direct signification but an oblique one." As James Edie summarizes the lectures' argument: "The child learns a language as an adult learns the style of a hitherto unknown work of art or music"; language thus is initially acquired "as a whole" or "as a *style* of expression which imposes itself and which contains an 'inner logic' that is grasped dumbly and inarticulately (by an *'esprit aveugle'*) prior to any ability to conceptualize the meanings for which it stands or which it enables us to express."[24]

Rejoinders

The turn to the pragmatics of speech has not gone unopposed among philosophers and social theorists; with varying intensity, qualms or objections have been raised both regarding ordinary language or speech-act theory and the existentialist focus on expressiveness. In the former domain, Searle's classification of speech acts (as found in *Expression and Meaning*) has elicited relatively mild reservations from Jürgen Habermas, who is otherwise a supporter of linguistic pragmatics. In Habermas' view, Searle's taxonomy is promising due to its potential linkage with the notion of "validity claims" inherent in discursive exchanges. "In depicting illocutionary force in terms of the correlation between language and world," he observes, "Searle relies on the validity conditions of assertive and directive utterances; thus he derives the theoretical criteria for classifying speech acts from the dimension of validity." The flaw of the mentioned taxonomy is said to result from Searle's tendency to mingle "validity" and "success" criteria and, more importantly, from his subordination of interpersonal communication to individual intentionality, reflected in the varying "directions of fit" (or "word-world" matchings):

"The model of a solitary agent relating to the external-objective world by means of linguistically mediated directions of fit does not leave room for intersubjective communication among speakers attempting to reach a consensus on some topic." The slighting of communicative interaction, according to Habermas, is particularly evident in the case of "declaratives" tied to "institutional facts"; for in such instances "the speaker does not at all refer to the objective world, but acts in accordance with the legitimate norms of society, while simultaneously initiating new interpersonal contacts." As should be noted, these and related comments are meant not to undermine Searle's approach, and speech-act theory in general, but to place it on a more solid footing: basically, we read, the stated difficulties "can be avoided if we start from the premise that the illocutionary goals of speech acts are accomplished through intersubjective recognition of power and validity claims, and if we further accept normative rightness and subjective truthfulness as claims on a par with truth, while diversifying the respective actor-world relations."[25]

Stronger objections have been voiced by more ontologically inclined thinkers, including "post-structuralists" weary of modern "subjectivity." Clearly, no elaborate effort is required to detect behind notions like "direction of fit" or "word-world" correlation familiar epistemological tenets, particularly the "analytic-synthetic" distinction and the logical-empiricist bifurcation of logic (or logical language) and sense data— tenets which, in turn, can be traced to traditional metaphysical assumptions regarding mind-matter and subject-object polarities.[26] Critical considerations along these lines have been articulated forcefully by Jacques Derrida in an essay entitled "Signature Event Context" (1977). In his essay, Derrida's main quarrel was with distinctive—though unavowed— metaphysical presuppositions animating ordinary language theory in general, and especially with its treatment of language as a means of intentional action or performative utterance. "All of the difficulties encountered by Austin in an analysis which is patient, open, aporetical, in constant transformation," he wrote, ultimately "strike one as having a common root: Austin has not taken account of what—in the structure of *speech* (before any illocutionary or perlocutionary specification)— already entails that system of predicates I call *graphematic* (or textual) and consequently blurs all the oppositions which follow." One of the "essential elements" presupposed but not sufficiently explored by Austin was subjectivity or "classically, consciousness: the conscious presence of the intention of the speaking subject in the totality of his speech acts. As a result, performative communication becomes once more the communication of an intentional meaning." In traditional epistemology and metaphysics, consciousness and subjective intention typically served as loadstone designed to stabilize meanings through the univocity of language use—a stabilizing effort also evident in Austin's portrayal of "felicity" conditions which aims at a perfect meshing of speech and its context. Among his success criteria "we necessarily find once more those of an exhaustively definable context, of a free consciousness present to the total operation, and of absolutely meaningful speech master of itself: the teleological jurisdiction of an entire field whose organizing center remains *intention*." In Derrida's view, once the stabilizing anchor is removed, once the full sway of language—including the duplicity of intentions and the porousness of contexts—is recognized, the program of speech-act theory is bound to appear problematic; in this case, he commented, "the category of intention will not disappear; it will have its place, but from that place it will no longer be able to govern the entire scene and system of utterance."[27]

With regard to existentialism or existential phenomenology, the stress on expressiveness has been questioned by numerous philosophers—among them such quasi-existentialist thinkers as Gadamer and Heidegger. In his essay on "Man and Language" (cited in the opening chapter) Gadamer differentiates the nature or "being" of language sharply from consciousness or subjective intentionality. Although agreeing that language essentially "consists in what is said in it," speaking in his view does not coincide with self-expression or self-enactment. The reason for this noncoincidence resides in language's tendency to transgress or overreach human intentions. While representing "the real mark of our finitude," he writes, language in a sense "is always beyond us. The consciousness of the individual is not the standard by which the being of language can be measured; indeed, there is no individual consciousness at all in which a spoken language is actually present." Contrary to existentialist construals of speech (and also to the tenor of much of speech-act theory) the essay contends that "no individual has a real consciousness of his speaking when he speaks. Only in exceptional situations does one become aware of the language in which he is speaking: it happens, for instance, when someone starts to say something but hesitates because what he is about to say seems strange or comical." On the basis of these considerations, Gadamer depicts as an "essential feature of the being of language" its nonsubjectivity or "I-lessness." Elsewhere he comments, in a similar vein: "The subjective starting point, so natural to modern thought, leads us wholly into error. Language is not to be conceived as an autonomous projection of the world by subjectivity—either the subjectivity of individual consciousness or that of the spirit of a people."[28]

In a more nuanced manner Gadamer's argument was articulated and anticipated by Heidegger. In his essay on "Language" (1950) Heidegger asks specifically: "What does it mean to speak?" And he continues: "The current view declares that speaking is the activation of speech (and hearing) organs. Speech is the audible expression and communication of human feelings which in turn are guided by thoughts." According to the essay, "this characterization of language takes three points for granted: First and foremost, speaking is expression. The idea of speech as an utterance or expression (*Äusserung*) is the most common; it already presupposes the notion of something internal that utters or externalizes (ex-presses) itself." Secondly, speech is regarded "as an activity of man" and finally, human expression is seen "always as a presentation and representation of the real and the unreal." As Heidegger comments: "If we take language to be an utterance or externalization, then we give an external notion of it, and this at the very moment when we explain it by recourse to something internal." Differently put: "If attention is fastened exclusively on human speech, if speaking is taken simply as the voicing of the inner man, and if speech so conceived is regarded as language itself, then the nature of language can never appear as anything but an expression and activity of man." What is ignored in this treatment is that "human speech is not self-subsistent." Similar thoughts are stated also in "The Way to Language" (1959) where we read: "Speaking must have speakers, but not simply in the way as an effect must have a cause. Rather, speakers have in language their abode"—that is, they obtain their cues and their speech from language and thus, in a sense, speak "out of language." As Heidegger adds: "We do not merely speak *the* language—we speak *by way of* it. We can do so only because (or to the extent to which) we have already listened to language. What do we hear there? We hear language speaking."[29]

Expression and Interpretation

The tenets of speech pragmatics and existential self-disclosure can be transferred without great difficulty to the domain of textual interpretation, provided the activities of speaking and hearing are expanded to encompass writing and reading as well. Just as, in the analytical and existentialist view, speech tends to be governed by speaker's goals (within concrete contextual limits), textual meaning may be said to depend chiefly on author's intentions (again within concrete historical settings); moreover, corresponding to the linkage of speaking and hearing, authorial purpose may be correlated with a (more or less adaptive) intentionality on the part of reader or interpreter. A transfer along these lines is in fact encouraged by the discussed philosophers. In the confines of speech-act theory, the primacy of authorial intent is strongly championed in Searle's *Expression and Meaning*. In discussing the status of "fictional discourse" —treated as "nonserious" discourse in which the author "pretends *as if*" something were the case or happening—he writes: "Now *pretend* is an intentional verb, that is, it is one of those verbs which contain the concept of intention built into it." This initial insight "leads immediately to our second conclusion: the identifying criterion for whether or not a text is a work of fiction must of necessity lie in the illocutionary intentions of the author." Broadening his comments to cover texts in general, Searle adds: "There used to be a school of literary critics who thought one should not consider the intentions of the author when examining a work of fiction. Perhaps there is some level of intention at which this extraordinary view is plausible"; but "at the most basic level it is absurd to suppose a critic can completely ignore the intentions of the author, since even so much as to identify a text as a novel, a poem, or even as a text is already to make a claim about the author's intentions." In reviewing existentialism I previously quoted Sartre to the effect that words and sentences only gain meaning if "placed within the point of view of the author who saw the thing (or point) to be expressed." More dramatically the same thought is articulated by Gusdorf who states that "the whole of human experience in its militant sense may be understood as a striving for expression." Such is also "the way of the writer: the discipline of expression frees him from the spectres which haunt him."[30]

In his overview of critical approaches to literature, Hayden White presents existentialism basically as a reaction to the "Inflationary" type of exegesis sponsored by New Critics and formalists. "It was the inflation of art at the expense of life," he notes, "that drew the ire of the existentialist critics" at the time; embroiled in the agonies of the war and postwar period, existentialists "regarded the pervasive formalism of the Inflationary mode as unresponsive to the human needs and desires which inspired artistic creativity in the first place." Countering the purely receptive-aesthetic enjoyment of timeless texts, writers in this camp "insisted on opening up once more the basic questions" which other literary theorists "had begged or simply not asked, such questions as 'Why write?', 'Why read?', and 'Why criticize?' " In White's view, the basic thrust of existentialist thought was to see literary production, like other forms of activity, as an outgrowth and reflection of human life or the human condition. Particularly in Sartre's work, he asserts, "the distinction between writing and criticizing" — we might add: between speaking and writing as well — "is hardly made; the one activity is indistinguishable from the other. Both writing and criticizing are conceived as ways of closing the gap not only between literature and life, but also between art and work, thought and action, history and consciousness." Among existentialists and their supporters, "criticism, like writing in general, was viewed as action not contemplation, as violent not pacific," as creative not receptive — "although Sartre, like Camus, desired that it would not be all these things."[31]

The concern with authorial intent — a concrete-historical rather than a speculative or hypothetical intent — is not restricted to the rise of existentialism in the postwar period, but reverberates in many recent and contemporary works on literary theory. A case in point is Peter Juhl's *Interpretation*, subtitled *An Essay in the Philosophy of Literary Criticism*. As Juhl indicates, a central aim of his study is "to show that there is a logical connection between the meaning of a literary work and the author's intention or, to put it differently, that to understand a literary work *is*, in virtue of our concept of the meaning of a literary work, to understand what the author intended to convey or express." In cases of ambiguous texts or utterances, he adds, "the author's intention logically determines which of the linguistically possible interpretations of a text is correct," with the result that "a claim about the meaning of the text is at least in part a claim about the author's use of the words in question." Although presented as a logical or analytical proposition, the study's thesis is also said to accord with ordinary critical practice. To be defensible, we read, the proposed outlook "must account in some plausible manner for the sorts of things critics and ordinary readers alike actually do in interpreting a work, what they take into account in arriving at an interpretation." An important side-claim connected with the thesis is that interpretation has to deal not with an "implied" or hypothetical (or philosophically presupposed) author but with a concrete individual and his actual intentions. "How we view the story, the situation, or events presented in a work, or what we take to be expressed or suggested by it," Juhl notes, "is determined not by our picture of the so-called implied author, but rather by our picture of the real, historical person. If a literary work conveys or expresses certain propositions, then — or so I shall argue — the real author is committed to the truth of those propositions and to the corresponding beliefs." This focus on concrete intent in his view also solidifies the linkage between literature and real-life situations and experiences: "It follows that, in an important sense, literature is not autonomous, that the connection between literature and life is a good deal closer than the implied-author doctrine" would "lead us to believe."[32]

In the domain of political-theoretical exegesis, a leading contemporary champion of authorial intent is Quentin Skinner — whose writings are approvingly cited in *Interpretation* on repeated occasions. Together with Juhl, Skinner treats exegesis as the deliberate recovery of the meaning of texts, a recovery which "presupposes the grasp of what they were intended to mean, and how this meaning was intended to be taken." Strongly inspired by ordinary language and speech-act theory, he construes texts as modes of meaning expression and writing or text-production as a type of purposive utterance or "linguistic action" — whose comprehension, as in the case of all actions, has to respect the "special authority of the agent over his intentions." Actually, exegetic comprehension in his view involves a two-tiered alignment with authorial goals; as he states, interpreters must try "to understand both the intention to be understood, and the intention that this intention should be understood, which the text itself as an extended act of communication must at least have embodied." Again in accordance with Juhl, Skinner focuses on the actual-historical rather than a philosophically constructed author. Particularly in reading a work of the past, he notes, the student of the history of ideas must pinpoint concretely "what its author, in writing at the time he did write and for the audience he intended to address, could in practice have been intending to communicate." To accomplish this goal, historical interpretation has to take into account the concrete historical setting of a text as well as the linguistic conventions operating at the time—but in such a manner that contextual factors and linguistic rules emerge as further indices, rather than obstructions of authorial intent. "The appropriate methodology for the history of ideas," he concludes, "must be concerned, first of all, to delineate the whole range of communication which could have been conventionally performed on the occasion of the given utterance and, next, to trace the relation between the given utterance and this wider linguistic context as a means of decoding the actual intention of the given writer."[33]

Views of this kind are echoed—sometimes with modified accents—in the writings of several present-day political theorists and interpreters, most notably in John Pocock's *Politics, Language and Time*. In line with Skinner, Pocock credits ordinary language analysis not so much with subverting as with giving new impulses to the study of political thought—by revealing texts as purposive utterances or performative expressions in prevailing historical settings. According to analysts (and some historians of science), he states, "men think by communicating language systems" which "help constitute both their conceptual worlds and the authority-structures, or social worlds, related to these," with the consequence that individual thinking and writing "may now be viewed as a social event, an act of communication and of response within a paradigm-system, and as a historical event, a moment in a process of transformation of that system and of the interacting worlds." More strongly than Skinner, Pocock stresses the role of linguistic contexts—of the fact that "paradigms" available to a writer may "take precedence over questions of his 'intention' or the 'illocutionary force' of his utterance"—but only to underscore the difficulty and need of concretizing authorial intent; for, "to know a language is to know the things which may be done with it, so that to study a thinker is to see what he attempted to do with it." Basically, the task of political exegesis in his view is "to identify the 'language' or 'vocabulary' with and within which the author operated, and to show how it functioned paradigmatically to prescribe what he might say and how he might say it." In a more subdued and circumspect manner, a similar outlook is also endorsed by John Gunnell, in *Political Theory: Tradition and Interpretation*, who writes that "there is good reason to designate poltical theory as an activity and to discuss the political theorist as a kind of actor," provided one admits "that these are ideal typifications and not pre-existent historical objects." In a "very fundamental sense," he adds, "the criterion for distinguishing political theory as a particular kind of creative activity and body of literature is the degree to which the vision of the theorist is inseparable from the problem of restructuring political society in terms of that vision. Like that of the artist, it is a vision that demands incarnation and requires public expression."[34]

Verbal Praxis and Politics

Regarding the actual formulation of a "vision" meant to restructure society, of course, writers and theorists differ in terms of boldness and ingenuity; as Gunnell recognizes, the notion of political theory as "the creative mind's encounter" with public issues is an ideal-typical model that permits varying degrees of approximation. This diversity is readily apparent among the discussed philosophers. In the case of ordinary language thinkers, political visions and aspirations are relatively diffuse and implicit; yet, the stress on speaker's and author's intentions—one may conjecture—should entail a broadly liberal outlook concerned with the free articulation and pursuit of chosen ends. Actually, the conjecture is borne out in Searle's case; his book *The Campus War* (1970) counseled a moderate-liberal position with respect to student unrest and university reform during the Vietnam era. By comparison, existentialists have been more explicit or outspoken on political issues; in addition to writing philosophical treatises, most members of the existentialist movement— certainly most of its French spokesmen—elaborated in detail on their preferred political perspective and the theoretical reasons sustaining this perspective. Although commonly endorsing a mixture of freedom and social responsibility, individual writers espoused distinct versions of existentialist politics—ranging from the defense of a near-libertarian posture (in the case of the early Sartre) over sponsorship of a democratic-socialist conception (Merleau-Ponty) to the advocacy of an existentialist Marxism emphasizing spontaneous social "praxis" (later Sartre).[35] Since these versions have been discussed extensively in the literature, I shall not dwell on them further; instead, I want to conclude by casting a brief glance at a specifically political thinker at least loosely affiliated with existentialism: Paulo Freire.

According to his own account, Freire's views have been shaped by a number of mentors, among them "Sartre and Mounier, Erich Fromm and Louis Althusser, Ortega y Gasset and Mao, Martin Luther King and Che Guevara, Unamuno and Marcuse"; but the existentialist theme of creative self-enactment is clearly one of his central preoccupations. Probably his most widely known book is *Pedagogy of the Oppressed* (1970), which offers as one of its major contributions a speech pedagogy or education in communicative discourse (termed "dialogics"). As Freire affirms, human beings—as distinguished from animals—are creatures of "praxis" who "not only live but exist" and whose "existence is historical." While animals "live out their lives on an atemporal, flat, uniform 'prop', men exist in a world which they are constantly re-creating and transforming"; whereas the former are "beings-in-themselves," completely "immersed" in the world, the latter "emerge from the world, objectify it, and in so doing can understand it and transform it with their labor." Praxis in his portrayal is a combination of "action and reflection" aiming at "transformation of the world"; moreover, it is intimately connected with speaking or with what Freire calls "the word." "Within the word," he writes, "we find two dimensions, reflection and action, in such radical interaction that if one is sacrificed—even in part—the other immediately suffers. There is no true word that is not at the same time a praxis; thus, to speak a true word is to transform the world." Authentic speech—as distinguished from mere "verbalism" or "idle chatter"—is said to be constitutive of human existence or the source of genuine humanity: "Human existence cannot be silent, nor can it be nourished by false words, but only by true words, with which men transform the world. To exist, humanly, is to *name* the world, to change it." What matters most to Freire, however, is that speech cannot be the prerogative of intellectuals or an educated elite; for, in the end, no one can speak in lieu of or *"for* another, in a prescriptive act which robs others of their words." Rather than being a badge of distinction, speech is (or must become) a universally shared attribute of mankind: "While to say the true word—which is work, which is praxis—is to transform the world, saying that word is not the privilege of some few men, but the right of every man."[36]

5

Transcendental Hermeneutics
and Universal Pragmatics

Os justorum liberabit eos . . .

The focus on speech and communicative interaction has exerted a pervasive impact on contemporary language philosophy—so much so that
Hacking feels justified (with good reason) to designate our era as the
"Heyday of Sentences." Yet, the spreading of a notion or the broadening
of its sway frequently implies its transformation; the reception of speech
pragmatics is no exception. As previously indicated, the turn to
pragmatics was prompted chiefly by antiepistemological motives: the intent to salvage or liberate language from a narrow preoccupation with
logical or referential univocity—a preoccupation, however, which rests
on deep-seated philosophical convictions. In the preceding chapter I
alluded to the linkage between speech and rhetoric and between the latter
and "commonsense" argumentation, and also to the long-standing "intramural warfare" between philosophy and common sense; in some
measure, rather than subsiding, this warfare or tension has resurfaced in
the meantime in the context of pragmatics itself. Under philosophical
auspices, the concern with speech readily appears as a lapse into contingent cultural patterns to the detriment of universally binding yardsticks of thought and action. Moreover, even on a commonsense level,
a mere shift of accent from competence to performance or from *langue*
to *parole* does not seem to impair the importance and legitimacy of both
sides of the mentioned polarities. As a result, efforts have been afoot for
some time to inject universal, invariant, or "transcendental" standards
into communicative interaction—the latter seen both from the angle of
speech or illocutionary initiative and from the perspective of reciprocal
listening and interpretation (or "hermeneutics"). Given pragmatic
premises, the invoked standards are likely to have strongly normative
connotations in the sense that even the pursuit of (empirical) knowledge
is found to obey norms of a practice of inquiry.

To some extent, the reemergence of universal aspirations cuts across
philosophical schools of thought, especially across the dividing line between Anglo-American and Continental thought. Among speech-act
theorists, John Searle has been slowly moving away in recent years from

115

Austin's pragmatism and descriptivism in the direction of universal parameters of speech. As he noted in his *Expression and Meaning,* after listing the main categories of speech acts: "But any philosopher is bound to feel that where there are categories there ought to be a transcendental deduction of the categories, that is, there ought to be some theoretical explanation as to why language provides us with these and with only these. The justification of these categories," he added, "in terms of the nature of the mind has to wait for the next book." Actually, in the confines of Anglo-American philosophy, the most prominent spokesman during recent decades for a revival of transcendentalism or transcendental analysis has been Peter Strawson—known chiefly for such publications as *Individuals* (1959) and *The Bounds of Sense* (1966). In his writings, Strawson appealed strongly to the Kantian legacy, especially to Kant's stress on the "apriori conditions of possibility" of inquiry, action, or experience. To be sure, as incorporated into linguistic analysis, Kantianism assumes a somewhat reduced or watered-down cast—which has been described as a "minimalist interpretation of the transcendental." According to this interpretation, the investigation of a domain of experience presupposes a categorial or conceptual framework integrating discrete elements into a coherent pattern; to the extent that a given field exhibits consistently a distinct framework, the latter may be termed its condition of possibility and hence "transcendental." What is missing in this version is Kant's broader goal of a genuine "transcendental deduction," that is, his effort to show how categories are grounded necessarily in transcendental consciousness or in the "transcendental synthesis of apperception." In Strawson's "descriptive metaphysics," transcendental analysis simply relies on the judgments of concrete individuals regarding the coherence of a field of experience and its categorial premises—judgments invariably imbued with an experimental character: instead of enjoying a deductive status, a conceptual structure qualifies as transcendental as long as its necessity and universality have not been successfully refuted.[1]

Comparatively speaking, universal or transcendental concerns have always been cultivated more diligently and persistently in Continental thought. In our own period—and bypassing more orthodox modes of neo-Kantianism—such concerns have emerged primarily in two settings: those of existential phenomenology and of "critical theory" (the latter representing a confluence of the Kantian tradition of critical philosophy and critical strands in Marxism). In the first setting, a transcendental or at least "quasi-transcendental" type of analysis can be found in Heidegger's early work, and especially in *Being and Time* (1927): building upon, but also departing from Husserl's transcendental perspective, the study delineated universal conditions of possibility of human existence or

"*Dasein*," conditions pinpointed in a set of pragmatic-existential categories. Later, in the context of French phenomenology, similar "quasi-transcendental" ambitions are discernible in Ricoeur's phenomenological "hermeneutics," marked by the effort to reconcile Husserlian teachings with existentialist themes. In the setting of "critical theory," the chief contemporary spokesmen are Jürgen Habermas and Karl-Otto Apel—the former committed to the theoretical project of a "universal pragmatics," the latter to the development of a "transcendental hermeneutics." The following discussion will be restricted to central arguments advanced by the mentioned Continental thinkers. As in preceding chapters, I intend to move along a spectrum, this time a spectrum of increasing transcendentalism (in the traditional sense): starting from the existential-categorial frameworks of Heidegger and Ricoeur, I shall proceed to Habermas's partially empirical universalism and conclude with a glance at Apel's more rigorously transcendental (and quasi-Kantian) outlook.

Dasein and Speech: Heidegger

In Heidegger's *Being and Time*, language-related issues were integrated into the broader and more encompassing effort to capture the basic structure of existence or *Dasein*—the latter seen as gateway to the exploration of the "meaning of Being." Tied to this overarching goal, relevant comments were scattered throughout the different portions of the study; for present purposes, however, the central and most instructive arguments can be found in the section entitled "*Dasein* and Speech; Language." From the vantage point of Husserlian phenomenology wedded to the postulate of meaning invariance, the section performed a decisive, pragmatic-existential "turn": instead of concentrating on formal-syntactical or logical-cognitive properties of language, the focus of analysis was placed squarely on "speech" as existential-human capacity and its underlying premises and constitutive elements; as the opening paragraph affirmed: "The existential-ontological foundation of language is speech" (*die Rede*). In performing this turn, Heidegger appealed explicitly to the Greek formulation of human nature as "*zoon logon echon*"—a phrase which he translated as "the being that speaks" rather than as "*animal rationale*" (mainly because of the long-standing absorption of "logos" and reason by logic and logical-empiricist inquiry). As portrayed in the section, one should note, "speech" was not merely a synonym for "ordinary" or everyday talk—which could easily degenerate into idle chatter (*Gerede*); rather, it was anchored in, or linked with, universal categorial presuppositions of *Dasein*, in particular with *Dasein*'s basic "disposition" or "attunement" (*Befindlichkeit*) and with its "understanding" (*Verstehen*) of itself and of the world. In Heidegger's words: "Speech is existentially on an equally basic or primordial footing as disposition and understanding." Viewed on a categorial plane, speech embodied the "articulation" of understanding or the intelligibility of *Dasein*; most importantly, it was not simply a contingent endowment, but constitutive for human existence, that is, for man seen as a creature of "care" searching for meaning in the world. "The attuned intelligibility or intelligible attunement of being-in-the-world," we read, "expresses itself in speech; in this manner, the entire meaning-complex of intelligibility is *put into words*."[2]

Apart from probing categorial underpinnings, the section examined in detail the various dimensions and implications of speech—an examination which, in many respects, anticipated by several decades tenets of later "speech-act theory" (as discussed in the preceding chapter), including the distinction between locutionary content and illocutionary force. As Heidegger noted, speech or speaking occurs in many diverse forms: it can assume the modes of "assenting or refusing, demanding or warning, of pronouncing, consulting or interceding, or else of 'making assertions', or of talking in the sense of 'giving a talk'." Whatever its mode, speaking is always a "speaking about (something)"; but, as Heidegger continued, "the *about* of speech has not necessarily, and regularly not at all, the character of a predicative or propositional assertion. A command also is issued about or regarding something; a wish has its 'about', and so does intercession" (and so on). Thus, according to *Being and Time*, speech always contains a thematic ingredient or worldly reference—briefly termed "the spoken about" (*das Beredete*)—which is variously embedded in modes of speaking and whose presence is due to its structural significance: the fact that speech "helps to constitute the open disclosedness of being-in-the-world." Thematic content or reference, however, does not exhaust the structure of speech which, in Heidegger's view, also embraces speech performance, the speaker's relation to an addressee, and the utterance (or speech act) as a whole. Speech performance, in his portrayal, was closely related to the speaker's (illocutionary) intent—but not in a straightforward or subjectivist sense. What surfaces in the performative act, he stated, is indeed the "self-expression" of the speaker, but a self-expression which needs to be construed existentially as a structural manifestation of being-in-the-world: "In speaking *Dasein* expresses itself, not in the sense that an 'interior' is initially segregated from the external world, but because as being-in-the-world *Dasein* is already 'outside' itself in the mode of understanding." Similar considerations applied to the speaker-addressee relationship. Summarizing his conception of speech, Heidegger listed four main "constitutive" or structural elements: "the 'about' of speech (*das Beredete*), the utterance as such (*das Geredete*), the communication to an addressee (*Mitteilung*), and the speaker's self-disclosure (*Bekundung*)." These elements, he added, were not merely "empirical properties" of a given language, but rather "existential characteristics lodged in the structure of *Dasein*, characteristics which render something like language ontologically possible."[3]

While thus anticipating or at least intimating later analytical teachings or insights, *Being and Time* deviated from "speech-act theory" through a number of distinctive accents or arguments which are not commonly found in ordinary language studies. Foremost among these accents—above and beyond the categorial orientation—was the stress on the linkage between speaking and listening and on the correlation between speech and silence. Listening or hearing, from Heidegger's perspective, was not simply a passive or subsidiary mode of communicative interaction; rather, in his words: "Listening is constitutive for speech itself." As presented in the section, the constitutive role of listening was due to *Dasein*'s categorial quality of understanding—which, in the case of interaction, implies a reciprocity of understanding and thus a mutual attentiveness and attunement. "Listening," we read, "manifests the existential openness of *Dasein* as co-being with and for others. Listening even constitutes the primary and authentic openness of *Dasein* for its innermost possibilities, as exemplified in the listening to the voice of a friend." An equally important role was attributed to silence. "Whoever keeps silent in a dialogue," Heidegger wrote, "can make himself on occasion better understood, that is, contribute more to reciprocal understanding than someone who incessantly talks." Actually, talkativeness was likely to lead to idle chatter (*Gerede*) which, in turn, tended to obscure understanding or else to foster the "sham clarity and real unintelligibility of the trivial." Keeping silent, on the other hand, was not equivalent to being dumb or speechless; on the contrary, a dumb or speechless person "has not only not demonstrated his ability to keep silent, but entirely lacks the possibility to demonstrate anything of the sort." In the same manner, someone who "by nature is accustomed to say little does not thereby maintain silence or prove his ability to do so"; generally stated: "Who never says anything can also at the proper moment not keep silent." Seen in this light, speech and silence were no so much antithetical as mutually constitutive or reciprocal conditions of possibility: "Only genuine speech renders possible genuine silence; to be able to keep silent, *Dasein* must have something to say—that is, have at its disposal a rich and authentic disclosedness of itself."[4]

To round out this review of *Being and Time* one further aspect should briefly be mentioned. After having devoted the bulk of his discussion to speech (*Rede*), Heidegger at the end of the cited section turned to "language" (*Sprache*) in the broader sense, and particularly to the question of its ontological status or "mode of being." Is language, he queried, "a mundane ready-to-hand utensil, or does it have *Dasein*'s status, or is it neither of the two?" As the section pointed out, recent decades have witnessed the emergence of a complex linguistic philosophy or linguistic science, but "the mode of being of its subject matter remains obscure; even the horizon in which the question might be raised is veiled." In order to make some headway in this domain, the section concluded, philosophical inquiry "will have to abandon 'linguistic philosophy' in order to probe the 'things themselves' and thus to promote a conceptual clarification of the relevant issues." With respect to this kind of inquiry — which, one might add, increasingly became the focus of Heidegger's later writings — *Being and Time* was merely designed to serve as a prolegomenon or initial roadmap, a map indicating "the ontological 'topos' or topology of this phenomenon within *Dasein*'s structural mode of being."[5]

Existence and Hermeneutics: Ricoeur

In Heidegger's own description, the general approach followed in *Being and Time* could be characterized as a "hermeneutical" phenomenology, that is, a phenomenology seeking to grasp various modes of being through an interpretation of their meaning and ontological status. A broadly similar approach — though with a heavier dose of transcendental-philosophical and epistemological concerns — has been formulated some four decades later by Paul Ricoeur. Rather than summarizing his sprawling opus I want to concentrate for present purposes on an article entitled "Existence and Hermeneutics" which succinctly captures his basic posture (and which serves as lead essay in his book *The Conflict of Interpretations*). As Ricoeur points out, the central aim of his essay is to clear a path leading from (Husserlian) phenomenology to hermeneutics — defined as the interpretive understanding of meaning — and thus to help bring about a "renewal of phenomenology through hermeneutics." After sketching briefly the history of Western and particularly modern hermeneutical inquiry, the essay asserts that there are essentially two ways of "grounding hermeneutics in phenomenology" or of grafting "the hermeneutic problem onto the phenomenological method": namely, a "short route" identified with Heidegger's "ontology of understanding" or "analytic of *Dasein*," and a "long route" proceeding toward existential understanding *via* a deliberate epistemology of interpretation — which is the one adopted by Ricoeur. In Heidegger's *Being and Time*, he observes, the question "On what condition can a knowing subject understand a text or history?" is replaced by the different question: "What kind of being is it whose being consists of understanding?" — a question exceeding the confines of (traditional) epistemology. On Heideggerian premises, we are

told, "one must deliberately move outside the enchanted circle of the problematic of subject and object and question oneself about being"; treated
in this manner, hermeneutical understanding is "no longer a mode of
knowledge but a mode of being, the mode of that being which exists
through understanding," that is, *Dasein*. Once this route is taken, Ricoeur
adds, transcendental phenomenology is no longer of primary significance;
for ultimately, it is "against the early Husserl, against the alternately
Platonizing and idealizing tendencies of his theory of meaning and intentionality, that the (Heideggerian) theory of understanding has been erected." Although claiming to share "the desire" for the latter perspective and
acknowledging the "extraordinarily seductive power of this fundamental
ontology," the essay opts for the longer route—chiefly for cognitive and
methodological reasons: "In this way we will continue to keep in touch
with the disciplines which seek to practice interpretation in a methodical
manner, and we will resist the temptation to separate *truth*, characteristic of understanding, from the *method* put into operation by disciplines
which have sprung from exegesis."[6]

As outlined in the essay, the long route presents itself as a kind of wind-
ing road (or detour) proceeding through three main stages: namely, from
the domain of "semantics"—concerned with meaning contents—over the
stage of "reflection" and self-reflection to the destination of existential
understanding. Regarding the first stage, Ricoeur invokes the testimony
of diverse interpretive procedures, ranging from literary criticism to psychoanalysis, in support of the view that meaning contents should be seen
as complex "expressions of life" whose analysis requires attention to their
multi-layered "architecture"—exemplified chiefly in "double" and "multiple" meanings which he terms "symbolic" expressions. Construed in
this sense, an interpretive semantics has to be concerned with the "shown-
yet-concealed" or with the interlacing of "primary, literal" with "secondary and figurative" significations; in his words, it embodies "the work of
thought which consists in deciphering the hidden meaning in the apparent meaning, in unfolding the levels of meaning implied in the literal
meaning." According to the essay, the advantages of departing from this
stage are primarily methodological and epistemological in character.
Semantic analysis, we read, first of all "keeps hermeneutics in contact
with methodologies as they are actually practiced" in interpretive disciplines. More importantly, the approach "assures the implantation of
hermeneutics in phenomenology at the level at which the latter is most
sure of itself, that is, at the level of the theory of meaning developed in
the *Logical Investigations*." To be sure, Ricoeur adds, Husserl at that
point "would not have accepted the idea of meaning as irreducibly nonunivocal"; in fact, he "explicitly excludes this possibility"—which is the
reason "why the phenomenology of the *Logical Investigations* cannot be

hermeneutical." Yet, despite this divergence, the linkage between hermeneutics and Husserlian thought is said to persist on the level of semantic inquiry: "If we part from Husserl, we do so within the framework of his theory of signifying expressions."[7]

Taken by itself, however, semantic analysis is insufficient for hermeneutics; if this were the terminal point, significations would tend to "close in" on themselves and hermeneutics could not properly qualify "as philosophy." Thus, a further step is required, the step of "reflection" which forges a "link between the understanding of signs and self-understanding"; for it is "in the self that we have the opportunity to discover an existent" searching for meaning. In relating "symbolic language to self-understanding," Ricoeur asserts, "I think I fulfill the deepest wish of hermeneutics"; for, all hermeneutical inquiry aims at "self-understanding by means of understanding others." In a sense, the reflective step involves a "Cartesian" turn, that is, a return to the "*cogito*"—but the latter now has an existential rather than purely cognitive cast. "Hermeneutics," we read, "must be grafted onto phenomenology, not only at the level of the theory of meaning expressed in the *Logical Investigations*, but also at the level of the problematic of the *cogito*." Yet, while embracing the Cartesian legacy, one also has to realize that "the graft changes the wild stock": for, just as the inclusion of symbolic expressions in semantics "forces us to abandon the ideal of univocity," it must "now be understood that by joining these multivocal meanings to self-knowledge we profoundly transform the problematic of the *cogito*." Viewed as a purely cognitive capacity, the traditional *cogito*, in Ricoeur's judgment, is "a truth as vain as it is invincible" or "like a first step which cannot be followed by any other" —at least so long as the subject has not dispersed itself in the world through self-enactment or symbolic self-disclosure; moreover, the *cogito*'s "truth" tends to be permeated with falsehood, that is, with "false consciousness" or self-deception. Notwithstanding these flaws of Cartesianism, however, the reflective step is portrayed as crucial to hermeneutics for cognitive-philosophical motives: only by means of this step is it possible to uncover "the principle of a logic of double meaning"—which is not simply a formal logic but a "transcendental logic" established "at the level of conditions of possibility." By virtue of this reflective grounding, "the logic of double meaning proper to hermeneutics can be called transcendental."[8]

As suggested by the transformation of the *cogito*, reflection does not yield a completely unmediated or self-sufficient subjectivity as source of meanings; rather, its "internal reform" is precisely what justifies in the end "our discovering there a new dimension of existence" or existential understanding—a discovery coinciding with the third and final stage of the sketched route. In order to reach this destination of his inquiry,

Ricoeur enlists primarily the help of Freudian psychoanalysis. Philosophically construed, he argues, psychoanalysis makes two main contributions to this last move: namely, first, "a true dismissal of the classical problematic of the subject as consciousness," and next, "a restoration of the problematic of existence as desire." Freudian depth analysis, the essay states, involves a "critique of consciousness" which in turn "points to (existential) ontology"; its exegesis of dreams, myths, and symbols "always contests to some extent the pretension of consciousness in setting itself up as the origin of meaning." In this manner, psychoanalysis engenders a hermeneutics "free from the prejudices of the ego"; in fact, it induces or is liable to induce a "true ascesis of subjectivity," leading to "the real loss of the most archaic of all objects: the self." Of course, this loss in Freudian teachings is only preparatory to a therapeutic recovery: "All of psychoanalysis speaks to me of lost objects to be found again symbolically. Reflective philosophy must integrate this discovery with its own task: the self (*le moi*) must be lost in order to find the 'I' (*le je*)" — namely, in the mode of existential desire and energy. Once the boundaries of consciousness are transgressed, human existence emerges as "desire and effort" (*conatus*); as a result, the *cogito* "is no longer the pretentious act it was initially" but appears "as *already* posited in being." Yet, desire and effort are not simply empirical-instinctual forces outside the circle of interpretation; although glimpsed "behind the enigmas of consciousness," existence remains a "being-interpreted" entangled in the "movement of deciphering to which it gives rise." From the angle of a psychoanalytically refined hermeneutics, meanings thus are not so much conscious products as the expressions of "existence" on its path through loss and self-recovery; what its analysis discovers is "existence as desire, and this existence is revealed principally in an archaeology of the subject."[9]

Discourse and Communicative Competence: Habermas (1)

Transcendental preoccupations — with still more pronounced epistemological and normative overtones — have arisen also in the context of "critical theory," a perspective only marginally influenced by phenomenology and most strongly indebted to critical philosophy and critical Marxism (in addition to more recent accretions like speech-act theory and generative linguistics). Although cultivated by a broader school of thought, the critical framework today is most prominently represented by Jürgen Habermas, whose opus in a bold sweep spans the social sciences as well as philosophy and the humanities. Without denying the occurrence of a "linguistic turn" at some point in his intellectual career, it seems fair to say that Habermas has been concerned with language from the beginning, especially with the practical function of communication or communicative interaction. One of his earliest publications (1962) analyzed the status of the "public sphere" (*Öffentlichkeit*) in modern Western society, noting in particular the progressive decay of public debate and deliberation during the last hundred years—a decay attributed mainly to the rise of technocracy and of a consumption-oriented economy governed by private utility maxims. A subsequent book, entitled *Theory and Practice* (1963), inserted this decay into a broader account of the history of Western philosophy since antiquity, an account focusing on the relation between theoretical and practical reason and on the steady decline or atrophy of the latter in modern and recent times. Language in these studies, one should note, figured chiefly as a means of practical communication rather than an autonomous topic of inquiry. Something like a categorial mode of analysis, with closer attention to language as such, began to emerge during the following years—and initially in the confines of strictly epistemological investigations. In several respects, Habermas's *Knowledge and Human Interests*(1968) stood in marked contrast to dominant logical-empiricist canons of the period: the study first of all signaled a "pragmatic" shift within epistemology, by linking types of knowledge with underlying human orientations termed "cognitive interests"; those interests, furthermore, were given a transcendental or quasi-transcendental anchorage—through the claim that types of cognition reflect a categorial (and not randomly variable) structure of human existence or experience. Seen as a categorial structure, existence in Habermas's portrayal exhibited three main dimensions: those of man's relations with nature, with his fellow-man, and with himself. While, in the first dimension, cognition aimed at the appropriation of nature's bounty for human goals (and thus was guided by a "technical interest"), the second domain was animated by the purpose of reaching reciprocal understanding among individuals (in accordance with a "practical interest"); in the last area, finally, the quest for knowledge involved a search for self-knowledge, a search necessitating a struggle against both internal and external "blinders" or constraints (thus reflecting an "emancipatory interest"). Language and speech played a role primarily in the last two fields: namely, first, as an instrument of communicative interaction; and secondly, as a "therapeutic" medium facilitating the transition from a distorted-repressive to a rational and liberated mode of self-knowledge.[10]

In Habermas's own assessment, *Knowledge and Human Interests* was not a *summa* or capstone of his thought but rather a "prolegomenon" to a full-fledged social theory, and more concretely, a launching pad for more detailed inquiries centered on various issues raised in the study. As he realized, one of the unresolved or relatively obscure aspects of the study was the status of cognitive interests—a realization which prompted him to clarify the notion of "quasi-transcendental" categories hovering midway between the accomplishments of a transcendental subjectivity and empirical endowments. Closely linked with this notion was the issue of the genesis of structural categories, that is, the question of their "ontogenetic" and "phylogenetic" development over time—an issue which impelled him to devote closer attention to cognitive and developmental psychology (as practiced by Piaget and Lawrence Kohlberg), to the literature of social and political evolution, and also to the methodology of "rational reconstruction" aimed at uncovering deep-seated competences and rule-systems (as advocated again by Piaget and Chomsky). At the same time, the empirical and genetic connotations of this quasi-transcendental approach conjured up the danger of historicism or the contingency of human knowledge—a danger which motivated Habermas to formulate the concept of "discourse" as the arena of knowledge validation, in differentiation from routine interaction in everyday situations. As he pointed out in a new edition of *Theory and Practice* (1971), "discourses require the suspension of everyday practical constraints, a suspension intended to render inoperative all motives except that of a cooperative readiness to reach understanding and to separate questions of validity from those of genesis." Since truth or validity, he added, is "distinguished from mere certainty by its claim to be absolute, discourse is the condition of the unconditioned." The concept of "discourse," however, is clearly a linguistic category which needed to be analyzed within the context of contemporary language philosophy—with the result that language as such imposed itself with growing intensity as an inescapable topic of study. This turn to language was reinforced by problems arising in the field of human self-knowledge and emancipation: for, how could the transition from distorted to rational or nonrepressive understanding be made intelligible without recourse to a theory of undistorted speech and linguistic communication—a theory which in turn presupposes procedures of rational reconstruction?[11]

The first deliberate steps by Habermas into the terrain of language philosophy and linguistic theory occurred in two essays, published in 1970, which revolved around the notion of "communicative competence." The first essay, entitled "On Systematically Distorted Communication," took its point of departure from the issues of self-knowledge and psychoanalytic therapy discussed in the last section of *Knowledge and Human Interests*. As Habermas observed, the task of disentangling seriously deformed or "systematically distorted" speech and meaning patterns requires resources which exceed the bounds of everyday communication and commonsense understanding. The ordinary " 'hermeneutic' consciousness of translation difficulties," he wrote, "proves to be inadequate when applied to systematically distorted communication; for in this case, incomprehensibility results from a faulty organization of speech itself." Obvious examples of systematic distortion were pathological speech disturbances or defects; however, more interesting and significant instances were those "which appear in speech which is not conspicuously pathological," that is, in cases of "pseudo-communication" where participants themselves "do not recognize any communication disturbances." In cases of this kind, ordinary understanding had to be replaced with a relatively systematic-theoretical analysis undertaken by a neutral observer, since only the latter "notices that the participants do not understand one another." According to the essay, a prominent model for such an analysis was provided by Freudian psychoanalysis, an approach encompassing a broad spectrum of meaning deformations ranging from pseudo-communications and Freudian "slips" over dreams to neurotic and psychotic speech pathologies. With particular reference to neurotic disturbances, Freud's model specified three main criteria for detecting meaning deformations: first, on the level of language, deviation from recognized linguistic rules manifest, for example, in "condensation, displacement, absence of grammaticalness"; secondly, on the behavioral level, prevalence of stereotyped behavior patterns, compulsory repetition, and the like; and lastly, on a holistic-existential level, incompatibility of expressions and meanings in the sense that "the usual congruency between linguistic symbols, actions and accompanying gestures has disintegrated." Drawing on recent linguistic reinterpretations of Freudian theory, the essay proposed to redefine the therapeutic-analytical situation in terms of processes of "desymbolization" and "resymbolization"— the former denoting the banishment of a traumatic experience from ordinary awareness and the insertion of private meanings in the resulting semantic gap. Seen in this context, the analyst's efforts were basically designed to dissolve the opacity of private meanings and thus to achieve a "resymbolization," that is, "the re-entry of isolated symbolic contents into public communication."[12]

As Habermas elaborated, a consistent linguistic reconstruction of psychoanalysis depended on a number of theoretical premises or requisites of which he listed mainly three (all of which were closely tied to traditional "subjectivity" and the attendant subject-object dichotomy): first, a conception of ordinary, nondistorted communication; secondly, a developmental theory of symbolization; and lastly, a theory of meaning deformation construed in terms of deviant socialization. In Habermas's portrayal, ordinary or "normal" communication was characterized primarily by these features: congruence between linguistic expressions, actions, and gestures; adherence to publicly sanctioned linguistic rules; recognition by speakers of the "categorial difference between subject and object," between "outer and inner speech," and between private and public realms; and finally maintenance of a functioning "intersubjectivity" coupled with the cultivation of a stable "ego-identity" among participants. Symbolization from a developmental perspective involved basically "two genetically successive phases" of meaning formation: namely, an archaic or "prelinguistic" and a mature or "linguistic" phase. Archaic meaning patterns or "palaeosymbols," Habermas noted (partially echoing Ricoeur), lack "all characteristics of normal speech" and "do not fit into a system of grammatical rules"—a trait entailing a distinct "privatism" of meaning in lieu of its public stabilization. "The privatism of prelinguistic symbol-organization, so striking in all forms of speech pathology," we read, "originates in the fact that the usual distance between sender and addressee, as well as the differentiation between symbolic signs, semantic content, and items of reference has not yet been developed; thus, the distinction between reality and appearance, between the public and the private sphere cannot yet be clearly sustained with the help of palaeosymbols (*adualism*)." The significance of this two-phase theory for psychoanalytic therapy resided in the mentioned processes of desymbolization and resymbolization, whereby a traumatic event is initially "excommunicated from public communication and banished to the archaic level of palaeosymbols" in order to be later reintegrated into "common linguistic usage." According to the essay, these two requisites were linked with still more basic assumptions regarding meaning deformations—assumptions underlying Freud's three-layered model of the psyche: "All three categories—ego, id, and superego— reflect fundamental experiences typical of systematically distorted communication." Rigorously applied, Freud's structural model could be "reduced to a theory of deviant communicative competence"—a theory which, together with its corollary concept of "communicative competence," was still undeveloped (or only barely developed) in the literature.[13]

Habermas's subsequent writings in the field of language theory set themselves mainly the task of filling this gap. The second of the two essays of 1970, entitled "Towards a Theory of Communicative Competence," shifted the focus somewhat abruptly from psychoanalysis to generative linguistics and ordinary language analysis; as outlined in the essay, the notion of "communicative competence" involved basically a critical adaptation and combination of Chomsky's category of "linguistic competence" with central tenets of Austin's and Searle's speech-act theory. Regarding generative grammar, Habermas saw its advance over previous linguistic approaches in Chomsky's stress on "the creativity of the speaker and the grammaticalness of language," and particularly in the discovery that "the competent speaker must possess a knowledge grossly disproportionate to his empirical information," in other words, that he "must know more than he can have learned in his previous con-

tacts with his linguistic environment." To explain this asymmetry between knowledge and learning experience, Chomsky had to rely on a
number of presuppositions among which the essay mentioned mainly
these: existence of an "abstract linguistic system" composed of generative
rules; the "innate" character of this system, more precisely its development out of the "interaction of phase-specific stimulus conveyance and
organic maturation processes"; the presence of "linguistic universals" in
the depth structure of the system; and finally, the possibility of deriving
surface structures from deep structures by means of transformational
rules. While accepting many of Chomsky's insights, Habermas found
generative grammar and its key concept of "linguistic competence"—
defined as "the mastery of an abstract system of rules, based on an innate
language apparatus"—flawed by several defects. Summarily assessed, the
approach in his view was too closely tied to a technical "information
model of communication," a model in which, prior to concrete interactions, senders and receivers are presumed to be equipped with the same
linguistic program or code. What this model neglects, the essay noted,
is essentially the "pragmatics" of speech, that is, the possible emergence
of meaning out of actual speech performances and thus the process of
progressive reciprocal understanding. "If general linguistics," we read,
"restricts itself to giving a rational reconstruction of the abstract system
of linguistic rules which the ideal speaker has in mind, as it were, prior
to all communication, and if the theory of language performance
analyzes solely restrictive extra-linguistic conditions for applying
linguistic competence, then not only grammar and phonetics but semantics, too, would have to be developed independently of the pragmatic
dimension of language performance."[14]

In an effort to counter or remedy the sketched flaws, Habermas proceeded to outline a scheme of "semantic universals" which went beyond
Chomsky's model by incorporating both intersubjective and experientially induced meaning patterns. "Some meanings," he wrote, "are *a priori*
universal in as much as they establish the conditions of potential communication and general schemes of interpretation; others are *a posteriori*
universal, in the sense that they represent invariant features of contingent
scopes of experience which, however, are common to all cultures. For
that reason we differentiate between semantic universals which process
experiences and semantic universals which make this processing possible
in the first place." In addition, "intersubjectively universal" patterns were
said to be those "fixed on structures which first develop with the cultural
level of linguistic communication itself," while "monologically universal"
meanings refer to "structures of the solitary human organism prior to all
communication." For the further development of Habermas's own
perspective, the notion of "intersubjective universals"—subsequently

termed "dialogue-constitutive universals"—proved to be of decisive importance (while the distinction between a priori and a posteriori patterns tended to merge in the domain of "quasi-transcendental" categories). Regarding the presumed independence of "innate" linguistic rules from cultural learning experience, the essay pointed to the testimony of anthropology and comparative ethno-linguistics, and especially to the study of kinship systems: "An intercultural comparison of the kinship vocabulary shows clearly that this same semantic field is differently classified depending on the prevailing status system, that is, on the specific definition of the age-, sex-, and descent-linked primary roles." More broadly, semantic meaning patterns were generally connected with cultural conditions or with the "non-exceedable common context of the society to which the speakers belong"—a connection which could be demonstrated even in the case of Chomsky's model.[15]

Coupled with the expansion and diversification of the notion of linguistic rules or universals was a more basic transformation of Chomskyan linguistics: the broadening of "linguistic competence" to make room for intersubjective, communicative experience. "The general competence of a native speaker," Habermas asserted, "does not extend merely to the mastery of an abstract system of linguistic rules"; rather, "producing a situation of potential ordinary-language communication is itself part of the general competence of the ideal speaker." Differently phrased: "In order to participate in normal discourse the speaker must have at his disposal, in addition to his linguistic competence, basic qualifications of speech and symbolic interaction which we may call *communicative competence*." The latter term denoted basically the "mastery of an ideal speech situation," that is, a situation manifesting the "ideal" or universal parameters of communication. To elucidate this conception further, the essay turned to speech-act theory and especially to Austin's distinction between locutionary and illocutionary speech components. Utterances, Habermas observed, "have, in addition to the meaning of their propositional content, a meaning which is linked to the speech situation as such. This, following Austin, we can call their 'illocutionary force'." Seen on a structural level, expressions in his view were not simply aspects of contingent interactions, but reflected the "universal pragmatic power" of utterances: "They explain the meaning of certain idealized features of speech situations in general, which the speaker must master if his competence is to be adequate for participating at all in situations of potential speech." Thus, rather than coinciding with empirically variable contexts, speech situations could be shown to exhibit a universal linguistic structure composed of equally universal ingredients. Appealing to Searle's notion of "constitutive rules," Habermas named the latter ingredients "constitutive universals" and more particularly discourse- or "dialogue-constitutive universals": "It is the dialogue-constitutive universals (as we now prefer to say) that establish in the first place the form of intersubjectivity between any competent speakers capable of mutual understanding." Accordingly, communicative competence was "defined by the ideal speaker's mastery of the dialogue-constitutive universals, irrespective of actual restrictions under empirical conditions."[16]

Turning to a more detailed review of linguistic interactions, the essay sketched a tentative classification of constitutive universals—which, in many respects, resembled Heidegger's fourfold scheme of speech components. The first category in this list embraced terms or phrases which are indispensable to speech or discourse itself, such as personal pronouns, "deictic" expressions, forms of address, and the like. The main accent of the essay, however, rested on three types or categories of utterances which were said to "mark the basic differentiations which are fundamental for any speech situation"—types having to do respectively with thematic content (Heidegger's "spoken about"), speaker's self-disclosure (Heidegger's *Bekundung*), and speaker-addressee relations (*Mitteilung*). In Habermas's portrayal, the first type of performative acts—called "constatives" at one point—concentrated on "the truth value of utterances according to the prototype of 'to claim' and 'to dispute' "; the second mode—termed "representatives"—involved "the self-representation of persons according to the prototype of 'to reveal' and 'to hide'," while the third kind—labeled "regulatives"—referred to "the normative status of rules according to the prototype of 'to prescribe' and 'to follow'." In terms of traditional metaphysical vocabulary, constatives were said to demarcate the dimensions of "being and appearance" and thus to permit the "differentiation between a public world of intersubjectively acknowledged interpretations and a private world of personal feelings and impressions," while—reflecting the dichotomy of "being and (internal) essence"—representatives were claimed to support the distinction between a "communication on objects" and the expression by speakers of "their own selves"; manifesting the dualism of "what is and what ought to be," regulatives finally sustained the "differentiation between valid (normative) rules which are intentionally followed, and regularities of observable events which can be stated empirically." As viewed in the essay, the preceding classification was not merely a descriptive exercise, but carried distinct evaluative (and even political) implications: to be fully operative, the structure of communication required "ideally" competent speakers, that is, speakers able to perform all types of speech acts without discrimination or constraint. Genuine discourse, we read, "is determined by a symmetrical relation between I and You (We and You), I and He (We and They). An unlimited interchangeability of dialogue roles demands that no side be privileged in the performance of these roles: pure intersubjectivity exists only when there is complete symmetry in the distribution of assertion and denial, revelation and concealment, prescription and conformity, among the partners of communication."[17]

Universal Pragmatics: Habermas (2)

The reviewed papers were intended as preparatory explorations anticipating the formulation of a more systematic perspective in which the concepts of "communicative competence" and "dialogue-constitutive universals" would coalesce into a theory of "universal pragmatics." A decisive step in this direction occurred with the publication (in 1976) of Habermas's monograph entitled "What Is Universal Pragmatics?" In its opening paragraph the study specified as its overriding task or ambition the identification and reconstruction of the "universal conditions of possible communicative understanding" (*Verständigung*). Couched in this manner, Habermas recognized, his approach was closely akin to the legacy of transcendental philosophy, as revived in our time chiefly by Karl-Otto Apel—an outlook focusing on the a priori premises of speech which speakers must share or have recognized whenever they perform or respond to utterances. Reformulating and modifying Apel's concern with the "normative conditions of the possibility of understanding," the study proposed to concentrate on the "validity basis of speech"—a concept reflecting the assumption that "anyone acting communicatively must, in performing any speech action, raise universal validity claims and suppose that they can be vindicated or redeemed." To flesh out this concept, a nuclear model of speech performance was employed: "I say something about something to someone in a language"—a model which, analyzed into its ingredients, yields the four (Heideggerian) components of (1) a linguistic utterance, (2) made about something (a theme or content) (3) by a speaker (4) in relation to a hearer. According to Habermas, validity claims could be directly linked with this scheme. "Insofar as he wants to participate in a process of reaching communicative understanding," he wrote, a speaker "cannot avoid raising the following—and indeed precisely the following—validity claims: He claims to be (1) *uttering* something understandably; (2) giving *something* to understand; (3) making *himself* thereby understandable; and (4) coming to an understanding *with another person*." Thus, he added: "The speaker must choose a *comprehensible* expression so that speaker and hearer can understand one another"; he must "have the intention of communicating a *true* proposition (or a propositional content whose existential presuppositions are satisfied) so that the hearer can share his knowledge"; he must "want to express his intentions *truthfully* so that the hearer can believe his utterance (or trust him)"; and finally, he must "choose an utterance that is *right* so that the hearer can accept it and both can concur in the utterance with respect to a recognized normative background." More briefly put, communicative understanding is "based on a recognition of the corresponding validity claims of comprehensibility, truth, truthfulness, and rightness."[18]

As Habermas acknowledged, his language theory—oriented toward a "universal pragmatics"—deviated radically from prevailing or conventional approaches, and particularly from such twentieth-century perspectives as logical empiricism and structural linguistics. "The logical analysis of language that originated with Carnap," he observed, "focuses primarily on syntactic and semantic properties of linguistic formations. Like structural linguistics, it delimits its object domain by first abstracting from the pragmatic properties of language, subsequently introducing the pragmatic dimension in such a way that the constitutive connection between the generative accomplishments of speaking and acting subjects, on the one hand, and the general structures of speech, on the other, cannot come into view." What was chiefly neglected in such approaches was the possibility of giving a systematic or "formal" account of the "generative accomplishments" of speakers—an account matching in logical rigor the analyses of syntactic and semantic properties. Although legitimate for some purposes, the bifurcation between *langue* and *parole*, he affirmed, "is not sufficient reason for the view that the pragmatic dimension of language from which one abstracts is beyond formal analysis." Habermas at this point entered into detailed methodological considerations regarding the status and meaning of "formal" inquiry, further defined as "reconstructive" analysis or the method of "rational reconstruction" (to which I can only allude here briefly). Applied to the field of language theory, "rational reconstruction" stood mainly in opposition to empiricist linguistic investigations; generally speaking, reconstructive procedures were said to be "not characteristic of sciences that develop nomological hypotheses about domains of observable events; rather, they characterize sciences that systematically reconstruct the *intuitive knowledge of competent subjects*." Appealing to Gilbert Ryle's distinction between "know-how" and "know-that," the study argued that rational reconstruction first of all yields a theoretical knowledge or "second-level know-that" about the "implicit rule consciousness" (or know-how) of competent speakers; more importantly, the procedure uncovers the "evaluative accomplishment" of rule competence, that is, the ability of speakers to differentiate between grammatical and ungrammatical as well as between meaningful and meaningless utterances. "The rule consciousness of competent speakers," we read, "functions as a court of evaluation, for instance, with regard to the grammaticality of sentences." As indicated, however, grammatical comprehensibility was not the only yardstick of speech; to the extent that universal validity claims can be shown to undergird intuitive evaluations, "reconstructions relate to pretheoretical knowledge of a general sort, to *universal capabilities*."[19]

In the area of linguistics, Habermas noted, a fruitful reconstructive strategy has been employed by Chomsky, with chief reference to syntax and syntactic-grammatical rules; moving beyond narrowly empiricist confines, the goal of the latter's inquiries was "an explicit description of the rules that a competent speaker must master in order to form grammatical sentences and to utter them in an acceptable way." While conceding the "great merit" of Chomsky's work, however, Habermas—as on previous occasions—found it necessary to deviate from generative grammar in several important respects. One modification concerned the postulated correlation between grammatical theory and an innate "mental grammar" operative "in the mind" of speakers—which he toned down in favor of a weaker "maturationist" view of cognitive and linguistic development. More important for his own overall perspective was the change in the scope of reconstruction. According to Habermas, Chomsky's approach is capable only of grasping the grammaticality of sentences and the linguistic intelligibility of utterances. "The grammaticality of a sentence means," he wrote, that "the sentence, when uttered by a speaker, is *comprehensible* to all hearers" who have mastered the relevant grammatical rules. In the context of universal validity claims, such comprehensibility is "the only one of these universal claims that can be fulfilled immanently to language." However, the purpose or "telos" of communicative interaction exceeded these intra linguistic bounds. Thus, as indicated, the validity of a "propositional content" depended on "whether the proposition stated represents a fact," just as the validity of an "intention expressed" rests on "whether it corresponds to what is actually intended by the speaker," and the validity of the "utterance performed" on "whether this action conforms to a recognized normative background." Consequently, "whereas a grammatical sentence fulfills the claim to comprehensibility, a successful utterance must satisfy three additional validity claims: it must count as *true* for the participants insofar as it represents something in the world; it must count as *truthful* insofar as it expresses something intended by the speaker; and it must count as *right* insofar as it conforms to socially recognized expectations." In order to encompass this broader scope of interaction, Chomsky's "linguistic competence" had to be replaced by a broader theory of "communicative competence" predicated on a "universal-pragmatic" analysis of speech. To the extent that utterances reflect the structural dimensions of factual "representation, expression, and legitimate interpersonal relation," we read, "what is expressed in them is precisely the communicative competence for which I am proposing a universal-pragmatic investigation."[20]

In developing and fleshing out this kind of reconstructive investigation, the study (again) enlisted the help of speech-act theory as formulated by Austin and Searle: "The discussion of the theory of speech acts has given rise to ideas on which the fundamental assumptions of universal pragmatics can be based." Relying on Austin's distinction between locutionary content and illocutionary force, Habermas mentioned as a chief contribution of speech-act theory its emphasis on the "double structure of speech"—the aspect that communication occurs simultaneously on two levels, those of intersubjectivity and propositional information exchange—a structure revealing the "inherent reflexivity" of language: "The peculiar reflexivity of natural language rests in the first instance on the combination of a communication of content—effected in an objectifying attitude—with a communication concerning the relational context in which the content is to be understood—effected in a performative attitude." While borrowing from analytical teachings in this and numerous other respects, Habermas (as before) departed from Austin's conception in several important details, and particularly in two: first, by extending the notion of "meaning" to cover both thematic content and illocutionary "force" (thus reducing the nonrational overtones of the latter term); and secondly, by modifying the Austinian classification scheme by moving beyond the narrow confines of "truth-falsity" and "happiness-unhappiness" criteria. Invoking the nuclear structure of communication as reflected in the noted validity claims, the study proposed a systematic and "universal-pragmatic" taxonomy of speech functions and corresponding speech acts or modes of linguistic interaction. On the functional level, the following chief types of language use were listed in the study: a "cognitive," an "interactive," and an "expressive" type, the first emphasizing propositional content, the second concerned with interpersonal speaker-hearer relations, and the third with intentional self-disclosure. Correlated with these functional categories were distinct types of speech acts, labeled "constative," "regulative," and "expressive" acts (or "avowals"). In Habermas's words, the difference between functional modes and speech acts derives "from stressing one of the validity claims universally inhabiting speech, that is, from the fact that in the cognitive use of language we raise truth claims for propositions and in the interactive use we claim (or contest) the validity of a normative context of interpersonal relations," while the expressive use relates to "the truthfulness with which a speaker utters his intentions" or "the transparency of a subjectivity representing itself in language." The fourth claim of comprehensibility was equally raised in all three functional modes and utterances; for "every speech act must fulfill the presuppositions of comprehensibility."[21]

The sketched taxonomy or typology, Habermas noted, could be further correlated with standards regarding the success or failure of speech acts, as outlined in Searle's recent writings. Building on such Searlean criteria as "preparatory," "essential," and "sincerity rules," the study argued that communicative success was predicated on a complex, inter-related set of "commitments" or "engagements" on the part of speakers, undertaken in such a way that hearers can rely on them. "The bond," we read, "into which the speaker is willing to enter with the performance of an illocutionarily act means a guarantee that, in consequence of his ut-terance, he will fulfill certain conditions." Thus, the illocutionary point or "force" of successful speech could be said to reside "in the fact that it can move a hearer to rely on the speech-act-typical commitment of the speaker." The basic thesis advanced in the study at this point was that successful communication implies the rationality of reciprocal expecta-tions, a rationality tied to the possibility of validation: "In the final analysis, the speaker can illocutionarily influence the hearer and vice-versa, because speech-act-typical commitments are connected with cognitively testable validity claims—that is, because the reciprocal bonds have a rational basis." The specific commitments undertaken by speakers in communicative interactions, Habermas added, consisted in the will-ingness to live up to the validity claims implicit in speech, claims varying with functional modes: "In the cognitive use of language, the speaker proffers a speech-act-immanent *obligation to provide grounds*," im-plemented by recurring to "the experiential source from which he draws the certainty that his statement is true." On the other hand, "in the in-teractive use the speaker proffers a speech-act-immanent *obligation to provide justification*," that is, to indicate "the normative context that gives him the conviction that his utterance is right." Finally, in the ex-pressive use, the speaker's engagement involves the *"obligation to prove trustworthy*, to show in the consequences of his action that he has ex-pressed the intention actually guiding his behavior." The stipulated com-mitments and obligations could be tested and redeemed either directly, in the context of the ongoing communication itself, or else indirectly: namely, by means of "theoretical" and "practical" discourses (in the case of constatives and regulatives) or through subsequent actions or interac-tions (in the case of expressive acts).[22]

Pulling together the diverse strands of the preceding arguments, the concluding section of the study delineated a comprehensive "model of linguistic communication," a model designed to pinpoint the "systematic place of language." Drawing on the discussion of validity claims, the sec-tion specified this "systematic place" by means of a series of demarcations or differentiations. "Language," Habermas affirmed, "is the medium through which speakers and hearers realize certain fundamental demar-cations. The subject demarcates himself: (1) from an environment that he objectifies in the third-person attitude of an observer; (2) from an environment that he conforms to or deviates from in the ego-alter attitude of a participant; (3) from his own subjectivity that he expresses or conceals in a first-person attitude; and finally (4) from the medium of language itself. For these domains of reality I have proposed the somewhat arbitrarily chosen terms: *external nature, society, internal nature,* and *language*." As used by Habermas, the phrase "external nature" (or "external reality") designated the "objectified segment of reality that the adult subject is able (even if only mediately) to perceive and manipulate." By "society" (elsewhere called "normative reality") the study referred to "that symbolically prestructured segment of reality that the adult subject can understand in a non-objectifying attitude, that is, as one acting communicatively (as a participant in a system of communication)." Under the rubric of "internal nature" Habermas subsumed "all wishes, feelings, intentions, and the like, to which an 'I' has privileged access and can express as its own experiences before a public." Language itself was enmeshed in the same system of demarcations. "Finally," we read, "I introduced the linguistic medium of our utterances as a special region; precisely because language (including non-propositional symbol systems) remains in a peculiar half-transcendence in the performance of our communicative actions and expressions, it presents itself to the speaker and the actor (preconsciously) as a segment of reality *sui generis*." The entire model highlighted the universal structural features of communicative pragmatics, by showing how "grammatical sentences are embedded, by way of universal validity claims, in three relations to reality," relations corresponding to the "pragmatic functions of representing facts, establishing legitimate interpersonal relations, and expressing one's own subjectivity."[23]

Transcendental Hermeneutics: Apel

Among the numerous distinctions and demarcations introduced in Habermas's study, one further and more general boundary might briefly be mentioned: the differentiation between his outlook and traditional transcendentalism, especially as espoused by Karl-Otto Apel. Reviewing various adaptations of Kantian philosophy in our time, the study criticized as too weak the "minimalist interpretation" adopted by Strawson — a strategy entailing the "renunciation of the concept of the constitution of experience and of an explicit treatment of validity problems" — while faulting Apel for his excessively Kantian fervor. In trying to profile more clearly his own approach, Habermas offered two main reasons for his reluctance to embrace Apel's vocabulary of a "transcendental hermeneutics" or "transcendental pragmatics." The first reason had to do with the difference between transcendental "constitution" and pragmatic "genesis" (or generation). Linguistic utterances, he conceded, could indeed be targets of a conceptual analysis of transcendental or a priori premises; such analysis, however, was unable in his view to uncover their genesis in universal structures of competence. "The idea underlying transcendental philosophy," he wrote, "is—to oversimplify—that we constitute experiences by objectifying reality from invariant points of view"; but "I do not find any correspondent to this idea under which the analysis of general presuppositions of communication might be carried out: Experiences are, if we follow the basic Kantian idea, constituted; utterances are at most generated." The second point concerned the a priori quality of transcendental knowledge in the Kantian sense. From the perspective of rational reconstruction, Habermas observed, "the distinction between drawing on a priori knowledge and drawing on a posteriori knowledge becomes blurred. On the one hand, the rule consciouness of competent speakers is for them an a priori knowledge; on the other hand, the reconstruction of this knowledge calls for inquiries undertaken with empiricial speakers—the linguist procures for himself a knowledge a posteriori."[24]

Habermas's reservations notwithstanding, Apel's outlook actually is far from being a refurbished version of transcendentalism; while accepting crucial ingredients of Kant's teachings, his approach also revises and transforms transcendental philosophy—in the direction of a more strongly linguistic and communicative conception of reflection. Apel's perspective is explicated in a number of writings, particularly in *Towards a Transformation of Philosophy* (1973) and a string of subsequent essays, including a longer monograph (of 1976) entitled "Speech-Act Theory and Transcendental Pragmatics (with Reference to the Question of Ethical Norms)"—on which I shall briefly focus for present purposes. In this essay, the notion of a "transcendental" pragmatics or hermeneutics is elaborated by means of a critical confrontation with contemporary empiricist language philosophy and empiricist linguistics. According to empiricism, Apel notes, transcendental philosophy is vitiated or rendered impossible by the circumstance that transcendental reflection necessarily presupposes language or linguistic communication as an empirical premise. Countering this argument the essay contends that the pregiven status of language does indeed transform and expand the task of transcendental inquiry—but without undermining its basic function. "There cannot be, let us grant, a transcendental philosophy," we read, "which in its inquiry would not also have to presuppose contingent facts (which today are targets of empirical science)"—an admission which does not impair the autonomy of its "a priori claims" from empirical experience. What the recognition of language entails, in Apel's view, is the need to revise transcendental reflection: to cover not only the conditions of possibility of solitary cognition but also the a priori conditions of communicative interaction and intersubjective discourse. What this revision "practically" means, he writes, is "that transcendental philosophy construed as a transcendental pragmatics of language and communication takes its departure—in a move more radical than Kant's—from a reflection on the *unsurpassable conditions of possibility of discursive argumentation*." In other words: Kant's transcendental "synthesis of apperception" is replaced or rather augmented by the universal "synthesis of symbolic interpretation" and communicative understanding.[25]

As the essay thus recognizes, transcendental reflection in our time—rather than coinciding with Kantian apriorism—has to take into account and integrate the lessons of the "linguistic turn" in contemporary thought. To illustrate the implications of this turn, and also to specify more clearly the direction of his own views, Apel—like Habermas—appeals to generative grammar and to the teachings of ordinary language and speech-act theory. What he finds attractive in the former is primarily the distinction between deep and surface structures and the assumption of a generative endowment not entirely converging with empirical linguistic conventions. It is chiefly the meaning and status of this endowment which marks the point of divergence. According to Apel, the source of man's communicative capacity must be located "not in a Chomskyan 'linguistic competence' rooted in empirically fixed and explicable linguistic 'universals' and innate-genetic aptitudes," but rather in a more broadly reflective competence "which we have to postulate as the condition of possibility of a linguistic transcendence of mere 'anthropological' faculties." A constituent feature of this reflective competence is intersubjective communication or speech pragmatics (viewed again not in an empirical or biological genetic sense). Regarding speech-act theory, the essay applauds Searle's turn to speech performance and the interpretation of "meaning" in terms of various (constitutive or regulative) rules; what is seen as defective in this outlook, however, is the insufficient elucidation of the "rule-governed" character of linguistic behavior. In Apel's judgment, meaning in Searle's approach tends to be tied either to syntactical structures or else to contextual or conventional rules operative in a given linguistic community. Actually, he writes, the "rules of language" in a pragmatic sense refer "not primarily to language-conventions seen as empirical 'institutional facts' present in a social-historical situation, nor do they refer primarily to 'speech' construed as empirical implementation of language-conventions; rather, they point to the *universals of human speech capacity* as such."[26]

The appeal to "universals" of speech and to a universal communicative competence approximates Apel's argument to Habermas's perspective—but without producing a complete convergence. In terms of the essay, the difference between a transcendental and a universal pragmatics resides mainly in the latter's tendency to break off philosophical reflection in favor of a recourse to ultimate empirical facts or processes. Although properly emphasizing the universal dimension of speech, we read, Habermas fails to take into account the distinction "between an *instinctual apriori* amenable to empirical explanation and the necessary postulate of a *transcendental apriori* relating to the premise of a semiotic-communicative competence capable of transcending even innate restrictions of possible language-generation." What is slighted or neglected in this manner is the reflective grounding of empirical premises—the aspect that "the universal-pragmatic conditions of communication can be elucidated as *non-empirical* requisites only through reflection on the conditions of possibility of argumentative discourses." Apel in this context also chides the procedure of "rational reconstruction" for its implicit empiricist bias; especially in the domain of language, he asserts, the "empirical-universal" reconstruction of competences needs to be replaced or at least supplemented by "the paradigm of a renewed and expanded transcendental philosophy" dedicated to the reflective exploration of the "linguistic-communicative conditions of possibility of a synthesis of symbolic world-interpretation." The need for such exploration is clearly illustrated in the case of normative theory—which, in its absence, tends to lapse into hypothetical axioms or a "naturalistic fallacy": "It should be obvious that the attempt to demonstrate (with the help of speech-act theory and the notion of 'communicative competence') the possibility of grounding ethical norms can be successful only if we are able to uncover in the universal-pragmatic rules of communication a non-empirical, that is, a *transcendental-normative* core."[27]

Rejoinders

Transcendental modes of analysis—whether of the existential or the quasi-Kantian variety—have not been immune from critical assessments or evaluations. In the case of Heidegger, his later ontological "turn" (*Kehre*) involved at least an implicit distancing from the categorial existentialism presented in *Being and Time*—for which reason I shall not dwell here on evaluative commentaries. Regarding Ricoeur, the most problematic (and perhaps vulnerable) aspects of his approach concern the juxtaposition of layers of understanding—termed "semantic," "transcendental," and "existential" levels—and the differentiation between the so-called "short" and "long" routes of inquiry; since I intend to comment on these aspects at a later point, I shall not elaborate on them further presently. With respect to Apel, the preceding portrayal is probably too condensed and summary to permit a fair assessment of his views—although his other writings do not deviate from, but rather amplify and corroborate the thrust of the discussed essay. Accordingly, what I propose to do in the present context is to focus briefly on Habermas's arguments—arguments which clearly are at the center of attention in contemporary debates regarding the status and prospects of a quasi-transcendental or universal-rational type of inquiry.[28]

Habermas's publications can be and have been scrutinized from diverse angles and at different theoretical junctures (among which I can select here only a few for purposes of illustration). One controversial facet of his arguments concerns the status of psychoanalysis or psychoanalytic therapy both in *Knowledge and Human Interests* and in the paper on "systematically distorted communication." Much of the controversy has centered on the feasibility of applying or extending the Freudian model to larger social-political contexts—an issue which is not directly or only marginally relevant at this point. In the field of language theory, the debate can be narrowed to concentrate on the character and significance of the Freudian "unconscious" seen as an arena of "archaic symbol-organization." In Habermas's paper, archaic or palaeosymbols are presented basically as linguistic deformations or deviations from "normal" syntactical and semantic rules. Viewed in this manner, archaic meanings are characterized chiefly in a negative or privative sense, namely, in terms of the deficiency or absence of grammaticality and of the regular "dualisms" between subject and object and between public and private spheres; the task of therapy on this account consists in the removal of these deformations and thus in the "emancipation" of the subject from presubjective and prelinguistic modes of symbolization. In some measure, Ricoeur's existential hermeneutics can be seen as a corrective to this view—to the extent that his notion of an "archaeology of the subject" implies the latter's emergence out of a topography "separate from the place where immediate consciousness reigns" and which maintains its influence on the process of ego-formation. A more radical departure from an ego- or subject-centered approach can be found in Jacques Lacan's reinterpretation of Freudian teachings. As Anthony Giddens notes, in a passage directly confronting Habermas's and Lacan's conceptions: "Lacan reads 'Wo es war soll Ich werden' not as a therapeutic injunction of psychoanalytic practice (see, by contrast, Habermas's model of psychoanalysis as critical theory), not as implying that 'the ego must dislodge the id', but as a developmental formula: 'it' precedes 'I' and the latter always remains bound to the Other."[29]

As previously indicated, a noticeable corollary of Habermas's linguistic turn has been the switch—at least on the level of methodological strategy—from Freudian depth psychology to generative or depth linguistics. This switch has been accompanied by the replacement or augmentation of critical self-reflection by the procedure of "rational reconstruction," and also by the shift from a reflective-historical hermeneutics to a "formal analysis" of competences in Chomsky's vein, a shift only partially qualified by the concern with intersubjective communication. As Apel notes, notwithstanding the stress on pragmatics, Habermas's concept of "communicative competence" remains largely patterned on Chomsky's analysis of universal categories and genetic endowments. Given this indebtedness to Chomskyan views, however, universal pragmatics is liable also to inherit some of the quandaries besetting structural and generative linguistics (which have been outlined in an earlier chapter): quandaries relating to the focus on meaning invariance and univocity and, more generally, to the substitution of a "Kantian unconscious" for Freudian depth motivations. The affinity with structuralism also conjures up a number of well-known polarities — *langue* versus *parole*, competence versus performance, synchrony versus process — and the problem of their correlation given the tilt toward the first set of the opposed terms. In traditional philosophical vocabulary, the mentioned polarities correspond to the dichotomies of universalism and particularism, permanence and historical change. Habermas's essay on "communicative competence" still linked linguistic rules with historical settings and cultural-interpretive outlooks. "The conceptual hierarchies which the semantic analysis of a given common vocabulary discloses," we read, "change in accordance with the world view, that is, the global interpretation of nature and society which prevails in a social system at a particular stage of development. It is apparent that the examples presented by Chomsky and his colleagues are likewise guided by a global pre-understanding, though admittedly one that possesses a certain plausibility for us as sharers of the ontology governing the everyday understanding of enlightened members of our civilization." In later writings such references tend to vanish in favor of the stress on universal structures uncovered by means of "formal" or "reconstructive" analysis.[30]

The quandaries endemic to the structural-rationalist paradigm are partially mitigated, but in part also complicated and reinforced by the turn to ordinary language and speech-act theory. At the outset, one may question the feasibility of linking a framework focused on depth competences with a perspective emphasizing speech and communicative performance; as one may recall, the pragmatic shift inaugurated by Austin and Wittgenstein occurred largely as a reaction against the idealized rules extolled by logical-semantic analysis. In Habermas's case, the linkage of the two frameworks is accomplished by means of an accentuation (or restoration) of traditional subjectivity — a subjectivity functioning both as structural arena of depth competences and as the locus of performative utterances and communicative interactions. On the level of performance, the different modes of utterances or speech acts ultimately depend on the functional employment of language on the part of speakers; as the monograph on universal pragmatics states in discussing validity claims, it is essentially the speaker who must "choose a comprehensible expression," "have the intention of communicating a true proposition," "want to express his intentions truthfully," and finally "choose an utterance that is right." Seen in this light, all utterances—and not only "expressive" acts or "avowals"—are in a sense expressions of speakers' attitudes and engagements, a consequence which is liable to give rise to (previously discussed) criticisms addressed at the conception of speech as "expression." The reliance on subjectivity is particularly evident in the cited "model of linguistic communication" in which language is portrayed as a system of demarcations, more specifically as the medium through which "the subject demarcates himself" from external nature, society, internal nature, and language itself. The same reliance also surfaces in the definition of "intersubjectivity" as the level "on which speaker and hearer, through illocutionary acts, establish the relations that permit them to come to an understanding with one another."[31]

In connection with the "model of linguistic communication" one may also critically note the presentation of language as a "reality *sui generis*," that is, as a domain arrayed alongside the physical, social-normative, and internal spheres of reality. One question which immediately arises at this point is how language can simultaneously be a separate object domain and also serve as the medium for differentiating the several domains. A more important question, however, concerns the meaning—not further clarified in the essay—of the phrase "reality *sui generis*"; given the system of demarcations one can only surmise that language, like other aspects of the world, is also enmeshed in the subject-object relations familiar from traditional philosophy. In this context, one may recall Heidegger's comments in *Being and Time* where he asked whether language is "a mundane ready-to-hand utensil" or whether it has *"Dasein's* status" or perhaps is "neither of the two"—and also his conclusion that language's "mode of being" so far "remains obscure" and that "even the horizon in which the question might be raised is veiled." In comparison with Heidegger's treatment one may also note the relatively scant attention given by universal pragmatics to listening and to silence—seen not merely as adjuncts but as constitutive features of speech. In the words of *Being and Time*, "only genuine speech renders possible genuine silence" just as silence provides the nourishing soil of speech.[32]

Interpretation and Critique

In turning to textual exegesis (with particular reference to social-political thought), I have to proceed here without the trusted guide

whose assistance I invoked in preceding chapters: Hayden White's overview of literary-exegetic approaches makes no mention of "transcendental" or universal-pragmatic arguments. Fortunately, his guidance is less
crucial at this juncture, due to the close proximity of the discussed
frameworks and textual interpretation. Probably it is not exaggerated to
say that among all the reviewed perspectives none are more closely tied
to exegesis than those presented in this chapter—as is evident already
from their designations or self-descriptions. The title "hermeneutics,"
whether linked with existential or quasi-transcendental premises, clearly
points to the task or labor of interpretation involved in the search for
understanding; in lieu of a narrow concern with canonical-textual meaning or authorial intent, hermeneutical conceptions thus accentuate the interpreter's or reader's contributions, including his critical acumen needed
for the assessment of a text's long-range signficance. To be sure, the
precise role assigned to the interpreter varies among the discussed
thinkers. While, under existential auspices, exegesis basically denotes the
clarification of deep-seated "pre-understandings" in the light of textual
analysis, transcendental (or universalist) views tend to underscore the
reader's constructive and evaluative achievements. Notwithstanding
these differences, however, hermeneutical inquiry—pursued on a
reflective-categorial level—invariably implies a creative tension and thus,
in a sense, a blending of interpretation and critique.

The connection between "pre-understanding" and interpretive clarification (sometimes called the "hermeneutic circle") is most fully elaborated in *Being and Time*, both with respect to textual and to general existential exegesis. As Heidegger indicates there, human existence is simultaneously "projected" and a "project"—projected by various cultural, intellectual, and linguistic configurations which, however, are never fully
constraining. In seeking to comprehend both the world and himself, man
initially must find his bearings in a native tongue with its everyday meanings and pre-understandings; but "authentic" existence also transcends
common sense in favor of reflective-ontological insight. As one commentator points out, if man as speaker or interpreter "brings meaning to light
in an *authentic* way, then he takes 'something' out of the night of hidden-
ness and posits it within a horizon of intelligibility" which, to be sure, "is
already there and which is enclosed in the language spoken to him in a
certain culture." Although always enmeshed in a "determinate language,"
human existence is "thereby not necessarily conditioned"; rather, "that
onto which ek-sistence projects itself and the world is not yet determined.
The new meaning that man can always force to 'light up' therefore always originates, as it were, in a 'realm of emptiness'."[33] The stress on
reflective-authentic insight is also present in Ricoeur's approach. His
essay on "Existence and Hermeneutics" (as mentioned) portrays exegesis

as "the work of thought which consists in deciphering the hidden meaning in the apparent meaning, in unfolding the levels of meaning implied in the literal meaning." The essay also strongly accentuates the interpreter's role in the clarification of meaning—including his task, on a reflective level, to overcome the "internal warfare" of competing perspectives. While unable to avoid the *"risk* of interpretation" or to escape the "dialectic" of exegetic views, we read, a reflective-philosophical hermeneutics carries "the diversity of hermeneutic methods back to the structure of the corresponding theories," thus preparing itself "to perform its highest task"—which consists in "showing in what way each method expresses the form of a theory" and how "each interpretation is grounded in a particular existential function."[34]

In referring to this "highest" interpretive ambition Ricoeur speaks of critical exegesis or the "critical function" of hermeneutics. No doubt, among contemporary exegetic approaches, the interpreter's critical role is nowhere more forcefully extolled than in the confines of "critical theory," and especially in Habermas's writings. Without denying the importance of everyday semantic and hermeneutical understanding, Habermas from the beginning insisted on the need to move beyond commonsense meanings in the direction of underlying structures and genetic capacities. As presented in *Knowledge and Human Interests*, the distinctive character of both psychoanalysis and "critical" social inquiry resided in the combination of hermeneutical understanding with theoretical-scientific explanation aimed at grasping unintelligible constraints. The distrust of ordinary understanding persisted in the essay on "systematically distorted communication." The " 'hermeneutic' consciousness of translation difficulties proves to be inadequate," a cited passage states, "when applied to systematically distorted communication; for in this case incomprehensibility results from a faulty organization of speech itself." As long as we communicate in our ordinary or natural language, the essay continued, "we can never be neutral observers, simply because we are always participants"; our understanding on this level thus "can never be better than that of a partner in the communication." Freudian depth analysis, on the other hand, breaks through this barrier by explaining the genesis of traumatic events or scenes. "If we consider everyday interpretation within the range of ordinary language or translation from one language into another," Habermas observed, then psychoanalysis "differs from that hermeneutic understanding because of its explanatory power," that is, its ability "to 'explain' the Why, the origin of the symptomatic scene with reference to the initial circumstances which led to the systematic distortion itself." Accordingly, while "ordinary semantic analysis proceeds *ad hoc* from a traditionally determined pre-understanding which is tested and revised within the process of interpretation," depth analysis requires "a systematic pre-understanding which pertains to language and linguistic communication as such." Differently phrased, ordinary exegesis yielding hermeneutical understanding "makes use of the non-analyzed communicative competence of a native speaker"; by contrast, depth inquiry into systematic deformations affords an "explanatory understanding" predicated on "a theory of communicative competence."[35]

The differentiation between exegetic levels is continued in the monograph on universal pragmatics. In discussing the particular status of "rational reconstruction" or reconstructive inquiry, the study contrasts "two levels of explication of meaning." If the meaning of an action, gesture, or text is unclear, Habermas notes, explication is "directed first to the semantic content of the symbolic formation," in an effort to grasp the author's intent or purpose. Typically, on this level, exegesis explores "connections that link the surface structures of the incomprehensible formation with the surface structures of other, familiar formations." If exegesis along these lines is blocked or otherwise unsuccessful, the interpreter "may find it necessary to alter his attitude," that is, to exchange straightforward explication for a posture "in which he directs himself to the generative structures of the expressions themselves" or to the "rules" underlying symbolic formations. While "in normal paraphrase and translation" the interpreter grasps semantic meanings "in an ad hoc manner," his task is redefined once he "tries not only to *apply* this intuitive knowledge but to *reconstruct* it." Instead of clinging to surface structures in an attempt to comprehend meanings "*intentione recta*," exegesis at that point has to "peer through the surface, as it were, and into the symbolic formation to discover the rules according to which the latter was produced." The target of understanding at this deeper genetic level is no longer a symbolic content as such, but rather "the intuitive rule consciousness that a competent speaker has of his own language"—a rule consciousness probed in a theoretical-systematic manner. According to Habermas, this depth exploration is precisely the goal of "reconstructive understanding," that is, of "meaning explication in the sense of rational reconstruction of generative structures underlying the production of symbolic formations."[36]

Politics and Emancipation

Regarding the formulation of political vistas, a critical (existential or transcendental) hermeneutics is liable to encourage also the critique or critical assessment of society—that is, of habitual forms of interaction and institutionalized practices in favor of freer or more "authentic" modes of self-realization. In discussing the dimension of intersubjective relations, Heidegger's *Being and Time* outlines a distinctive type of in-

terpersonal "care" termed "anticipative-emancipatory solicitude," a
solicitude designed to foster and cultivate the freedom of fellow-humans
seen as "projects" of Being (potentially) transcending traditional constraints or external manipulation. A similar orientation can be found (at
least implicitly) in Ricoeur's argument where exegesis is portrayed as "an
aspect of *Dasein's* 'project' and of its 'openness to Being' " and where the
critical scrutiny of customary opinions, including habitual self-
understanding, ultimately yields a more genuine and unconstrained life-
form. It is again in Habermas's writings, however, that one finds the
most explicit articulation of a critical social-political theory. His essay on
"communicative competence" presents the notion of an "ideal speech
situation" as the yardstick of genuine interpersonal relations against
which to measure real-life constraints and distortions. Communicative
competence, he states, signifies "the mastery of the means of construction
necessary for the establishment of an ideal speech situation. No matter
how the intersubjectivity of mutual understanding may be deformed, the
design of an ideal speech situation is necessarily implied in the structure
of potential speech," since all speech presupposes or harbors validity
claims. Insofar as we master these means of construction, "we can con-
ceive the ideas of truth, freedom, and justice, which interpret each
other — although, of course, only as ideas." While serving as a standard,
Habermas adds, genuine intersubjectivity cannot be treated as an existing reality, given prevailing fissures and communicative deformations
"built into the social structure" and manifest in the "institutionalization
of political and economic power." Seen not as a pale utopia but as a concrete goal (immanent in speech), the standard generates a "practical
hypothesis" or imperative — from which "the critical theory of society
takes its point of departure."[37]

The prospects and implications of this imperative have been spelled
out by Habermas more fully in his *Toward a Rational Society*. The study
differentiates between two main types of "rationality" and corresponding
modes of "rationalization": namely, instrumental rationality fostering
scientific progress and the technical streamlining of productive forces,
and communicative rationality promoting the growth of interpersonal
understanding and its solidification in public institutions. According to
Habermas, the unfolding of productive forces can be a "potential for
liberation" only if it does not replace or thwart communicative rationalization; the latter, evident on the level of the "institutional
framework," can occur "only in the medium of symbolic interaction
itself, that is, through a removal of restrictions placed on communication." This removal, accordingly, constitutes the precondition of rational
advances in general: "Public, unrestricted, and nonrepressive discussion
about the suitability and desirability of action-orienting principles and

norms in light of the socio-cultural repercussions of developing sub-systems of instrumental conduct—such communication at all levels of political and repoliticized decision-making processes is the only medium in which anything like genuine 'rationalization' is possible." As Habermas adds, institutionalized discussion would involve a decline of normative "repressiveness" and "rigidity" and an increase in discursive reflexivity. Such changes, he writes, would not yield a perfection of technical mastery or a more smoothly functioning social system, but "would furnish the members of society with the opportunity for further emancipation and progressive individuation." More broadly phrased, the growth of productive forces "can at best support, but does not coincide with the intention of the 'good life'."[38]

6

The Rule of Metaphor

Welch einen weckruf jagt
Bläser mit silbernem horn
Ins schlummernde dickicht der Sage?*

Having discussed various epistemological treatments of language, and having subsequently glanced at both commonsense pragmatic and transcendental approaches, I would like to turn finally to the domain of poetry or poetic language. Although perhaps not set off from other perspectives by unmistakable boundaries, the domain in my view is sufficiently distinctive and unique to merit special consideration. Instead of lengthily elaborating on this view, I would like to plunge into the middle of the domain by looking at a poem—one specifically dealing with poetic language and thus likely to shed some inside light on the topic.

"The Word": A Poem

The poem I wish to consider was written by the German poet Stefan George and is entitled "The Word"; in English translation it reads as follows:

> Wonder or dream from distant land
> I carried to my country's strand
>
> And waited till the twilit norn
> Had found the name within her bourn—
>
> Then I could grasp it close and strong
> It blooms and shines the front along . . .
>
> Once I returned from happy sail,
> I had a prize so rich and frail,
>
> She sought for long and tidings told:
> "No like of this these depths enfold."
>
> And straight it vanished from my hand,
> The treasure never graced my land . . .

148

> So I renounced and sadly see:
> Where word breaks off no thing may be.

The poem belongs to George's later and more austere works, those written after the first World War.[1] Martin Heidegger repeatedly refers to this poem: his lecture titled "The Word" (1958) revolves around it, and it also serves as *leitmotif* in his longer essay on "The Nature of Language" (of the same year); in both instances Heidegger offers an extremely nuanced and penetrating interpretation of the poem's multiple facets and dimensions.[2] I do not intend to recapitulate his comments in the present context; nor do I propose to give a detailed exegesis of my own. I merely wish to highlight or allude to a few aspects.

George's poem, as one can readily see, deals with the poet's relation to the "word" or to language. Initially we find the poet very self-confident: he has an inspiration, a vision—"wonder or dream from distant land"—and he brings this inspiration to the "twilit norn" or (we might say) to his muse with the expectation that she will provide him with the proper words which will fit his inner vision like a glove. For a long time this arrangement works out quite well: language, handed to him by the "norn," obligingly serves as a means for the poet's creativity and self-expression. But then something happens. Once he has a particularly delicate inspiration—he returns "from happy sail" with a prize which is "rich and frail"—and again he approaches his muse: but this time she does not oblige; the proper words cannot be found on command ("no like of this these depths enfold"). So, the poet is challenged and upset in his creative mastery; he undergoes a sobering experience and learns some kind of "renunciation."

Clearly, there is much more in the poem than the skeleton outline I have just sketched. What is this "more," and why should it matter? Why does the poet not simply give the straightforward report I have just extracted? Why—even on the edge of despair—does he insist on writing a poem? Why, even in the midst of "sadness," does he continue to depend on the "norn" and her not completely reliable cooperation? Why does he still put his trust so faithfully in the "word" and in language? These questions clearly touch at the heart of poetry. However, I think their implications are broader—broader than "poetry" seen as a specialized occupation or art form: the questions also touch at the heart of language. The poet's special attentiveness or faithfulness brings into view a dimension of language which is likely to be overlooked by epistemology in its various forms and also by a straightforward "pragmatics" (even in its transcendental version): it is a dimension obscured by the conception of language as a cognitive instrument and also by talk about language "use" and even about speech as a mode of human self-expression and self-disclosure.

Poetry and Metaphors

To gain access to this dimension, perhaps we should look a bit more closely at the poet's language in the cited lines. What do we find? Presumably talking about a poetic inspiration, George says: "Wonder or dream from distant land I carried to my country's strand." These lines, it seems, are not couched in "literal" language or do not carry "literal" meaning; so, we may ask, is he offering "figurative" speech and "figurative" meanings? Again, presumably referring to another inspiration, the poet writes: "Once I returned from happy sail, I had a prize so rich and frail." Obviously, we may say, the poet has not really been voyaging or sailing across any sea; so, what we apparently have again is figurative speech. Actually, when we look further, we discover that the entire poem is a string of such "figurative" phrases and meanings. Since the sense of the phrases is not literal, are we to conclude that the poet is simply "imagining things," that he is concocting—perhaps wilfully and arbitrarily—images and symbolic expressions? The opposite of literal speech is commonly called figurative or else "metaphorical" language. To be sure, not all figures of speech are "metaphors" in the strict or technical sense of the term—as there are also such figures or "tropes" as metonymy (where one name stands for another), synecdoche (where a part stands for the whole), simile, and others. Yet, if we do not insist on being too technical—or if we use the term in a "synecdochical" fashion—we might say that all figures of speech are types of metaphors (or at least closely related to metaphorical language).

Irrespective of technical-terminological issues, the linkage between poetry and metaphor has always been close and intimate—and has been recognized and explored by commentators since classical antiquity. In his *Poetics* Aristotle offered a definition of metaphor which exerted a lasting influence through the ages. "Metaphor," he wrote, "consists in giving the thing a name that belongs to something else, the transference being either from genus to species, or from species to genus, or from species to species, or on grounds of analogy." We may disregard (for the time being) that Aristotle speaks here of "giving the thing a name" and thus seems to focus exclusively on isolated nouns; probably we have to expand this conception to include not only individual nouns, but also phrases or sentences and even, as in our previous example, a poem as a whole. In the passage Aristotle defined metaphor as a "transference" or *"epiphora"* and thus as a movement (the Greek term *"metaphora"* derives from *"metapherein"* which, like *"epipherein"*, means moving or carrying something from one place to another, thereby transferring or displacing it). We may note in this context—and it has been noted in literature—that Aristotle's definition explained the term "metaphor" itself metaphorically: namely, by presenting it as an *"epiphora"*, that is, a spatial movement or change of location—a movement which literally can apply only to spatial objects rather than to words or names. However this may be, metaphor in Aristotle's treatment signified the displacement or transposition of a name (or names) from one usage or context to another: typically from ordinary, current or literal usage to an unusual or "alien" terrain. To some extent, this aspect of displacement and unfamiliarity is also present in another passage in *Poetics* to which I alluded in the opening chapter and which reads: "It is a great thing, indeed, to make a proper use of the poetic forms, as also of compounds and strange words. But the greatest thing by far is to be a master of metaphor: it is the one thing that cannot be learnt from others; and it is also sign of genius, since a good metaphor implies an intuitive grasp of the similarity in dissimilars." Paraphrasing this statement one might say that metaphorical language involves the ability of the poet or speaker to transfer himself into alien terrain, or to move back and forth between usages and contexts, in an effort to discover (manifest or latent) resemblances and distinctions.[3]

Aristotle's praise of metaphor is somewhat untypical of philosophical assessments of poetic language; nor, it seems fair to note, should one exaggerate the significance of the praise in Aristotle's overall perspective. Even more than in the case of rhetoric, the relationship between philosophy and poetry has traditionally been marked by tension if not enmity. For illustrative purposes, I want to draw attention briefly to an instructive high point of this tension at the beginning of modernity: Thomas Hobbes's differentiation between genuine philosophy and "absurd" speech. Although himself a prolific coiner of metaphors—as attested in his portrayal of the state as a "Leviathan" or "mortal God," and of civil strife as "Behemoth"—Hobbes rigorously refused to grant such figures philosophical status. As defined in *Leviathan*, philosophical reason or reasoning was equivalent to counting or "reckoning (that is, adding and subtracting) of the consequences of general names agreed upon, for the marking and signifying of our thoughts"; sharply put: "In what matter soever there is place for addition and subtraction, there is also place for reason; and where these have no place, there reason has nothing at all to do." To count as rational or philosophically meaningful language had to be tailored to logical counting operations, whereas departures from this rule invariably led to absurdity or absurd speech: "For words are wise men's counters, they do but reckon by them; but they are the money of fools." A prominent manner of lapsing into absurdity resided for Hobbes in "the use of metaphors, tropes, and other rhetorical figures, instead of words proper." For, he added, "though it be lawful to say (for example) in common speech 'the way goes or leads hither or thither', 'the proverb says this or that' (whereas ways cannot go, nor proverbs speak), yet in reckoning and seeking the truth such speeches are not to be admitted."[4]

Metaphor: From Epistemology to Pragmatics

My aim here is not to offer a historical overview of theoretical treatments of poetry, and its connection with metaphor, since antiquity. Leaping briskly beyond intervening epochs, I want to concentrate rather on the fate of poetry and metaphor in our own age. In light of discussions in preceding chapters, it should come as no surprise that poetic and metaphorical language has not fared too well at the hands of professional philosophers, at least during the first part of this century (the so-called "Heyday of Meanings"). Among epistemologists, a quasi-Platonic preoccupation with univocity and apodictic meaning tended to engender an aversion to, or distrust of, figurative and metaphorical expressions—a distrust readily manifest both among empiricists and rationalists. In the logical-empiricist camp, Gottlob Frege early on insisted on the primacy of sense and reference and their mutual correlation—a correlation not to be found in poetic language; in contrast to objective-scientific propositions, poetic statements in his view reflected only the internal-subjective imagination and feelings of the poet. The bifurcation of emotion *versus* cognition or of internal *versus* objective domains was reinforced and fleshed out further by Rudolf Carnap who reserved "sense" (or meaning) entirely for epistemic endeavors. Differentiating strictly between the "representative" or cognitive and the "expressive" function of language, Carnap subsumed both poetry and metaphysics under the latter category. "Metaphysical propositions," he wrote, "are neither true nor false, because they assert nothing, they contain neither knowledge nor error, they lie completely outside the field of knowledge, of theory, outside of truth or falsehood; but they are, like laughing, lyrics, and music, expressive." The emotive-expressive use of language was particularly evident in the case of poetry. "The aim of a lyrical poem in which occur the words 'sunshine' and 'clouds'," he added, "is not to inform us of certain metereological facts, but to express certain feelings of the poet and to excite similar feelings in us. A lyrical poem has no assertional sense, no theoretical sense; it does not contain knowledge."[5]

To a degree, or in revised form, the emotion-cognition dualism survived the disintegration of logical empiricism as a solid paradigm—even in the case of writers otherwise critical of positivism. Thus, while generally sympathetic to the Wittgensteinian turn to pragmatics, Gilbert Ryle's *The Concept of Mind* (1949) presented poetic language as an exercise in "imaging" or "imagining" and the latter as a mode of "make-believe" in which real-life settings are employed in a "hypothetical manner." Similarly, distinguishing between cognitive (or "discursive") and aesthetic (or "presentational") types of symbols, Susanne Langer's *Philosophy in a New Key* (1942) depicted poetry as creative aesthetic symbolization and metaphors as particularly innovative poetic expressions (in contrast to literal-contextual meanings): "Metaphor is our most striking evidence of abstractive seeing, of the power of human minds to use presentational symbols. Every new experience, or new idea about things, evokes first of all some metaphorical expression."[6] Echoes of these philosophical arguments can also be found in the works of literary critics or theorists. Thus, Ryle's concept of "hypothetical" presentation—together with the earlier inward-outward contrast—surfaces in perhaps the most well-known mid-century study of literary theory, Northrop Frye's *Anatomy of Criticism* (1957). Opposing two modes of language use, a "centrifugal" and a "centripetal" kind, Frye portrayed cognitive-scientific language as a centrifugal discourse directed "outward" from words to things, while poetry (and literature in general) was claimed to be characterized by an "inward" or centripetal movement toward an inner imaginative realm and the structure of language itself. "Verbal elements understood inwardly or centripetally," he wrote, are "as symbols, simply and literally verbal elements, or units of a verbal structure"—a structure operating in accordance with its underlying "hypothetical postulates." More broadly phrased, poetry or literature could be viewed as "a body of hypothetical structures" whose "final direction of meaning is inward." Some ten years later, in a study called *The Structure of Poetic Language*, the author—in a frankly Carnapian vein—affirmed that "the poetic sentence is objectively false, but subjectively true."[7]

Lingering positivist traces can be detected not only in general theoretical works, but also in studies specifically dealing with the role of metaphors. A prominent and illustrative example is Colin Turbayne's *The Myth of Metaphor* (1962). In large measure, the aim of the book was to debunk metaphor or at least the assumption that metaphorical expressions have a cognitive-referential significance. Relying on Ryle's notion of "make-believe"—and also on the latter's concept of "category-mistake"—Turbayne defined metaphor as a deliberate and pretended type of "sort-crossing" (a term denoting the "use of a sign in a sense different from the usual"). In employing metaphors, he stated, we are "aware, *first*, that we are sort-crossing, that is, re-presenting the facts of one sort in the idioms appropriate to another," and "*secondly*, that we are treating the world and man *as if* they belong to new sorts." The "as if" character of metaphors involved the aspect of make-believe or pretense—and also their potential danger since, due to a natural semantic drift, make-believe easily served as a stepping stone to belief. To counter this danger, the study insisted on a critical "unmasking" of metaphors, on the need to separate "mythical" abuse from deliberate pretense: "There is a difference between using a metaphor and being used by it, between using a model and mistaking the model for the thing modeled: the one is to make believe that something is the case; the other is to believe it." Believing metaphors was to become their "victim"—and thus "unknowingly, a metaphysician" who has "mistaken the mask for the face"; criticizing metaphors, on the other hand, was synonymous not with their elimination but only with their restoration as deliberate "hypotheses" or inventive devices. Once cognitive pretense was avoided, one may note, Turbayne's critique was not incompatible with a stress on creative self-expression—a possibility seized and developed in Philip Wheelwright's *Metaphor and Reality* (1962). Openly disavowing cognitive or referential ambitions, Wheelwright opposed the "block language" or "steno-language" predominant in a positivist-technological society to the vitality and fluidity of poetic-metaphorical language seen as outgrowth of inner creativity: "What really matters in a metaphor is the psychic depth at which the things of the world, whether actual or fancied, are transmitted by the cool heat of the imagination."[8]

As regards rationalist epistemology, poetry and metaphor have received a treatment not very dissimilar from that accorded under empiricist auspices (except for divergences deriving from affinities between "structure" and literary "form"). Given the stress on univocity and invariance of meaning, poetic language occupied only a subordinate or marginal place in Husserlian phenomenology. In the context of structural linguistics and anthropology, poetic-metaphorical expressions tended to be assimilated to logical complementarity or the interplay of structural elements. Saussure's *Course in General Linguistics* traced meaning variations to the placement of words in contextual configurations—especially to their insertion in the actual-sequential and a mental-hypothetical chain of signifiers, termed respectively "syntagmatic" and "associative" relations. Building upon this precedent, Levi-Strauss's *The Savage Mind* formalized the comparison between marriage and eating into a logical-structural correspondence. "The connection between them is not causal but metaphorical," he wrote. "Sexual and nutritional relations are at once associated even today"; but "how is this fact and its universality to be explained? Here again the logical level is reached by semantic impoverishment: the lowest common denominator of the union of the sexes and the union of eater and eaten is that they both effect a *conjunction by complementarity.*" Tentative steps beyond the confines of logical-structural reductionism were undertaken by the linguist Roman Jacobson, especially in his essay on "Linguistics and Poetics" (1960). While incorporating or adapting structuralist teachings, the essay attributed to poetic language a more strongly innovative and creative role. As in Saussure's study, signifiers were placed into a linguistic system of coordinates, a system formed by the intersection of "syntagmatic" and "associative" or "paradigmatic" chains—labeled now the "axis of combination" and the "axis of selection (or substitution)," respectively; but in poetic-metaphorical language the latter axis was given primacy over the former: "The poetic function projects the principle of equivalence from the axis of selection into the axis of combination." With this primacy the accent was simultaneously shifted from cognitive reference to the expressed "message"; in Jacobson's words, the poetic function "by promoting the palpability of signs, deepens the fundamental dichotomy of signs and objects."[9]

The waning of traditional epistemological vistas (during the "Heyday of Sentences") ushered in a sustained reassessment of poetic-metaphorical language by philosophers of different persuasions and backgrounds. In the present context, I want to draw attention briefly to three intellectual settings: first, that of a "holistic" or semantically refined empiricism; secondly, speech-act theory; and lastly, existential phenomenology and its offshoots. In the first domain, an important and influential new departure was signaled in Max Black's *Models and Metaphors* (1962). The central thesis of the study was based on analogy (and was thus itself in a sense metaphorical): namely, that—due to their fruitfulness in generating novel insights—metaphors function in language in a manner akin to the role of models in scientific inquiry. "A memorable metaphor," Black wrote (intending by that phrase an expression not readily reducible to literal meaning), "has the power to bring two separate domains into cognitive and emotional relation by using language directly appropriate to the one as a lens for seeing the other"; properly applied, such use tends to "enable us to see a new subject matter in a new way" or, more simply, "to *see new connections.*" In a similar manner, model-building contributes to scientific discovery and invention; models —particularly "theoretical" models—were said to be basically imaginative devices capable of paving the way to a reinterpretation of reality by providing a "new language" or a new way of talking about phenomena: "Use of theoretical models resembles the use of metaphors in requiring analogical transfer of a vocabulary. Metaphor and model-making reveal new relationships; both are attempts to pour new content into old bottles." Black's arguments were expanded and further sharpened in Mary Hesse's *Models and Analogies in Science* (1966). According to Hesse, scientific inquiry cannot solely rely on inductive or deductive procedures, but requires the help of inventive "redescription." In her words: "The deductive model of scientific explanation should be modified and supplemented by a view of theoretical explanation as metaphoric redescription of the domain of the explanandum." As she added: "Rationality consists just in the continuous adaptation of our language to our continually expanding world, and metaphor is the chief means by which this is accomplished."[10]

In contrast to the relatively instrumental view of language and metaphor still prevalent in holistic empiricism, speech-act theory emphasizes a broader notion of human intentionality manifest in different modes of speech. Moving beyond narrowly semantic confines, John Searle's *Expression and Meaning* (1979) champions a pragmatic-intentional conception of metaphor and linguistic utterances in general. In line with his preoccupation with literal meaning—an outgrowth of the "principle of expressibility"—Searle's study portrays both fictional and metaphorical statements as intentional deviations from literal usage (with the former being described as "nonserious" and the latter as "nonliteral" modes of utterances). Whereas fictional discourse reflects a particular "pretense" or "pseudo-performance" on the part of authors or speakers, the distinctive trait of metaphors is claimed to reside in the discrepancy between "speaker's utterance meaning" and literal "word or sentence meaning," a discrepancy attributable to "speaker's intentions." Building on a classification articulated by Black and others, the study differentiates between two major theories of metaphor or metaphorical meaning: namely, a "comparison" theory asserting the equivalence or exchangeability of literal and metaphorical expressions, and a "semantic" or "semantic interaction" model—endorsed by Black and Hesse—deriving meaning from the tension or interaction between literal context and figurative expression. In Searle's presentation, the first type links metaphors to "a comparison or similarity between two or more *objects*" while the second type focuses on the "verbal opposition" or tension between "two *semantic contents*, that of the expression used metaphorically, and that of the surrounding literal context" or framework. Translated into Fregean vocabulary, the comparison approach manifests a concern with reference, the interaction model a concern with semantic meaning—in the sense that the former construes metaphor as "a relation between references" and the latter as "a relation between senses and beliefs associated with references." While finding some merit in the interactionist stress on beliefs, *Expression and Meaning* ultimately rejects both types because of their neglect of pragmatic-illocutionary aims. "The proponents of the interaction view," we read, "see correctly that the mental and semantic processes involved in producing and understanding metaphorical utterances cannot involve references themselves, but must be at the level of intentionality"; their shortcoming, however, consists in clinging to semantic correlations instead of "speaker's utterance meaning."[11]

Among the mentioned intellectual settings, none has engendered a more extensive literature on fiction and poetry than existential phenomenology and hermeneutics; James Edie's book on *Speaking and Meaning: The Phenomenology of Language* (1976) is a prominent and illustrative work in this genre. Moving (cautiously) from a Husserlian perspective in the direction of an existential hermeneutics, Edie makes room for the role of multiple or "polysemic" meanings, including metaphorical expressions. As in the case of speech-act theory, metaphoricity or "surplus" of meaning is ascribed chiefly to the intentionality or intentional purpose of the speaker; however, intentionality is construed in a more existential sense—such that it captures or encompasses man's precognitive, perceptual encounter with the world. In Edie's presentation, metaphor is tied to "the primordial attempt to articulate in language the structure and meaning of the perceptual world"; especially the more basic or "root metaphors" are said to be "derived from the lived experience of bodily processes, from perceptual experience, from sensation, from lived-space and lived-time." Viewed under existential-phenomenological auspices, precognitive perception carries distinct purposive connotations: "That man must, first of all, speak in terms of his primary perceptual experience is an immediate result of the intentional structure of experience"; it is essentially because of his purposive and "perceptual insertion in the world that man adopts a certain *metaphorical economy* in his language, using primary perceptual categories to designate experiences of a more complex and derivative nature." In assessing the linguistic status of metaphors, Edie—together with Searle—places the accent squarely on the pragmatic dimension of speech, as contrasted to syntax and formal-logical structure. We must distinguish, he writes, "words as they occur in *la langue* and words as they are actually used in historical speech-acts, in *la parole*." Given the stability of syntax, "metaphor can arise only on the level of *la parole*," that is, "only when we try actually to put experience into words." At this juncture, "human intentions enter in and we get a new sense of 'usage'," a usage deviating from the habitual or literal meaning of terms.[12]

The affinities with speech-act theory extend to general theoretical preferences. Like the former, *Speaking and Meaning* differentiates between two main theories of, or approaches to, metaphor, a differentiation predicated basically on the role or attitude of the speaker. In the first type—Searle's "comparison" model—the speaker adopts a chiefly receptive stance, by registering or accentuating existing similarities or resemblances among various objects which "can be substituted for one another in endlessly fascinating ways." Metaphors in this category tend to take the form of similes, verbal images, and parables which may "reveal unexpected but immediately recognizable truths." In the second type—basically a merger of the "interaction" model with innovative "utterance meaning"—the speaker is assigned a more active and imaginative role. Metaphor in this case involves an act of discovery and invention, that is, the creation of new meanings through symbolic juxtaposition and interaction. In Edie's words: "Here the emphasis has to be on *synthesis* and the manner in which some metaphorical usages not only bring together and juxtapose different images or experienced objects but also make us see what has not before been seen and force on us a new perspective." As he adds, metaphorical expressions of this type reflect an intentional reorganization of experience; with their help, "we filter one field of experience through another, and thus create new realms of meaning and thereby enable ourselves to see what before could not be seen."[13]

The Rule of Metaphor: Ricoeur

It would not be difficult to cite additional pertinent studies culled from various intellectual contexts. Instead of proliferating examples, however, I would like to focus at this point on one prominent text originating in the domain of existential phenomenology and hermeneutics: Paul Ricoeur's *La métaphore vive* (1975), translated as *The Rule of Metaphor*. Widely acclaimed by both literary critics and philosophers, Ricoeur's book is impressive for a number of reasons: among them its comprehensive range or coverage and its innovative theoretical approach. In addition to offering a broad historical account of the treatment of poetry, rhetoric, analogy, and metaphor from classical antiquity over the Middle Ages to modernity, *The Rule of Metaphor* contains a detailed review of recent and contemporary writings on these topics, a review judicious both in its selection and critical assessments. Regarding its general orientation, Ricoeur's approach in my view represents a blending—a very ingenious and unconventional blending, to be sure—of competing theoretical frameworks. In terms of Searle's and Edie's categories, the study basically seeks to combine or reconcile the virtues of "comparison" theories—ultimately dating back to Aristotle—with more recent "interaction" or tension models. Aristotelian sympathies or affinities are evident throughout the book. Concerning the definition of metaphor, Ricoeur deviates from Aristotle's focus on isolated nouns and their substitution, in favor of a broader attentiveness to phrases, sentences, and texts. What he finds congenial in Aristotle's outlook is chiefly the concern with concrete similarities and more generally with "reference"—although he proceeds to reinterpret or reformulate this concern in such a manner that "reference" and poetic "mimesis" denote not simply a description of reality but a creative re-description and disclosure. "My whole aim," he writes, "is to do away with the restriction of reference to scientific discourse"; properly construed, "the literary work through the structure proper to it *displays* a world, (but) only under the condition that the reference of *descriptive* discourse is suspended." It may be, indeed, he adds, "that the metaphorical statement is precisely the one that points out most clearly this relationship between suspended reference and displayed reference. Just as the metaphorical statement captures its sense or meaning as metaphorical midst the ruins of the literal sense, it also achieves its reference upon the ruins of what might be called (in symmetrical fashion) its literal reference."[14]

A question immediately conjured up by this formulation concerns the appropriateness of the employed terminology. Is the term "reference" subtle enough, one may ask, to convey the aspect of display or disclosure? Sensitive to this query, Ricoeur takes recourse at this point to a suggestion made by Roman Jacobson: namely, that the "poetic function" of language does not so much "obliterate the reference but makes it ambiguous" — with the result that poetic statements exhibit not only a "split addresser" and a "split addressee" but also a "split reference." Finding in the last phrase a confirmation of his view regarding the relation between "suspended" and "displayed" reference, he proceeds to apply the notion to metaphorical expressions. "It is within the very analysis of the metaphorical statement," he affirms, "that a referential conception of poetic language must be established, a conception that takes account of the elimination of ordinary language and patterns itself on the concept of split reference." In relying on the split character of reference, *The Rule of Metaphor* seeks not to relinquish but to recapture or reconstruct the traditional theory of comparison, including the Aristotelian dictum that "to metaphorize well is to see (or perceive) the similar in the dissimilar." As Ricoeur grants, "seeing" in this context no longer signifies direct vision or perception, but only a kind of "metaphorical seeing" or a "seeing as"; correspondingly, metaphor denotes no longer a straightforward discovery of existing similarities, but also a mode of invention — or rather a mixture of discovery and invention. "Does not the fittingness, the appropriateness of certain verbal and non-verbal predicates," he asks, "indicate that language not only has organized reality in a different way, but also made manifest a way of being of things, which is brought to language thanks to semantic innovation? It would seem that the enigma of metaphorical discourse is that it 'invents' in both senses of the word: what it creates, it discovers; and what it finds, it invents."[15]

At this point the study shifts attention to the "interaction" or tension model of metaphor, as espoused by Black and others. The chief merit of Black's argument is seen in his insistence "that metaphor creates the resemblance rather than finding and expressing it," and more generally in his portrayal of poetic discourse as a kind of model-building or "heuristic fiction." As Ricoeur points out, "the creation of heuristic fiction is the road to redescription" of reality—a redescription which "unites manifestation and creation" and which, in his view, even grasps the essence of the Aristotelian "mimesis," especially when the latter is joined with the corollary notion of "mythos" construed as a poetic plot or tale. "As for *mimesis*," he asserts, "it stops causing trouble and embarrassment when it is understood no longer in terms of 'copy' but of redescription" whose effectiveness depends on "the invention of the *mythos*"—a conjunction particularly evident in the case of metaphorical expressions: "In service to the poetic function, metaphor is that strategy of discourse by which language divests itself of its function of direct description in order to reach the mythic level where its function of discovery is set free." In addition to the stress on discovery, Ricoeur also accepts (in principle) Black's notion of a tension between different semantic levels or contents: especially between metaphorical "focus" and literal "frame," or between "tenor" and "vehicle." To be sure, interactionist categories are not simply endorsed or incorporated without revision. Just as it expands and refashions the "referential" component of comparison theories, *The Rule of Metaphor* broadens and deepens the concept of symbolic tension—to the point where the semantic domain (strictly defined) is transgressed. In outlining its own view of metaphor and "metaphorical truth," the study initially identifies three kinds of tensions said to be operative in poetic statements: namely, first, a tension "within the statement," that is, between focus and frame or between "principal" and "secondary subject"; secondly, an exegetic tension between a literal interpretation which fails and a metaphorical intepretation "whose sense emerges through non-sense"; and thirdly, a tension "in the relational function of the copula" or between the similarity and dissimilarity of compared items or expressions.[16]

Exploring the topic of poetic tension more thoroughly, Ricoeur feels impelled to move beyond the three mentioned types which, he says, essentially "remain at the level of meaning immanent to the statement." The dimension he seeks to uncover concerns the copula, but no longer in its "relational" or comparative but its existential or (what one may call) ontological sense. "In the most radical terms possible," he affirms, "tension must be introduced into metaphorically affirmed being. When the poet says that 'nature is a temple where living columns rise . . . ,' the verb *to be* does not just connect the predicate *temple* to the subject *nature* along the lines of the threefold tension outlined above. The copula is not only relational; it implies besides, by means of the predicative relationship, that *what is* is redescribed: it says *that* things really are this way." To grasp the thrust of this redescription, according to Ricoeur, one has to probe beneath the relational and purely referential function of the copula. "Is there not," he asks, "a metaphorical sense of the verb *to be* itself, in which the same tension would be preserved that we found first between words (between 'nature' and 'temple'), then between two interpretations (the literal and the metaphorical), and finally between identity and difference?" And he answers: "In order to elucidate the tension deep within the logical force of the verb *to be,* we must expose an 'is not', itself implied in the impossibility of the literal interpretation, yet present as a filigree in the metaphorical 'is'. Thus, the tension would prevail between an 'is' and an 'is not'." What this analysis discloses is that poetic-metaphorical tension affects not only the "compared terms," nor even "the copula in its referential function, but the existential function of the verb *to be.*" In Ricoeur's view, this existential tension in the copula reveals the "inescapably paradoxical character" surrounding metaphor and any metaphorical concept of "truth." "The paradox," he writes, "consists in the fact that there is no other way to do justice to the notion of metaphorical truth than to include the critical incision of the (literal) 'is not' within the ontological vehemence of the (metaphorical) 'is'. In doing so, the thesis merely draws the most extreme consequence of the theory of tension."[17]

Metaphor and Metaphysics

As can be seen, Ricoeur's conception of metaphor clearly advances beyond the boundaries of straightforward comparison as well as a strictly semantic tension or interaction, by pushing his probe to the heart of the copula, *The Rule of Metaphor* unearths a poetic dimension commonly ignored in other approaches. Given its radical thrust, the reader of the study might expect the analysis of metaphor to yield significant implications on a broader theoretical or philosophical plane; surprisingly, this expectation is largely disappointed. In fact, Ricoeur not only seems reluctant to draw the consequences from his inquiry, but subsequently proceeds to repudiate or at least drastically qualify some of its main insights. Previously I had occasion to raise doubts regarding the notion of "reference." Is reference, I queried, still an appropriate term in the case of a comparison or comparative procedure where similarities are invented or created—or at least as much invented as found? Similar doubts, I believe, beset the portrayal of "existential tension." Is it still feasible and legitimate to juxtapose a "literal 'is-not' " to a "metaphorical 'is' "—when we have just been told that what is at issue is the copula in its existential rather than its relational or referential function? Is it still possible to speak of a "metaphorical" or figurative truth in application to the relation of "an 'is' and an 'is not' "? Are we here not in the dimension of an ontological (or ontic-ontological) difference between being and non-being, presence and absence—rather than that of a difference between beings?

The qualification (and virtual recantation) of the analysis occurs in the final chapter of the study, entitled "Metaphor and Philosophical Discourse" and devoted to a discussion of philosophical inferences deriving from the sketched view of poetic language. In the course of that chapter, following a renewed historical recapitulation, Ricoeur confronts the issue of the relation between metaphor and metaphysics. As he notes, the issue has been raised on at least two occasions by Martin Heidegger. The first reference is contained in the latter's *Der Satz vom Grund* (1957) where, in the middle of an inquiry into the "principle of sufficient reason," the question is put forth whether thought and thinking can properly be called a "hearing" and "seeing" or whether this can only be done in a "metaphorical, transferred sense"? In tackling this question, Heidegger draws a parallel between the "metaphorical" transfer from the literal (hearing and seeing) to the figurative level of meaning (thinking) and the "metaphysical" transfer from the sensible (or visible) to the non-sensible (or invisible) domain. Finding that both kinds of transfer have been closely interlaced in the tradition of Western thought, he states: "The metaphorical exists only within the bounds of the metaphysical." The second instance is found in the essay on "The Nature of Language" to which I referred at the beginning of this chapter. Pointing to some lines by Hölderlin which contain phrases depicting language as "the flower of the mouth" or treating "words like flowers," Heidegger comments in that essay: "It would mean that we stay bogged down in metaphysics if we took Hölderlin's phrase here 'words like flowers' as being a metaphor." As he adds, the phrase signals no transfer or simple "break in the vision," but rather "the awakening of the largest view; nothing is 'adduced' here, but on the contrary the word is released back into the source of its being."[18]

Reacting to Heidegger's observations, Ricoeur criticizes the linkage of metaphor and metaphysics as implausible or unconvincing; in fact, the remainder of his final chapter is devoted chiefly to the task of vindicating the autonomy of a "philosophical discourse" seen as heir to traditional metaphysical thought. Regarding the juxtaposition of sensible and non-sensible realms as indicative of the "root meaning" of metaphysics (in *Der Satz vom Grund*), the chapter counters: "I am afraid that only a reading forced beyond any justification can make Western philosophy lie on this Procrustean bed." What particularly disconcerts or irritates Ricoeur in this context is an essay by Jacques Derrida entitled "White Mythology" which—proceeding beyond "Heidegger's restrained criticism"—engages in (what Ricoeur calls) an "unbounded 'deconstruction'" of metaphysics. In Derrida's presentation, traditional philosophy is basically an abstracted and deceptive system or "mythology" which has disguised its links with, and origins in, metaphor. In his words: "It is metaphysics which has effaced in itself that fabulous scene which brought it into being, and which yet remains, active and stirring, inscribed in white ink, an invisible drawing covered over in the palimpsest." Seen in this light, traditional philosophy thus appears as "a white mythology which assembles and reflects Western culture" and in which Western man takes his *"logos"* or the *"mythos* of his idiom" for "the universal form of that which it is still his inescapable desire to call reason." From the transfer or transposition characteristic of metaphor, metaphysics in Derrida's view has inherited a host of dichotomies which it treats as absolute logical categories or ideal schemata. "The movement of metaphorization (the origin and then the effacing of the metaphor, the passing from a proper sensible meaning to a proper spiritual meaning through a figurative detour)," he writes, "is nothing but a movement of idealization"—a movement bringing into play well-known traditional oppositions such as those between nature and spirit, freedom and necessity, and between "the sensible and the intelligible, the sensible and sense itself." It is this set of polarities which circumscribes "the possibility of metaphysics; and the concept of metaphor so defined belongs to (it)."[19]

I do not wish to dwell further on Derrida's essay and his perhaps somewhat "unbounded" stress on the metaphoricity of metaphysics and of metaphor itself. Probably it would be helpful at this juncture to recall, in its broad contours, Heidegger's view of "metaphysics." In Heidegger's usage, the term signifies basically the theory of "being" or of the "beingness of beings" (though one which fails to reflect on the sense and possibility of its undertaking): a theory which identifies "being" either with an array of substances or essences and their correlation or else with a set of cognitive representations anchored in a knowing subject.[20] From this vantage point, "metaphysical" transfer or transposition means then either a move from one substantive realm to another (for instance, from the sensible to the intelligible, the phenomenal to the noumenal), or else a move from an "inner" subjectivity to the "outer" world of objects and their connections; correspondingly, "metaphorical" transfer designates either the acknowledgment of existing similarities between beings or realms or the invention of resemblances through creative imagination. Without forcing past thought into a needlessly "Procrustean" mold, there are grounds for asserting that these modes of transfer have indeed been central to dominant strands of traditional philosophy (thus warranting the linkage between metaphor and metaphysics). Ricoeur's own approach, in fact, pays tribute to the same legacy—as is evident both in *The Rule of Metaphor* and in some of his earlier writings. Thus, his essay on "Existence and Hermeneutics" presented multiple or "symbolic" meaning

as arising from the fact that "meanings overlap, that the spiritual meaning is 'transferred' from the historical or literal meaning because of the
latter's surplus of meaning." In another essay of the same period Ricoeur
expressed himself even more pointedly: "The symbol, I said, is constituted from a semantic perspective such that it provides a meaning by
means of a meaning. In it a primary, literal, worldly, often physical
meaning refers back to a figurative, spiritual, often existential, ontological meaning which is in no way given outside this indirect designation." In the language of "our medieval symbolists," he added, "what is
primary is the translation, the transfer from the visible to the invisible by
means of an image borrowed from sensible realities; what is primary is
the semantic constitution under the form of the 'similar-dissimilar' at the
root of symbols or figures."[21]

In a modified form, this legacy still reverberates in *The Rule of
Metaphor*, particularly in the emphasis on the literal-figurative bifurcation and in the effort to salvage "living metaphor" from routine usage.
To be sure, as indicated, the "similar-dissimilar" distinction is joined in
the study with a stronger accent on creative tension and the role of
metaphors as heuristic models. Yet, one may ask: can the final thrust of
the study still be reconciled with traditional notions of transfer and comparison? More specifically: can the tension located in the "existential
copula" still be captured in terms of a comparative transposition? Is the
relation between "is" and "is not" or between being and non-being (or
nothing) a relation between realms of being linked by a similarity of
dissimilars—or is it the result of a heuristic invention generated by a
model-builder? What emerges here, I think, is a certain restrictiveness or
inadequacy of the traditional notion of metaphor (and of metaphysics as
well)—a conclusion rendering it advisable to place at least a question
mark behind the (English) title of Ricoeur's study, so that it reads *The
Rule of Metaphor*? Returning to Heidegger's comments: their aim in my
view is not simply to eliminate metaphor in favor of literal meaning, nor
else to unleash a boundless stream of metaphoricity, but rather to show
the limits of both metaphor and metaphysics, as traditionally
understood, by means of a fuller attentiveness to poetic language and to
language in general. That this is indeed their aim is suggested by additional observations in *Der Satz vom Grund* (observations passingly
acknowledged by Ricoeur). After having pointed out that seeing and
hearing are not purely sensible-physical processes—such that the meaning of sensible seeing and hearing could then be transposed to a non-
sensible level—Heidegger elaborates on his statements as follows: "Their
purpose is to warn us not to jump to the conclusion that the talk of thinking as a hearing and seeing is a mere metaphor, and thus take it too light-

ly."[22] The expression "mere metaphor" here is not meant to denigrate metaphor, nor as a plea for the creation of richer or "living" figures of speech; rather, it calls into question the notion of metaphor as transfer and seeks to transgress it into a new direction—that of a dimension of language allowing metaphor (and metaphysics) to operate in the first place.

Heidegger's writings frequently refer or allude to the latter dimension. His essay on "Language" (1950) observes that poetry or poetic "naming" involves not merely a referential word-world relationship or the application or transfer of words to things. Such naming, he states, does not simply "deck out" familiar objects and events "with the words of a language"; rather, it "calls them into the word," that is, into language and thus (in a sense) into "being"—where "being" carries not an ontic-empirical but an ontological significance, intimating a disclosure of meaning veiled in "non-being" and concealment. As the essay continues, such a calling "into the word" establishes a resonance between nearness and distance; it always calls "back and forth, here and there—here into presence, there into absence." In the same context, Heidegger ascribes to the tension between presence and absence—that is, to the dimension of ontological "difference"—a generative and sustaining quality. Abandoning the term "metaphor" in favor of *"diaphora"* he defines the latter as a "carrying" process which both separates and reconciles contesting elements. "The intimacy of the difference," we read, "is the unifying bond of the *diaphora*"; this "difference carries (out) world and things by *letting* them *be*" (namely, as world and things). In the essay on "The Nature of Language" this letting-be is further portrayed as a gift or a giving, more particularly as a gift of language. Properly thinking about the matter, Heidegger writes, "we may never say of the word (or language) that it 'is' (on an ontic level), but rather that it 'gives'—not in the sense that words are given by an 'it', but that the word itself gives." What, however, "does the word give?", he continues. "According to poetic experience and the most ancient tradition of thought, the word gives Being."[23]

Reflections of this kind are not restricted to Heidegger's later writings on language, but are foreshadowed in some of his earlier works. Thus, his lectures on "The Origin of the Work of Art" (1936) link language—particularly poetic language—closely with "being" seen as a space or region inhabited by or sustaining ontological difference. According to the lectures, a chief distinguishing trait of an artwork resides in its manifestation of being—in the fact "that the unconcealment (disclosure) of being has happened here and continues to happen ever anew," differently put: "that the work as such *is* rather than is not." Construed as a "language-work," poetry poignantly illustrates this aspect of disclosure. In Heidegger's presentation, poetic language "initially creates an open space for the manifestation of beings as beings." Instead of merely serving as a vehicle of communication, such language — by "naming" them for the first time — "allows beings to gain a voice (or 'come to word') and thus their mode of appearance; only this naming bestows on beings their proper sense of 'being'." Disclosure of being, however, signifies not merely an empirical-ontic occurrence, but a shift of level or a sea-change bringing into view a basic ontological and non-antithetical difference, contest, or "strife" — the strife between being and non-being, presence and absence as well as between meaning and non-meaning, "world" and "earth." As we read in the lectures: "In setting up a world and positioning the earth, the artwork is an instigation of this (ontological) strife. The point of this instigation is not that the work should instantly settle and dissolve the conflict in an insipid harmony, but that the strife may remain a strife: setting up a world and positioning the earth, the work accomplishes this strife." In terms of a later passage, the essence of being (or "truth") is "in itself the primal strife through which that open arena is won into which beings protrude and from which they in turn recoil."[24]

Although perhaps most vividly captured in his writings, the foregoing views are not the exclusive trademark of Heidegger's thought; as it seems to me, broadly compatible observations have been advanced by a number of contemporary thinkers, most notably by Merleau-Ponty and Michel Foucault. Thus, commenting on poetic and metaphorical expressions, the former's posthumous treatise on *The Visible and the Invisible* (a rephrasing of ontological difference) voiced the belief that "there is or could be a language of coincidence, a manner of making the things themselves speak," an idiom of which the philosopher "would not be the organizer" since its words would cohere "by virtue of a natural intertwining of their meaning, through the occult trading of the metaphor — where what counts is no longer the manifest meaning of each word and of each image, but the lateral relations, the kinships that are implicated in their transfers and their exchanges." To which the attached "Working Notes" added: "A 'direction' of thought — this is not a *metaphor*" properly speaking, since "there is no *metaphor* between the visible and the invisible"; at this juncture "*metaphor* is too much or too little: too much if the invisible is really invisible, too little if it lends itself to transposition." Pushing the correlation of the visible and invisible to the point of ontological contest or "strife," Foucault's *Language, Counter-Memory, Practice* contemplates the possibility of a thought and language radically "transgressing" metaphysical antitheses in the direction of "nonpositive affirmation." "Contestation," he asserts, "does not imply a generalized negation, but an affirmation that affirms nothing, a radical break of transitivity." From an ontological vantage point, "to contest is to proceed until one reaches the empty core where being achieves its limit and where the limit defines being. There, at the transgressed limit, the 'yes' of contestation reverberates."[25]

Hermeneutics and Deconstruction

As in preceding chapters, I would like to conclude this discussion of poetic and metaphorical language by exploring briefly its implications for social and political thought, and first of all for textual exegesis. In the latter domain, the last few decades have witnessed the emergence of a number of approaches variously indebted to aspects of Heidegger's work; probably the most prominent among them is the "philosophical" or ontological hermeneutics articulated by his student Hans-Georg Gadamer. As outlined chiefly in *Truth and Method* (1960), philosophical hermeneutics bears a broad affinity to the "tension theory" of metaphor mentioned on previous occasions. Relying on Heidegger's early thought —especially on the analysis of *Dasein* in *Being and Time*—Gadamer portrays "understanding" not primarily as an interpretative method, but rather as a structural-existential endowment, that is, as a categorial condition rendering possible both self-knowledge and the comprehension of texts. Seen from Heidegger's perspective, *Truth and Method* asserts, understanding is neither (as in Dilthey's case) a "resigned ideal of human experience" nor (as with Husserl) a "last methodological-philosophical standard opposed to the naiveté of natural life," but rather "the original mode of realization of *Dasein* construed as being-in-the-world." With regard to textual exegesis, understanding is said to be patterned on the "model of the dialogue or conversation between two persons," involving a process of question and answer; in fact, according to Gadamer, it is "more than a metaphor, it is a recollection of experiential evidence if the hermeneutical task is conceived as a conversation with the text." Due to the distance between life-worlds and the inevitable role of "prejudgments" in exegesis, this dialogical exchange involves first of all a "tension" or "polarity" between the text's demands and the interpreter's outlook—a tension described as "the true locus" of hermeneutical inquiry. Only by transcending the "particularity" both of the past and the present, and thus by perceiving the continuity of tradition behind apparent discontinuities, can genuine comprehension be achieved: "There is as little an isolated horizon of the present as there are historical contexts to be recovered; rather, understanding is always *the ongoing fusion of such presumably separate horizons.*"[26]

Despite the stress on dialogue or conversation, *Truth and Method* presents understanding not simply as the outgrowth of interpersonal communication; at least potentially, dialogical exchange and tension shades over into a more ontological — and less easily "fused" — strife and difference (although this tendency is not fully pursued). Countering historicist canons of exegesis, Gadamer rejects author's intention or the *"mens auctoris"* as the ultimate yardstick of interpretation. In his words: "Not only occasionally, but always, the meaning of a text transcends its author; that is why understanding is not merely a reproductive, but always a productive enterprise as well." More generally, textual exegesis in his view exceeds the bounds of interpersonal intentions. Hermeneutical interaction, he asserts, should not be misconstrued in the sense that the experienced text is viewed "as the meaning of another person treated as a 'Thou';" properly defined exegesis takes the text not "as the expression of another's life, but rather as a meaning-content detached from all bonds to intending individuals (an 'I' or a 'Thou')." What elevates textual "conversation" (and conversation in general) beyond individual intentions is the focus on a common topic or subject matter as well as the mediating effect of language. According to *Truth and Method*, the "miracle of understanding" consists not so much in a "mysterious communion of souls" but in a "sharing of common meaning"; the chief affinity between textual exegesis and actual conversation is said to reside in the fact that "both are concerned with a topic or 'object' placed before them: just as one interlocutor seeks to reach agreement with his partner concerning an issue, so the interpreter understands the 'object' discussed in the text." Understanding seen as a sharing of meaning, moreover, is essentially a linguistic accomplishment. A "guiding idea" of *Truth and Method*, we read, is "that the fusion of horizons occurring in understanding is the distinctive achievement of language" — a language which is "not a possession at the disposal of one or the other of the speakers." From a philosophical-hermeneutical perspective, language appears basically as "the medium (or middle ground) in which understanding and agreement between partners concerning a topic occurs."[27]

With its stress on language and topicality, Gadamer's hermeneutics approximates or anticipates Heidegger's position on interpretation (as outlined in his middle and later period) — although there is hardly a coincidence of views. Together with Gadamer, Heidegger deemphasizes and even brackets authorial intent. Thus, after citing a poem by Trakl, the essay on "Language" declares the author's name "unimportant," adding that a measure of the quality of a poem can be found in the degree to which "person and name of the poet can be ignored." As in the case of *Truth and Method*, Heidegger's writings shift attention from the communicative function of speech to the intrinsic character of language and its subject matter — but without attributing to the latter a commonsensical or object-status. As previously indicated, language (especially poetic language) in these writings is closely linked with thematic content—not in a merely denotative or predicative but a disclosing sense whereby words or names bestow "being" on things and thus allow them to come into their own. Like Gadamer, the essay on "Language" also treats language as a medium or "middle ground"; but in this case the term refers to a more ontological threshold or difference—that between "world" and "things," between meaning and non-meaning, between speech and silence. "Language speaks," we read, "by calling the evoked 'thing-world' and 'world-thing' into the middle or in-between of difference." Exegesis, against this background, means basically participation in the happening of difference, that is, in the ongoing disclosure and concealment of being. As one commentator notes, "interpretation is from now on forever inscribed and, as it were, at work in the project of the 'interpretation' that does not wish to interpet but, on the contrary, to let be, to let appear, and to let speak the language from which it, in the end, remains prohibited."[28]

Partly under the influence of Heidegger's later work, a mode of exegesis has recently come into vogue which is labelled "deconstructive" or "deconstructivist" and which in varying manners accentuates the simultaneously disclosing and concealing quality of language. In his (repeatedly invoked) overview of interpretive approaches, Hayden White describes this mode somewhat blandly and indiscriminately as the "absurdist moment" in literary studies, a moment stressing the evanescence and inconstancy of meaning and symbolization. "Absurdist criticism which originally arose in the thought of Paulhan, Bataille, Blanchot, and Heidegger primarily as a sickness unto death with language," he writes, "seizes upon this notion of abritrariness and, in the thought of Foucault, Barthes, and Derrida, takes it to its logical conclusion; these thinkers make of the arbitrariness of the sign a rule and of the 'freeplay' of signification an ideal." In White's presentation, this notion of "freeplay" stands opposed to previous critical exegetic perspectives for which language was "simply the medium embodying the literary message" rather than being treated as a "problem." The ambition of such earlier postures was "to penetrate through the medium, by philological analysis, translation, grammatical and syntactical explication, in order to get at the message, the 'meaning', the semantic level that lay beneath it." This orderly procedure, however, has recently been reversed. "Absurdist criticism, by contrast," we read, "treats language itself as a problem and lingers indefinitely on the surface of the text, in the contemplation of language's power to hide or diffuse meaning, to resist decoding or translation, and ultimately to bewitch understanding by an infinite play of signs." As White suggests, absurdist critics tend to cultivate an abnormal if not pathological brand of exegesis—as is evident in their reliance on "Nietzsche, Mallarmé, and Heidegger, all of whom treated language as the human problem par excellence, the disease which made 'civilization' possible and generated its mutilating 'discontents'."[29]

Other literary theorists have commented more patiently and judiciously on the "absurdist" or (better) "deconstructive" mode of interpretation. Thus, in a collection of essays devoted to the elucidation or illustration of this mode, Geoffrey Hartman places the accent on the decentering or dispersal of intended meaning. "Deconstruction, as it has come to be called," he observes, "refuses to identify the force of literature with any concept of embodied meaning and shows how deeply such logocentric or incarnationist perspectives have influenced the way we think about art. We assume that, by the miracle of art, the 'presence of the word' is equivalent to the presence of meaning. But," he adds, "the opposite can also be urged, that the word carries with it a certain absence or indeterminacy of meaning." In contradistinction to ordinary communication and even rhetorical discourse, literary or poetic language—on deconstructive premises—"foregrounds language itself as something not reducible to meaning: it opens a well as closes the disparity between symbol and idea, between written sign and assigned meaning." In referring to the interplay of presence and absence, opening and closure, Hartman's comments evoke the notion of ontological difference central to Heidegger's work—a difference which can assume diverse manifestations: "There is the difference, for instance, between sound and sense, which both stimulates and defeats the writer. Or the difference which remains when we try to reduce metaphorical expressions to the proper terms they have displaced. Or the difference between a text and the commentaries that elucidate it." Reverberations of the same ontological contest or strife are also evident in Derrida's position when he writes that "if we are to approach a text, it must have an edge" and when he defines a text as "no longer a finished corpus of writing, some content enclosed in a book or its margins, but a differential network, a fabric of traces referring endlessly to something other than itself, to other differential traces."[30]

Without a process of deliberate reception or borrowing, hermeneutics and deconstruction are not entirely alien to contemporary political exegesis. As it seems to me, echoes of Gadamer's arguments are present in Michael Oakeshott's conception of "political education" as an interpretive learning process involving induction into an ongoing dialogical practice. "Political education," he asserts in *Rationalism in Politics*, "is not merely a matter of coming to understand a tradition, it is learning how to participate in a conversation: it is at once initiation into an inheritance in which we have a life interest, and the exploration of its intimations." Hermeneutical in inspiration are also his observations on public language and its acquisition: "We do not begin to learn our native language by learning the alphabet, or by learning its grammar; we do not begin by learning words, but words in use; we do not begin (as we begin in reading) with what is easy and go on to what is more difficult; we do not begin at school, but in the cradle; and what we say springs always from our manner of speaking." Yet, although sensitive to historical continuity, Oakeshott is not a stranger to the "deconstructive" break-up of intentional meaning—as is manifest in his comment that in political activity "men sail a boundless and bottomless sea; there is neither harbor for shelter nor floor for anchorage, neither starting-place nor appointed destination. The enterprise is to keep afloat on an even keel." In a similar manner, deconstructive overtones can be detected in William Connolly's approach to political inquiry and discourse, especially in his portrayal of key political terms as "essentially contested concepts" and of politics itself as an ongoing practice of contestation. "Central to politics, as I understand it," Connolly states, "is the ambiguous and relatively open-ended interaction of persons and groups who share a range of concepts, but share them imperfectly and incompletely." Politics in this view "involves the clash that emerges when appraisive concepts are shared widely but imperfectly, when mutual understanding and interpretation is possible but in a partial and limited way, when reasoned argument and coercive pressure commingle precariously in the endless process of defining and resolving issues."[31]

Politics and Metaphor

The repercussions of Heideggerian thought—in both its historical hermeneutical and its deconstructive dimensions—extend from exegesis to the reconceptualization or productive rethinking of political experience. The significance of the existential-historical strand is clearly highlighted in John Gunnell's *Political Philosophy and Time* (1968), a study surveying the varying impact of temporal frameworks on "political vision" in the course of Western civilization. In Heidegger's early work, Gunnell notes in this study, man is portrayed as "a temporal being because of the intentional structure of consciousness and the universal structures of the human condition such as guilt, nothingness, death"—a portrayal which eludes the pitfall of historicism by its emphasis on "historicity" or the "ontological foundation" of temporal experience. "For Heidegger," he adds, "man and the self are grounded in time in their very being, and an ontological illumination of mankind and the individual must be conducted in terms of history and temporality." By virtue of its ontological moorings, existential analysis is said to bypass not only historicism but also the mere cultivation of past traditions in favor of the formulation of a new historical (and political) vision—a vision which, on the level of language, entails a "creative process of symbolic transformation" and the abandonment of "discursive speech" in favor of poetry and myth. In Gunnell's words: "For Heidegger the pre-Socratics and the post-traditional poetry of Hölderlin signify the pretheoretical and creative encounter with existence, the primordial experience of being, where the subject-object bifurcation and the dualism in general, including the poles of time and eternity, ontological and ontic, and language and object, that stem from the persistence of Aristotelian symbols can be overcome."[32]

The implications of Heidegger's post-existential writings have been probed by a number of political thinkers, most notably by Hannah Arendt. Concerning the status of traditional or "metaphysical" bifurcations, Arendt's *The Life of the Mind* contains some late-Heideggerian—and potentially "deconstructive"—observations. Reflecting on the sense of the thesis "that theology, philosophy, metaphysics have reached an end" in our time, she comments that what is at issue is "not that the old questions which are coeval with the appearance of men on earth have become 'meaningless', but that the way they were framed and answered has lost plausibility." Joining Nietzschean and Heideggerian insights regarding the demise of the "true world" of metaphysics, she affirms: "What has come to an end is the basic distinction between the sensory and the suprasensory, together with the notion, at least as old as Parmenides, that whatever is not given to the sense—God or Being or the First Principles and Causes (*archai*) or the Ideas—is more real, more truthful, more meaningful than what appears, that it is not just *beyond* sense perception but *above* the world of the senses. What is 'dead' is not only the localization of such 'eternal truths' but also the distinction itself." According to *The Life of the Mind*, the critique of "metaphysical fallacies" is not only a negative or debunking exercise since, rather than exhibiting "sheer nonsense," past metaphysical doctrines also contain clues or traces for a philosophical reorientation—in fact, "the only clues we have to what thinking means to those who engage in it." Correspondingly, the transgression of metaphysics is said to entail not only privative but also liberating and invigorating effects: "It would permit us to look on the past with new eyes, unburdened and unguided by any traditions, and thus to dispose of a tremendous wealth of raw experience without being bound by any prescriptions as to how to deal with these treasures."[33]

As a corollary of the critique of metaphysics, *The Life of the Mind* shifts the accent from rational categories to poetry and "poetic thinking," that is, a mode of reflection attuned to poetic language; in this connection, attention is also given to metaphor. As depicted in the study, metaphor basically supplies "the 'abstract', imageless thought with an intuition drawn from the world of appearances"—a service which is not merely ancillary but essential to philosophical thought: "All philosophical terms are metaphors, frozen analogies, as it were, whose true meaning discloses itself when we dissolve the term into the original context." According to Arendt, the discoverer of "this originally poetic tool" was Homer "whose two poems are full of all kinds of metaphorical expressions." Homer's example, however, was soon emulated by the founders of Greek philosophy—as is evident in "the two earliest, most famous and influential of all thought parables: Parmenides' voyage to the gates of day and night and Plato's Cave parable, the former being a poem and the latter essentially poetic, using Homeric language throughout." Viewed as an antidote to metaphysical antinomies, poetic and metaphorical language is said to offer "a kind of 'proof' that mind and body, thinking and sense experience, the invisible and the visible, belong together, are 'made' for each other, as it were." Against this background, the traditional "two-world theory" emerges as "a metaphysical delusion, although by no means an arbitrary or accidental one: it is the most plausible delusion with which the experience of thought is plagued." As Arendt concludes (in a statement not free of ambiguity): "Language, by lending itself to metaphorical usage, enables us to think, that is, to have traffic with non-sensory matters, because it permits a carrying-over, *metaphorein*, of our sense experiences. There are not two worlds because metaphor unites them."[34]

7

Language and Politics

... the rulers of the Gentiles lord it over them; not so among you. ...

*... paidos he basileia**

The preceding chapters have surveyed a complex linguistic panorama in our century, ranging from the "Heyday of Meanings" to the "Heyday of Sentences (or Discourses)" in its various manifestations. As will be recalled, the exploration was prompted not simply by curiosity but by political-theoretical concerns: chiefly the desire to discern the political relevance of the contemporary "linguistic turn." Inspired by classical definitions of man as both *homo loquens* or *zoon logon echon* and *zoon politikon*, the hope of the inquiry was to gain a better understanding of politics through an examination of language—that is, to find an answer to the query (adapted from Hacking): why does language matter to political philosophy? Glancing back over the successive steps of the inquiry, the journey so far seems to have yielded only disparate glimpses. As was noted in initial chapters devoted to the "Heyday of Meanings," language at the time was placed basically in the service of epistemology or the search for knowledge; from the vantage point of empiricist and rationalist construals, it functioned chiefly as a tool in scientific analysis (the investigation of empirical referents) or else as an arsenal of logical-syntactical structures. Turning from epistemology to pragmatics, subsequent chapters examined language as a medium of human speech, focusing first on ordinary-contingent modes of self-expression and next on speech seen as a quasi-transcendental endowment pregnant with universal, normative standards. Finally, the accent shifted to poetry and metaphor. Are all these aspects or dimensions of language simply isolated, disconnected elements? Must we leave *homo loquens*—and, by implication, political man—parcelled out among these fragments, or can we somehow discover a coherent bond or integrated fabric?

Conversation and Its Idioms

To be sure, by coherence at this point I do not mean a logically consistent or intentionally structured design, but only a loose and open-ended compatibility. In his *Philosophy and the Mirror of Nature* Richard Rorty has made a proposal along such lines regarding the correlation of philosophical positions. Distinguishing between "systematic" and "edifying" modes of philosophizing, Rorty presents the central aim of edification as "participating in a conversation rather than contributing to an inquiry" or "continuing a conversation" rather than "discovering truth." In contrast to the argumentative approach of systematic thinkers seeking to vindicate a given outlook, edifying thought is said to reflect a more flexible stance—one suffused with practical wisdom and a generous respect for difference: "One way of thinking of wisdom as something of which the love is not the same as that of argument, and of which the achievement does not consist in finding the correct vocabulary for representing essence, is to think of it as the practical wisdom necessary to participate in a conversation. One way to see edifying philosophy *as* the love of wisdom is to see it as the attempt to prevent conversation from degenerating into inquiry, into an exchange of views." A major advantage of the edifying, conversational mode over systematic inquiry, in Rorty's description, resides in the former's openness to reflective transformation, that is, to a general restructuring of the field of vision—an openness which also affects the assessment of human potential: "To see keeping a conversation going as a sufficient aim of philosophy, to see wisdom as consisting in the ability to sustain a conversation, is to see human beings as generators of new descriptions rather than beings one hopes to be able to describe accurately."[1]

As Rorty himself admits, his notion of edification is indebted in good measure to a contemporary political philosopher—Michael Oakeshott—whose writings have championed a similar posture for some time. In his essay "The Voice of Poetry in the Conversation of Mankind" Oakeshott attacked the tendency to construe thought and discourse exclusively in terms of a systematic inquiry or propositional argument. "There are philosophers," he noted, "who assure us that all human utterance is in one mode"; although recognizing "a certain variety of expression" and able to distinguish "different tones of utterance," these philosophers in fact "hear only one authentic voice." Particularly under the sway of modern epistemology, language and linguistic utterance, in Oakeshott's judgment, have increasingly been compressed into a one-dimensional mold, suffocating competing, nonsystematic idioms. In the words of the essay: "The view dies hard that Babel was the occasion of a curse being laid upon mankind from which it is the business of the philosophers to deliver us, and a disposition remains to impose a single character upon significant human speech. We are urged, for example, to regard all utterances as contributions (of different but comparable merit) to an inquiry, or a debate among inquirers, about ourselves and the world we inhabit." Irrespective of the proclivity or taste of inquirers for debate and for intersubjective corroboration or falsification, epistemology places discourse in a carefully circumscribed range of utterance: "While appearing to accommodate a variety of voices," inquiry actually admits "only one, namely, the voice of argumentative discourse, the voice of 'science', and all others are acknowledged merely in respect of their aptitude to imitate this voice."[2]

Against the constraining effects of epistemology, Oakeshott's essay espoused the vision of a diversity or multiplicity of idioms, a diversity whose common "meeting-place" was described as "not an inquiry or an argument, but a conversation." In contrast to the cognitive ambition to solve problems, we read, participants in a conversation "are not concerned to inform, to persuade, or to refute one another, and therefore the cogency of their utterances does not depend upon their all speaking in the same idiom; they may differ without disagreeing." According to Oakeshott, this open-ended mode of interaction was "the appropriate image of human intercourse — appropriate because it recognizes the qualities, the diversities, and the proper relationships of human utterances. As civilized human beings," he added, "we are the inheritors, neither of an inquiry about ourselves and the world, nor of an accumulating body of information, but of a conversation, begun in the primeval forests and extended and made more articulate in the course of centuries." As compared with the one-dimensional linearity of argumentation, conversation was portrayed as a polyphonic if not contrapuntal enterprise. In conversational settings, we are told, "thoughts of different species take wing and play around one another, responding to each other's movements." Above all, there is "no symposiarch or arbiter; not even a doorkeeper to examine credentials"; rather, "every entrant is taken at its face-value and everything is permitted which can get itself accepted into the flow of speculation." Without trying to restrict the number of potential voices or participants, Oakeshott's essay listed as the most prominent and "most familiar" idioms "those of practical activity, of 'science' and of 'poetry'": the first concerned both with the satisfaction of wants and the cultivation of moral conduct, the second with the search for universally valid knowledge, and the last with fostering contemplative imagination.[3]

Treated as a model of communicative interaction, conversational polyphony clearly is a captivating and attractive vision. One of the chief virtues of the model resides in its linguistic (and political) tolerance or liberality: conducted along Oakeshott's or Rorty's lines, conversational exchanges exhibit no privileged speakers, no "lead instruments," no first and second strings. Closely connected with this virtue is the model's open-endedness: although all participants are able to play a role, none is given the final word — mainly because there is no such final word. Despite these undeniable merits, however, I am troubled by the notion of sheer conversational "drift." In the absence of some common focus or "subject matter," what prevents conversation from turning into empty rhetoric or idle chatter? More broadly phrased: without presupposing some genuine attentiveness, how can conversation fail to decay into disconnected soliloquies? In large measure, this uneasiness derives from ambiguities surrounding the concept of "conversation": what is left somewhat unclear—both in Oakeshott's and in Rorty's presentations—is the character of the "voices" or participants and also the status of language itself. To the extent that the voices are treated as individual speakers or speaking "subjects," conversation readily shades over into a clash of idiosyncratic "expressions" if not into attempts at reciprocal manipulation (on the level of Oakeshott's "practical" idiom); if subjectivism is avoided, the result may be conceptual uniformity (patterned on the idiom of "science"). In either case, language functions basically as a means or instrument in the pursuit of ulterior motives (such as gain or information). To preserve the integrity of conversation and its idioms, added safeguards thus seem required. Is it possible to avoid random talk as well as routinized consensus—while still clinging to the spirit of conversational generosity and refusing to impose a "single character" on speech? As it appears to me, such an avenue is open provided we grant a certain preeminence in conversation to poetry or poetic language, that is, to the "rule of metaphor."

The Rule of Metaphor

At first blush, the suggestion of such a preeminence seems to run counter to the tenor of Oakeshott's position. In challenging the imperialist pretensions of particular idioms, his essay strongly insists that the "voices which speak in conversation do not compose a hierarchy"—adding that this "denial of a hierarchical order" was a clear "departure from one of the most notable traditions of European thought": the subordination of all endeavors to theoretical cognition (or the *vita contemplativa*). Yet, despite these assertions, conversation on Oakeshott's account is not devoid of internal lineaments or fibers preventing randomness. "As I understand it," he writes, "the excellence of this conversation (as of others) springs from a tension between seriousness and playfulness. Each voice represents a serious engagement," and "without this seriousness the conversation would lack impetus." However, this "tension" or tuning—avoiding both pedantry and frivolity—cannot be taken for granted, nor can it be simply ascribed to psychological dispositions of the participants; rather, its presence must be traced to the serious-playful quality of the conversational mode itself—a quality (one might argue) most clearly evident in poetic language. Moreover, in attempting to counter the "monotony" afflicting recent and contemporary conversation, Oakeshott himself appeals directly to that language—

declaring it an "opportune enterprise" to "consider again the voice of poetry." In fact, he notes, the enterprise is "not merely opportune, it is also 'philosophical' ": for, "the consideration of poetry becomes philosophical when poetic imagining" is shown to have "a specific place in the manifold of human activities."[4]

Poetic language, and its importance for conversation, are more explicitly recognized in Rorty's discussion of "edifying" discourse and thought. "The fear of science, of 'scientism', of 'naturalism', of self-objectivation," he writes, is "the fear that all discourse will become normal discourse. That is, it is the fear that there will be objectively true or false answers to every question we ask"—which is "frightening because it cuts off the possibility of something new under the sun, of human life as poetic" rather than merely cognitive. Distinguishing within edification between an interpretive-hermeneutical and a poetic (or deconstructive) strand, Rorty's study observes that "the attempt to edify (ourselves or others) may consist in the hermeneutic activity of making connections between our own culture and some exotic culture or historical period" or it may "instead consist in the 'poetic' activity" of coming up with "new aims, new words, or new disciplines, followed by, so to speak, the inverse of hermeneutics: the attempt to reinterpret our familiar surroundings in the unfamiliar terms of our new inventions." Given the definition of edification as the "project of finding new, better, more interesting, more fruitful ways of speaking" and the general opposition to systematic inquiry, the study's accent rests squarely on the latter activity—particularly because of its ability to rekindle the "wonder" or "puzzlement" presupposed in philosophical reflection as such. "Edifying philosophers," we read, "want to keep space open for the sense of wonder which poets can sometimes cause—wonder that there is something new under the sun, something which is *not* an accurate representation of what was already there, something which (at least for the moment) cannot be explained and can barely be described."[5]

In granting a special status to poetic language, however, one should be clear about the peculiar kind of "preeminence" attributed to it; simply put, preeminence in this context is by no means a synonym for predominance or mastery, but rather for a distilled form of gentleness and unconstraint. This quality derives chiefly from poetry's completely noninstrumental and nonmanipulative stance, a stance at variance with other treatments or dimensions of language. On empiricist and behaviorist premises, language—as has been shown—appears either itself as an empirical process (amenable to control) or else as a tool adapted to the gathering and dissemination of factual knowledge. From a rationalist perspective, in turn, language coincides basically with a matrix of logical and syntactical rules useful or required for cognitive endeavors. Under pragmatic auspices, finally, language serves either as a means for individual self-expression or self-articulation or else as a reservoir of universal norms shaping communicative interaction. Only in poetry is language itself able to obtain a hearing—independently of, or without directly promoting, the designs of human cognition, will, or desire. This "hearing," however, is liable to exact a price: the price of nonmastery and renunciation—akin to the poet's "renunciation" depicted in George's poem "The Word" (discussed in the preceding chapter). Seen in light of this surrender, poetic language does not properly speaking wield power, nor does it bestow power on anyone—although it is not devoid of a certain creative and enabling kind of potency. (These considerations prompt me, incidentally, to insert a second question mark in the title of the last chapter, so that it reads "The Rule? of Metaphor?")

Returning to Oakeshott's essay, one might say that poetry's preeminence inverts the notion of a linguistic "hierarchy"—if it does not entirely subvert or erode it. There is another aspect, however, casting doubt on this notion: in the case of poetry, what is granted preeminence is not really a "single" or particular voice—capable of subjugating other voices—but rather the voice of language itself, that is, the tissue rendering conversation possible in the first place. By not being subservient to ulterior motives, poetry makes room for the serious-playful character of language, thus sustaining the "tension between seriousness and playfulness" required in conversation; in Heideggerian terms, it alone is capable of "letting" language "be" or surrendering to the "being" of language (where "being" denotes neither a thing nor an intentional product). The same sustaining quality also affects the status of the participants or contributing voices in conversation by presenting them not merely as knowledge-seekers or as competent masters of speech and communication, but as serious-playful beneficiaries of language. In granting room to the integrity of language, poetry also lets human speakers "be"—beyond the confines stipulated by epistemologists and most pragmatists—by respecting the multidimensionality and unfathomable plurivocity of their various idioms.

Some Objections

The preference accorded to poetic language may give rise to a number of doubts or apprehensions, doubts which have been forcefully articulated by several leading contemporary thinkers. One such apprehension has to do with the effects of this preference on theoretical cognition and philosophical reasoning—an issue discussed (among others) by Ricoeur in the concluding portion of *The Rule of Metaphor*. According to Ricoeur, philosophy's integrity or viability depends in large measure on the distinction between metaphorical expressions, on the one hand, and conceptual and speculative discourse, on the other. "That there are philosophical terms," he asserts, "is due to the fact that a concept can be active as thought in a metaphor which is itself dead"; in fact, "no philosophical discourse would be possible, not even a discourse of deconstruction, if we ceased to assume what Derrida justly holds to be 'the sole thesis of philosophy', namely, 'that the meaning aimed at through these (metaphorical) figures is an essence rigorously independent of that which carries it over'." Although finding a "condition of *possibility*" in the "semantic dynamism of methaphorical utterance," speculative discourse is claimed to have "its *necessity* in itself, in putting the resources of conceptual articulation to work. These are resources that doubtless belong to the mind itself, that are the mind itself reflecting upon itself." As Ricoeur futher elaborates: "The *necessity* of this discourse is not the extension of its possibility, inscribed in the dynamism of the metaphorical. Its necessity proceeds instead from the very structures of the mind, which it is the task of transcendental philosophy to articulate. One can pass from one discourse to the other only by an *epoché*." Drawing on the Husserlian (and scholastic) distinction between imagination and rational "intellection," the chapter adds: "If the *imaginatio* is the kingdom of 'the similar', the *intellectio* is that of 'the same'. In the horizon opened up by the speculative 'same' grounds 'similar' and not the inverse."[6]

Turning to Heideggerian philosophy, and especially to his endeavor to cultivate a poetic (or poetically sensitive) mode of thinking, Ricoeur depicts the endeavor as both "attempt and temptation": namely, as "an attempt from which we must draw inspiration whenever it manifestly contributes to clarifying speculative thought" and as "a temptation we must shun when the difference between speculative and poetic discourse threatens once again to disappear." With specific reference to such key terms in Heidegger's later writings as "*Erörterung*" and "*Ereignis*," the chapter assigns to them a basically speculative-conceptual, as opposed to a poetic-metaphorical, status. "Even if *Ereignis* is called a metaphor," we read, "it is a philosopher's metaphor, in the sense in which the 'analogy of being' can, strictly speaking, be termed a metaphor, but one which always remains distinct from a poet's metaphor"; as a general principle, from the vantage point of philosophical discourse "the gulf cannot be bridged between the 'same' that is to be thought and poetic resemblance." To the extent that "poetic thinking" erases this gulf in an effort to "break with metaphysics" or "leap outside its circle," the chapter "regrets" this move and the entire "position assumed by Heidegger." In Ricoeur's presentation, the "price" exacted by this move is "the inescapable ambiguity of the later works, divided between the logic of their continuity with speculative thought and the logic of their break with metaphysics."

While the first logic places the later works in line with a philosophical reasoning that "unceasingly rectifies itself," the second logic is said to lead "to a series of erasures and repeals that cast thought into the void, reducing it to hermeticism and affectedness, carrying etymological games back to the mystification of 'primitive sense'. Above all, this second logic invites us to sever discourse from its propositional character."[7]

Ricoeur's observations are open to several comments or rejoinders. First of all, poetic thinking in Heidegger's treatment does not simply "erase" the distinction between poetry and thought, but rather preserves their distance and integrity—a distance which precisely supports their mutual affinity and attentiveness. This aspect is admitted by Ricoeur himself (passingly) when he cites these lines from Heidegger's *What is Philosophy?*: "Between these two there exists a secret kinship because, in the service of language, both intercede on behalf of language and give lavishly of themselves. Yet, between both there is at the same time an abyss for they 'dwell on the most widely separated mountains'." This passage, however, is not merely an isolated or untypical formulation, but is echoed in numerous other contexts. Thus, Heidegger's essay on "The Nature of Language" voices the hunch or suspicion "that the neighborhood of poetry and thinking is concealed in the farthest divergence of their modes of saying," adding: "We must discard the view that the neighborhood of poetry and thinking consists simply in a garrulous opaque blend of two kinds of saying, in which each clumsily borrows from the other." And at another point in the same essay we read that "in the last resort, poetry and thinking both need each other—each in its own fashion—in their respective neighborhood; in what region this neighborhood itself is located, each of them (thought and poetry) will define differently, but always so that they find themselves in the same domain. However, because we are caught in the prejudice nurtured through centuries that thinking is a matter of ratiocination, that is, of calculation in the widest sense, the mere talk of a neighborhood of thinking to poetry is suspect."[8]

Beyond this caveat regarding the relationship between the two modes of saying, Ricoeur's own argument inescapably drifts into the vicinity of poetic thinking. For, how can philosophical reason arise on top of metaphorical language without somehow being affected by the latter? In Ricoeur's own terms, how can "speculative discourse" find its possibility in "the semantic dynamism of metaphorical utterance" without being indebted to such utterance? More concretely: if metaphorical utterance jeopardizes (as we are told) such customary polarities as "inside" and "outside," subject and object, "finding" and "projecting" while opening up a "pre-objective world in which we find ourselves already rooted," how can speculative thought blithely reinstate these polarities and

categories—including "the mind itself" or the "structures of the mind"—
without dogmatic fiat? Above all, given the metaphorical "paradox of
the copula"—its correlation of being and non-being—how can reason
reign outside the confines of ontological difference? On the other hand,
if the relationship of discourses is construed as a complete "distanciation"
and bracketing (*epoché*), what prevents speculative thought from collaps-
ing into "ratiocination" and the cultivation of univocity—an outcome
conceded in Ricoeur's comments that speculative "interpretation is necessarily a rationalization that at its limits eliminates the experience that
comes to language through the metaphorical process," and that "reductive interpretations are consistent with the semantic aim characteristic of
the speculative order"? The untenability of this reductive outcome and
segregation becomes particularly obvious in Ricoeur's appeal to the Aristotelian maxim according to which philosophy should aim to "signify
things in act." Elaborating on the maxim, *The Rule of Metaphor* assigns
to speculative thought the task "to seek after the place where appearance
signifies 'generating what grows'" or where things emerge as "naturally
blossoming." But what kind of thought would be better suited to capture
and reflect this blossoming or genesis than a poetic or generative mode
of thinking?[9]

Another quandary besetting this mode—although one not unrelated to
the issue of rationalism—concerns the linkage between poetry (or poetic
thought) and aesthetics, and especially the former's possible affinity with
"aestheticism" or a socially and politically detached formalism. In several
of his writings, Habermas has ascribed such a proclivity to Heidegger's
work after the so-called "*Kehre*" (or reversal)—and more generally, to
post-Heideggerian intellectual postures leaning in the direction of "post-
modernism." The disclosure of the meaning of "being," he notes at one
point, "is supposed to be extracted by thought from the poetic word;
for a dialogue between the thinker and the poet Heidegger turns to
Hölderlin." This turn, he adds, is designed to counteract modern "subjectivism" and its attendant "will to power"; simultaneously, however,
the approach "leaves behind the validity claim of traditional philosophy."
In Habermas's presentation, Heidegger's thought "does not wish to be
understood 'as a valid statement or proposition', but only as 'a possible
occasion to open up a path for attunement'." This move is said to parallel
the intellectual development of some of his contemporaries—for example, that of the poet Gottfried Benn and his progressive fascination with
"the expressive world of art as pure form." Drawing the implications
from such an aesthetic move, Habermas concludes: "Perhaps Heidegger's
thought can be characterized indirectly by what it does not accomplish:
it relates as little to social-political praxis as it contributes to an interpretation of the results of science."[10]

The charge of aestheticism clearly needs to be taken seriously—although, in the end, I do not consider it cogent. As in Ricoeur's case, several rejoinders seem possible to the charge. For one thing, the assertion neglects the mentioned "inversion" of hierarchy: not occupying a "governing" position, poetry cannot possibly overrule or simply preempt other perspectives and modes of discourse. More importantly, Habermas's argument tends to leave crucial terms opaque or only conventionally defined; thus, it is by no means evident that Heideggerian thought (including its poetic dimension) makes no contribution to moral and political "praxis" or to the interpretation of "science"—provided the meaning of these terms is not merely taken for granted. The same opaqueness besets the key feature of the argument: the charge of "aestheticism," which seems to be identified with a retreat into subjective inwardness and detached formalism. Yet, few aspects mark Heidegger's opus more prominently than the break with traditional, subjectivist aesthetics. His lectures on "The Origin of the Work of Art" expressly criticize modern aesthetics for reducing the artwork to an object of subjective sensation or "experience"—retorting that such experience may be "the very element in which art vanishes." The same lectures also pointedly differentiate attentiveness to art from formalism, that is, from a "purely aestheticist appreciation of the formal aspects of a work, its qualities and attractions." Far from endorsing subjective-aesthetic self-enclosure Heidegger actually finds a crucial feature of art (and poetry) in its transgression of boundaries and enclosures—in its ability to shatter customary life-forms in favor of an openness to "being." In the words of the cited lectures, the more genuine the quality of an artwork, "the more plainly evident is the shock of the *being* of the work and the more completely unfamiliarity is inaugurated and the hitherto-familiar reversed." Unfamiliarity in this context, however, does not merely signify a "vaccum" or empty space, but rather the emergence of a possible historical world; accordingly, art and poetic language do not only instigate a formal "play," but rather (as Heidegger says at one point) a "world-play."[11]

The Gift of Language

It may be appropriate at this point to return to a notion mentioned in the preceding chapter: the conception of language as a "gift" or "giving," specifically as a gift of being or a giving which "lets" being "be." As it seems to me, this notion has important implications for the correlation of modes of discourse. Apart from unsettling familiar-conventional assumptions, poetic language displays a nurturing and sustaining quality—an aspect sometimes ignored or slighted by deconstructionists; while eroding metaphysical or "foundational" claims, its chief trait is its "giving virtue" or generosity. This trait is clearly acknowledged in Heidegger's writings; although emphasizing the ontological status of language—its role in the disclosure of being—his treatment does not simply preclude other linguistic dimensions. Thus, according to his *Letter on Humanism*, language can never be "grasped properly in terms of its symbolic structure, perhaps not even in terms of the character of signification"; in another passage the same *Letter* speaks even of the "liberation of language from grammar into a more original essential framework," a liberation "reserved for thinking and poetry." Elsewhere, however, grammar and empirical features are readily accorded their due. "We must not give grounds for the impression," Heidegger notes, "that we are here passing negative judgment on the scientific and theoretical investigation of language and languages. Such investigation has its own particular justification and its own importance; yet, scientific and theoretical information about language is one thing, undergoing an experience with language quite another." Similarly, turning to the pragmatic function of language he observes: "Do we wish to deny that man is the creature that speaks? By no means; we deny this as little as we deny the possibility to subsume linguistic phenomena under the rubric 'expression.' But we ask: in which sense or capacity does man speak?"[12]

Similar considerations can be extended to the various dimensions of language probed in the present study. Poetry or poetic thought, I want to suggest, sustains and nourishes these facets—although it does this not entirely innocently, that is, not without having deprived them of foundational pretense. Apart from this quiet (almost unnoticeable) dislodgment, however, such thought makes room for multiple and diverse enterprises, including epistemology and subjective and intersubjective pragmatics. Given its role in inaugurating the "world-play," poetic language does not simply bracket empirical "reality" or the cognitive need for "reference." To this extent I tend to concur with Ricoeur when he speaks about the "inalienable referential function" of both oral discourses and written texts. By addressing themselves "to anyone who knows how to read," he states, texts refer to a "world" which exists "in front of the text," that is, to a reality which "is 'the world of the text' and yet is not in the text." Radically construed, the notion of a world "in front of the text" points to a reality which, without being purely linguistic or symbolic, is not simply independent of language and the world-disclosure accomplished by language. A conception of this kind is not entirely unique to hermeneutical thought; an analogous view seems to be implied in Donald Davidson's comments on the "idea of a conceptual scheme." "In giving up dependence on the concept of an uninterpreted reality, something outside all schemes and science," Davidson writes, "we do not relinquish the notion of objective truth—quite the contrary. Given the dogma of a dualism of scheme and reality, we get conceptual relativity, and truth relative to a scheme. Without the dogma, this kind of relativity goes by the board. Of course, truth of sentences remains relative to language, but that is as objective as can be."[13]

The focus on linguistic-poetic world-disclosure is able to salvage not only empiricist concerns, but also elements of rationalist epistemology. The importance of syntactical-grammatical structures is stressed (I think over stressed) in Edie's *Speaking and Meaning*. "Syntax, in its abstract, formal purity," he affirms, "is utterly unaffected by semantics. Since it is free of both referentiality and contextuality, we are able on the level of syntax alone to discover strictly formal laws, strict synonymies, strict repeatabilities, strict idealities which words do not and cannot possess." However, syntactical laws can hardly operate or be articulated outside the range of "words" and their disclosing capacity. In a more subtle fashion, Ricoeur seeks to integrate "structuralist" features into his broader interpretive framework. "In the same way as the grammatical codes have a generative function," he argues, texts are predicated on "literary codes" endowed with a generative potency; this consideration leads him even to stipulate a "generative poetics" which "would correspond at the level of the composition of discourse (of the Aristotelian *taxis*) to the generative grammar in Chomsky's sense." These comments, it appears to me, are more persuasive if "generative" is understood more in the sense of disclosure than in terms of fixed a priori principles. Construed in the latter vein, generative poetics tends to succumb to Rorty's more general criticisms of Chomskyan epistemology—especially his argument that this epistemology requires "not just the premise that there is a fixed language of thought but the premise that our knowledge of the nature of that language is itself immune to correction on the basis of experience."[14]

A salvaging effort along similar lines, I believe, can also be directed at pragmatics in its various forms. For purposes of simplification, pragmatics in my view can be subdivided into ordinary, everyday talk, on the one hand, and "universal" or "transcendental" communication, on the other; the first mode conforms largely to traditional rhetorical and commonsense argumentation, while the second aims at the formulation of normative yardsticks of speech. Everyday talk commonly reflects the beliefs and intentions of speakers, but without violating prevailing linguistic conventions; on the whole, both the sense and reference of terms tend to be taken for granted on this level—though in a manner which remains fragile and open to challenge. Heidegger at one point presents everyday talk as a "forgotten and thus decayed mode of poetry," that is, as a form of speech which, while seemingly self-sufficient, remains secretly dependent on, and nourished by poetic language. The same nourishing effect can also be seen at work in the domain of ethics which, as Heidegger elsewhere remarks, is predicated on a concrete "ethos" or way of life attuned to ontological disclosure. The search for normative yardsticks is by no means barred in this perspective, although the emphasis is likely to be less on categorical principles than on concrete relationships; on the other hand, stipulation of yardsticks independently of a way of life is bound to carry a metaphysical tinge. Reviewing the endeavors of Habermas and Apel in this field, Rorty is appropriately "suspicious" of their attempt "to develop a 'universal pragmatics' or a 'transcendental hermeneutics' "; he even finds the "basic mistake" of such programs in the view "that we can get around overconfident philosophical realism and positivistic reductions only by adopting something like Kant's transcendental standpoint." As he adds, what is required and sufficient "to accomplish these laudable purposes is not Kant's 'epistemological' distinction between the transcendental and the empirical standpoints, but rather his 'existentialist' distinction between people as empirical selves and as moral agents."[15]

The giving quality of language can now be seen to provide sustenance or support to the main idioms mentioned in Oakeshott's "The Voice of Poetry in the Conversation of Mankind": chiefly to the idioms of "practical activity" and "science." As presented in that essay, the term "science" basically denotes an epistemological inquiry aiming at univocal meaning and knowledge. "Scientific investigation, the activity of being a scientist," Oakeshott writes, "is mankind in search of the intellectual satisfaction which comes from constructing and exploring a rational world of related concepts," that is, "a system of conceptual images related to one another consequentially and claiming universal acceptance as a rational account of the world we live in." As will be noted, science is here described as an activity, more specifically a discursive activity — with methodological rules seen not as a priori canons but as derivative from the practice: "The so-called 'methods' of scientific investigation emerge in the course of the activity and they never take account of all that belongs to a scientific inquiry; and in advance of scientific thought there are no scientific problems." The language adapted to scientific inquiry, according to the essay, is a streamlined, conceptual idiom which can readily be shared by the community of investigators. Science being "essentially a co-operative enterprise," we read, "all who participate in the construction of this rational world of conceptual images invoking universal acceptance are as if they were one man, and exactness is communication between them is a necessity." The goal of exactness is promoted largely through quantification, with the result that scientific discourse is "both narrower and more precise" than other idioms. For the sake of generating consensus and univocity, scientific terms or images are said to "become measurements according to agreed scales, relationships are mathematical ratios, and positions are indicated by numerical co-ordinates."[16]

In contrast to the "monodic" character of science, the voice of practical activity is subdivided by Oakeshott into two distinct (though related) modes of "imagining": namely, first, a narrowly pragmatic and commonsensical mode and, secondly, a more reflective and ethical mode. On the first level, practical life is governed basically by "desire and aversion" and its constitutive images are "pleasure and pain." Intersubjective relations on this level are described (perhaps in an excessively reductive fashion) as mundane and utilitarian: "Another self is known as the consumer of what I produce, the producer of what I consume, one way or another the assistant in my projects, the servant of my pleasure." According to Oakeshott, however, utilitarian contacts do not exhaust the "world of practice," since that world is composed "not merely of images of desire and aversion but also of images of approval and disapproval." What comes into view with approval and disapproval are moral awareness and ethical criteria. While "the merely desiring self can go no further than a disingenuous recognition of other selves," moral interaction presupposes "a genuine and unqualified recognition of other selves. All other selves are acknowledged to be ends and not merely means to our ends." The manifestations of practical activity are said to be either nondiscursive acts or discursive utterances; particularly on the narrowly pragmatic level, the appropriate linguistic idiom is described as a conventional language largely devoid of idiosyncratic features: "Its words and expressions are so many agreed signs which, because they have relatively fixed and precise usages, and because they are non-resonant, serve as a medium for confident communication. It is a language that has to be learned by imitation." In using the words or phrases of practical, everyday speech, we are told, participants do not seek "to enlarge their meaning, or to set going a procession of linguistic reverberations"; as a result, pragmatic language appears "like a coinage, the more fixed and invariable the value of its components, the more useful it is as a medium of exchange."[17]

Differentiating poetry from all other types of discursive practices, Oakeshott's essay presents "poetic imagining" as a "contemplative," that is, nonpurposive and nonmanipulative activity—more strongly, as an activity which coincides with contemplation: "I do not mean that poetic imagining is one species among others of contemplative imagining; I mean that the voice of contemplation is the voice of poetry and that it has no other utterance. And just as activity in practice is desiring and obtaining, and activity in science is inquiring and understanding, so poetry is contemplating and delighting." As employed in this context, contemplation is not equivalent to traditional metaphysics or the "voice of *theoria*," but rather to a special attentiveness to images and the activity of "image-making." In poetic language images are not tied to causal motives or ulterior ends: they are "neither pleasurable nor painful" nor targets of moral or cognitive assessment; differently put, "they provoke neither speculation nor inquiry about the occasion or conditions of their appearing but only delight in their having appeared." In view of its contemplative stance, the essay describes poetic imagining at one point as a "non-laborious" sort of activity, that is, an activity "which, because it is playful and not businesslike, because it is free from care and released from both logical necessity and pragmatic requirement, seems to participate in the character of inactivity." Seen as nonlaborious endeavor, such imagining is sharply at odds with both pragmatic and scientific genres of discourse; in Oakeshott's account, poetic words and images are in fact "not signs with preordained significances; they are not like chessmen behaving according to known rules or like coins having an agreed current value; they are not tools with specific aptitudes and uses." Exemplifying the serious-playful character of language, the poet—we are told—"arranges his images like a girl bunching flowers, considering only how they will appear."[18]

The differentiation of linguistic idioms or dimensions is not unique to the discussed essay. As it seems to me, Oakeshott's idioms find a loose parallel in Hannah Arendt's *The Life of the Mind*, especially in her categories of "thinking," "knowing," "willing," and "judging"—provided these categories are seen to stand not for mental faculties but rather for distinct modes of discourse. In Arendt's treatment, "knowing" is basically a synonym for cognitive-epistemic inquiry, while "willing" and "judging" (in one of its main uses) denote respectively the endeavors of moral self-enactment and commonsense interaction; "thinking," finally, signifies nonpurposive meditation. Relying on Kant's juxtaposition of "reason" and "intellect" (*Vernunft* and *Verstand*), the study equates the difference between the two faculties essentially with the distinction "between two altogether different mental activities, thinking and knowing, and two altogether different concerns: meaning, in the first category, and cognition, in the second." In Arendt's view, the two activities can and should by no means be collapsed—despite a longstanding tradition encouraging such a merger. "The basic fallacy, taking precedence over all specific metaphysical fallacies," she asserts, "is to interpret meaning on the model of (cognitive) truth." As distinguished from the meditative character of thinking, knowing is presented as a purposive, goal-oriented activity; its aim is to satisfy "our curiosity about the world" and to obtain an explanatory grasp of phenomena. According to *The Life of the Mind*, cognitive inquiry in this sense involves a complex interplay of intellect

and sense experience—an interplay reflected in the differentiation between two kinds of "truths," commonly termed "analytic" and "synthetic": "What science and the quest for knowledge are after is *irrefutable*
truth, that is, propositions human beings are not free to reject—they are
compelling. They are of two kinds, as we have known since Leibniz:
truths of reasoning and truths of fact." As the study adds, the Leibnizian
distinction is ultimately based on the age-old tension between necessity
and contingency according to which "all that is necessary, and whose opposite is impossible, possesses a higher ontological dignity than whatever
is but could also not be."[19]

For the sake of brevity, I shall not elaborate here further on the
faculties of "willing" and "judging"—the domains of morality and everyday life—but rather highlight some main traits of "thinking."[20] Although
marginally or subsidiarily involved in cognition, thinking is portrayed as
a purposeless enterprise. Whereas cognitive truth is "located in the
evidence of the senses," Arendt writes, this "is by no means the case with
meaning and with the faculty of thought, which searches for it; the latter
does not ask what something is or whether it exists at all—its evidence
is always taken for granted—but *what it means for it to be*," While the
desire to know, "whether arising out of practical or purely theoretical
perplexities, can be fulfilled when it reaches its prescribed goal," and
while cognitive endeavor "leaves behind a growing treasure of knowledge," thinking on the contrary "leaves nothing so tangible behind, and
the need to think can therefore never be stilled by the insights of 'wise
men'." In another passage, thinking is said to belong "among those *ener*
geiai which, like flute-playing, have their ends within themselves and
leave no tangible outside end product in the world we inhabit." As presented in the study, the thinking activity is closely akin to Heidegger's
mode of "poetic thinking"—as Arendt herself recognizes when, in commenting on Carnap's derision of metaphysics, she recalls Heidegger's
retort "that philosophy and poetry were indeed closely related; they
were not identical but sprang from the same source—which is thinking."
Arendt's study also comes close to the notion of an inverted hierarchy,
with some preeminence accorded to the least constraining faculty. While
refusing to "establish a hierarchical order among the mind's activities,"
she nonetheless voices the belief that "it is hardly deniable that an order
of priorities exists: It is inconceivable how we would ever be able to will
or to judge, that is, to handle things which are not yet and things which
are no more, if the power of representation and the effort necessary to
direct mental attention to what in every way escapes the attention of
sense perception had not gone ahead and prepared the mind for further
reflection as well as for willing and judging." In other words, she con-

cludes, "what we generally call 'thinking' " must somehow "prepare the particulars given to the senses in such a way that the mind is able to handle them in their absence."[21]

Homo Loquens and Politics

Traced through its various implications, poetic language accords a certain coherence to both *homo loquens* and politics—although a coherence which is far removed from the univocity of a "single character" or the stability of a "foundational" support. While clearly enmeshed in empirical processes and human purposes, language and politics are never simply "given," but rather modes of "giving." No one in recent times has stressed the connection of language and politics more eloquently than Arendt. In a passage cited in the opening chapter she asserts that "wherever the relevance of speech is at stake, matters become political by definition, for speech is what makes man a political being." In her portrayal, the Greek *polis*—that epitome of the *bios politikos*—basically "grew out of and remained rooted in the Greek pre-*polis* experience and estimate of what makes it worthwhile for men to live together (*syzen*), namely, the 'sharing of words and deeds'." However, not every "word" or "deed" in her judgment is equally political or an equally genuine testimonial to the meaning of politics. Appealing to Pericles' funeral oration, she places the true locus of politics at the boundary of mortality. "Men's life together in the form of the *polis*," she writes, "seemed to assure that the most futile of human activities, action and speech, and the least tangible and most ephemeral of man-made 'products', the deeds and stories which are their outcome, would become imperishable." It is precisely this boundary of mortality—differently phrased, the ontological play of presence and absence—which is most faithfully preserved in poetic language. This aspect seems to be expressly recognized in Oakeshott's comments that "in ancient Greece (particularly in Athens) 'politics' was understood as a 'poetic' activity in which speaking (not merely to persuade but to compose memorable verbal images) was preeminent and in which action was for the achievement of 'glory' and 'greatness'."[22]

To be sure, nothing would be less desirable—and less in harmony with the Greek legacy—than a simple "poeticizing" of contemporary politics. In a world torn asunder by individual, national-ethnic, and class cleavages and wedded to technological mastery, poetic imagining cannot simply be restored by fiat (least of all an aestheticist fiat). What such a world urgently requires is alertness to concrete political reality as it is experienced in everyday life—which is by no means synonymous with a complacent "realism." In Arendt's terminology, respect for empirical and cognitive "truth" is needed to guard against illusions and ideological distortions and to keep alive the sense of existing (and far from imaginary) deprivations and modes of suffering. At the same time, prevailing trends toward objectivism or objectification place a premium on linguistic and political pragmatics, that is, on the cultivation of general-public conversation and moral argument. Thus, a Habermasian critical posture—combining empirical analysis with universal normative yardsticks—seems a suitable stance in many respects in an age of technology and class division. Yet, although valuable and important for many purposes, epistemology and pragmatics are neither self-sufficient nor entirely adequate for political recovery. As I have tried to indicate, *homo loquens* is not merely a language-user—employing symbols to convey information or to express intentions—but is simultaneously maintained or sustained by language. Accordingly, the *bios politikos* cannot be preserved or recaptured through cognitive and practical-moral endeavors alone; in Arendtian vocabulary, the activities of "knowing" and "willing" must be undergirded and permeated by a more purposeless thoughtfulness or poetic thinking—which is the genuine abode of human freedom.[23]

Given its purposeless, playful character, however, such thinking cannot be instigated or instituted through planning or deliberate design. Shunning manipulative efforts, attunement to poetic thought demands patience, sobriety, and something like the "renunciation" mentioned in George's poem—which is not identical with despair; in line with this demand, man is bound to be over long stretches more a listener than a speaker or language-user. In our loquacious age, saturated with political slogans and advertisements, such listening is liable to be a difficult enterprise—especially if hearing also involves attentiveness to silence. As Heidegger comments at one point, language in our time "withdraws from man its simple and high saying; but its initial call or appeal does not thereby cease, it merely falls silent—a silence man assiduously avoids to heed." In his essay "Wherefore Poets?" Heidegger describes ours as a "needful" or "destitute" age, destitute primarily because of its forgetfulness of the gift of language and the ontological play of speech and silence. The same essay portrays Hölderlin and Rilke as preeminent poets in a destitute time, noting that such poets are particularly "venturesome" in that "their singing celebrates the integrity of the whole sphere of being." As Heidegger adds: "To be a poet in a destitute time means: to attend, singing, to the trace of the fugitive gods," to remain tenaciously "on the latter's tracks and thus to pave for other mortals a way to recovery." As regards the rest of us, he notes, "we must learn to listen to what *these* poets say—assuming that we do not mistake the temporality which conceals and shelters being, by confusing it with a clock time derived from the calculating dissection of phenomena."[24]

Citing a passage by Hölderlin, Heidegger elsewhere establishes a close connection between the gift of language and "friendliness" (a translation of the Greek *charis*):

> . . . As long as friendliness,
> in purity, still stays with his heart,
> man not unhappily measures himself
> with the godhead. . . .

What should emerge here at the latest (if it did not much sooner) is the affinity linking the poet's gift with love or friendship. Just as in the case of love, disclosure of being through language cannot be instigated at will and, once kindled, tends to mold or transform us in directions not of our choosing; although not a random occurrence and permeated by the "most gentle laws," poetic giving—again like love—cannot be reduced to syntactical or conventional "rules," mainly because such giving cannot routinely be replicated or repeated. In Oakeshott's pointed formulation, poetry is "a language without a vocabulary, and consequently one that cannot be learned by imitation." Oakeshott also links poetry closely with the "world *sub specie amoris*," as distinguished from the domains of utility, moral approval, and cognition—mainly because of the purposeless quality of both. "Friends and lovers," he writes, "are not concerned with what can be made out of each other"; and interaction among them "is, more than in any other engagement in practical imagining, 'whatever it turns out to be'."[25] To be sure, love is not entirely devoid of contest or contestation, that is, a subtle probing of reliability. In Heideggerian terms, disclosure of being also engenders ontological "strife" or conflict —the strife between absence and presence, being and nonbeing; however, instead of coinciding with destructive enmity, this rift yields rather a "loving struggle" in which harmony arises from respect for difference. To conclude, I want to cite another passage by Hölderlin (which Heidegger repeatedly invokes):

> Much, from the morning onwards,
> Since we have been a discourse and have heard from one another,
> Has humankind learned; but soon we shall be song.

Notes

Chapter 1: After Babel

1. This terminology is employed in Karl W. Deutsch, *The Nerves of Government: Models of Political Communication and Control* (New York: Free Press, 1963). As Deutsch asserts (p. 150): "If we can measure information, no matter how crudely, then we can also measure the cohesion of organizations or societies in terms of their ability to transmit information with smaller or larger losses or distortions in transmission." For the notion of "input" and "output" flows of information see David Easton, *A Systems Analysis of Political Life* (New York: Wiley, 1965). Compare also Melvin L. DeFleur, *Theories of Mass Communication* (2nd ed.; New York: McKay Company, 1970); Richard R. Fagen, *Politics and Communication* (Boston: Little, Brown & Co., 1966).

2. See, e.g., Paul E. Corcoran, *Political Language and Rhetoric* (Austin: University of Texas Press, 1979); Doris A. Graber, *Verbal Behavior and Politics* (Urbana: University of Illinois Press, 1976); J. Jeffery Auer, ed., *The Rhetoric of Our Times* (New York: Appleton-Century-Crofts, 1969); Brian Barry, *Political Argument* (London: Routledge & Kegan Paul, 1965); Hans D. Zimmermann, *Die politische Rede* (Stuttgart: Kohlhammer, 1969); Karin Dovring, *The Road of Propaganda: The Semantics of Biased Communication* (New York: Philosophical Library, 1959); Alexander L. George, *Propaganda Analysis: A Study of Inferences Made from Nazi Propaganda in World War II* (Evanston, Ill.: Row, Peterson, 1959); Harold D. Lasswell, Nathan Leites et al., *Language of Politics: Studies in Quantitative Semantics* (New York: Stewart, 1949).

3. Murray Edelman, *The Symbolic Uses of Politics* (Urbana: University of Illinois Press, 1964); *Politics as Symbolic Action: Mass Arousal and Quiescence* (New York: Academic Press, 1971); *Political Language: Words That Succeed and Policies That Fail* (New York: Academic Press, 1977). For a study by a sociologist paralleling Edelman's research compare Claus Mueller, *The Politics of Communication: A Study in the Political Sociology of Language, Socialization, and Legitimation* (Oxford: at the University Press, 1973). On the corrupting influence of totalitarian regimes see, e.g., Dolf Sternberger, Gerhard Storz and W. E. Süskind, *Aus dem Wörterbuch des Unmenschen* (Hamburg: Classen Verlag, 1957); on the relation of language and social class Denis Lawton, *Social Class, Language and Education* (London: Routledge & Kegan Paul, 1968); Basil Bernstein, "Language and Social Class," *British Journal of Sociology*, vol. 11 (1960), pp. 271-276.

4. Regarding language clashes in multilingual settings, especially in developing countries, see Joseph Bram, *Language and Society* (New York: Random House, 1955), pp. 43-58. Compare also Joyce O. Hertzler, *A Sociology of Language* (New York: Random House, 1965), pp. 247-259; David D. Laitin, *Politics, Language and Thought: The Somali Experience* (Chicago: University of

Chicago Press, 1977), Joshua A. Fishman, *Language and Nationalism* (New York: Newbury House, 1973).

5. According to Heidegger, *logos* encompasses both language and thought—where the latter term stands for "thought of Being" and ultimately for Being itself. See Martin Heidegger, *Unterwegs zur Sprache* (3rd ed., Pfullingen: Neske, 1965), p. 185. Compare also his comments (p. 11): "There is a doctrine which holds that, in contradistinction to plants and animals, man is *homo loquens*. The phrase signifies not only that, in addition to various other qualities, man also has the capacity to speak; rather, it implies that it is only language which enables man to be a human creature. In his capacity as speaker man is properly human; Wilhelm von Humboldt has taught us this. However, the question remains what is meant by 'man'." On *homo loquens* see I. Rauch and G. F. Carr, eds., *The Signifying Animal: The Grammar of Language and Experience* (Bloomington: Indiana University Press, 1980); George Steiner, *Extraterritorial: Papers on Literature and the Language Revolution* (New York: Atheneum, 1971), esp. pp. 58-101 ("The Language Animal").

6. Hans-Georg Gadamer, "Man and Language," in *Philosophical Hermeneutics*, trans. David E. Linge (Berkeley: University of California Press, 1976), pp. 59-60, 68 (translation slightly altered).

7. Hannah Arendt, *The Human Condition: A Study of the Central Dilemmas Facing Modern Man* (Garden City, N.Y.: Doubleday Anchor Books, 1959), pp. 4, 25-26, 175.

8. Arendt, *The Human Condition*, p. 257.

9. See Stanley Cavell, *Must We Mean What We Say? A Book of Essays* (Cambridge: at the University Press, 1976).

10. Gadamer, "Man and Language," p. 62.

11. *Hamanns Schriften*, ed. Friedrich Roth (Berlin: G. Reimer, 1842), vol. 7, p. 151. The letter is cited in Heidegger, *Unterwegs zur Sprache*, p. 13; for the notion that "language speaks" see pp. 180, 254.

12. Compare, e.g., Brand Blanshard, *Reason and Analysis* (London: Allen and Unwin, 1962); G. R. G. Mure, *Retreat from Truth* (Oxford: Blackwell, 1958).

13. Stanley Rosen, *Nihilism: A Philosophical Essay* (New Haven: Yale University Press, 1969), pp. xiii, xviii-xix. Regarding the differentiation between language and objects compare his statement (p. 47): "The main difficulty lies in the relation between the structure of speech and that of things. Ontologies of language, whether derived from Heidegger or Wittgenstein, desire to overcome the dualism inherent in the thesis of two structures, but the price they pay is to return to monism and so to silence. . . . My point is rather this: *if* there is to be rational speech, one must distinguish radically between the structure of speech and the structure of things, or, more simply, between speech and things."

14. Hilary Putnam, *Mind, Language and Reality* (Cambridge: at the University Press, 1975), p. 1. See also Jürgen Habermas, "Towards a Theory of Communicative Competence," *Inquiry*, vol. 13 (1970), pp. 371-372.

15. Ernest Gellner, *Words and Things: An Examination of, and Attack on, Linguistic Philosophy*, with a Foreword by Bertrand Russell (rev. ed., London: Routledge & Kegan Paul, 1979), pp. 49, 149, 235-36, 245-47. Regarding nihilism he commented (p. 239): "Anyone who goes to the centers of teaching

of this philosophy expecting epidemics of suicide, license, nihilism, *actes gratuits*, drug-taking, fast driving as the only escape from a meaningless world whose values are backed by nothing but custom and accident of language, is due for a big surprise. Nothing of the kind is concluded from the premises."

16. Richard Rorty, *Philosophy and the Mirror of Nature* (Princeton, N.J.: Princeton University Press, 1979), p. 276; Cavell, *Must We Mean What We Say?*, p. 95.

17. Gustav Bergmann, *Logic and Reality* (Madison: University of Wisconsin Press, 1964), p. 177.

18. Richard Rorty, "Introduction: Metaphilosophical Difficulties of Linguistic Philosophy," in *The Linguistic Turn: Recent Essays in Philosophical Method* (Chicago: University of Chicago Press, 1967), pp. 3, 13. The connection between ordinary language analysis and logical empiricism on a common epistemological plane seems dubious or overdrawn, especially in view of the essay's later comments on Wittgenstein.

19. "Introduction," pp. 33-38. Commenting on the last option Rorty stated (p. 37): "Such a project, which suggests that the study of language can lead us to certain necessary truths as well as to an Austinian empirical theory, holds out the hope that linguistic philosophy may yet satisfy our Platonic, as well as our Aristotelian, instincts."

20. "Introduction," p. 39. Among thinkers opposing traditional epistemology Rorty mentioned "philosophers as different as Dewey, Hampshire, Sartre, Heidegger, and Wittgenstein" (note 75).

21. *Philosophy and the Mirror of Nature*, pp. 257, 259, 264. Alongside Wittgenstein, Rorty places in the first category Wilfrid Sellars and Donald Davidson, while listing as spokesmen of the second type (or a mingling of the first with the second) such thinkers as Russell, Carnap, Quine, Putnam, and Michael Dummett. Regarding the linkage between an "immaterial eye" and an "immaterial I," Arendt comments that, in antiquity, "mathematical and ideal forms were not the products of the intellect, but given to the eyes of the mind as sense data were given to the organs of the senses; and those who were trained to perceive what was hidden from the eyes of bodily vision . . . perceived true being, or rather being in its true appearance. With the rise of modernity, mathematics does not simply enlarge its content . . . , but ceases to be concerned with appearances at all. It is no longer the beginning of philosophy, of the 'science' of Being in its true appearance, but becomes instead the science of the structure of the human mind." See *The Human Condition*, p. 242.

22. See Hans-Georg Gadamer, *Truth and Method* (New York: Seabury Press, 1975); Maurice Merleau-Ponty, *Signs*, trans. Richard C. McCleary (Evanston: Northwestern University Press, 1964), and *The Prose of the World*, trans. John O'Neill (Evanston: Northwestern University Press, 1973); also James M. Edie, "Was Merleau-Ponty a Structuralist?" *Semiotica*, vol. 4 (1971), pp. 297-323.

23. See especially Paul Ricoeur, *Freedom and Nature: The Voluntary and the Involuntary*, trans. Erazim V. Kohak (Evanston: Northwestern University Press, 1966).

24. Ricoeur, "From Existentialism to the Philosophy of Language," in *The Rule of Metaphor: Multi-Disciplinary Studies of the Creation of Meaning in*

Language, trans. Robert Czerny (Toronto: University of Toronto Press, 1977), pp. 315-16. The turn to symbolic exegesis is evident especially in *Fallible Man*, trans. Charles Kelbley (Chicago: Regnery, 1965), and *The Symbolism of Evil*, trans. Emerson Buchanan (New York: Harper and Row, 1967).

25. *The Rule of Metaphor*, pp. 317-322. As Ricoeur adds (p. 322): "Now the recapturing of the intentions of ordinary language experiences may become the major task of a linguistic phenomenology, a phenomenology which would escape both the futility of mere linguistic distinctions and the unverifiability of all claims to direct intuition of lived experience." Regarding his encounter with psychoanalysis see his *Freud and Philosophy: An Essay on Interpretation*, trans. Denis Savage (New Haven: Yale University Press, 1970); and regarding structuralism, *The Conflict of Interpretations: Essays in Hermeneutics*, ed. Don Ihde (Evanston: Northwestern University Press, 1974).

26. See, e.g., Albrecht Wellmer, " Communications and Emancipation: Reflections on the Linguistic Turn in Critical Theory," in *On Critical Theory*, ed. John O'Neill (New York: Seabury Press, 1976); Karl-Otto Apel, "Analytic Philosophy of Language and the 'Geisteswissenschaften'," *Foundations of Language*, Suppl. Series, vol. 5 (Dordrecht: Reidel, 1967); Jacques Derrida, *Of Grammatology*, trans. Gayatri C. Spivak (Baltimore: Johns Hopkins University Press, 1976); Michel Foucault, *The Archaeology of Knowledge*, trans. A. M. Sheridan Smith (New York: Random House, 1972).

27. George Steiner, *After Babel: Aspects of Language and Translation* (Oxford: at the University Press, 1975).

28. Ian Hacking, *Why Does Language Matter to Philosophy?* (Cambridge: at the University Press, 1975), pp. 6-7, 10, 160.

29. *Why Does Language Matter to Philosophy?*, esp. p. 16. Hacking elaborates explicitly the implications of "mental discourse" for Hobbes' political theory (p. 25): "The public discourse of politics is, in his opinion, entirely parasitic upon mental discourse. Indeed it is instructive to compare the thrust of his theories of the state and of speech. In the case of the state, individuals are constituted prior to a state that makes sense and exacts obligations only in terms of the needs of individuals and the contracts into which they enter. Likewise, Hobbesian mental discourse is constituted prior to the public discourse that is derived from it."

30. Karl-Otto Apel, *Towards a Transformation of Philosophy*, trans. Glyn Adey and David Frisby (first German ed. 1973; London: Routledge & Kegan Paul, 1980), pp. 93-95 (translation slightly altered). Apel's tripartite scheme is roughly akin to the "Delta factor" outlined by Walker Percy in *The Message in the Bottle* (New York: Farrar, Straus and Giroux, 1954), pp. 3-45.

31. Apel, *Die Idee der Sprache in der Tradition des Humanismus von Dante bis Vico* (first ed. 1963; 3rd ed., Bonn: Bouvier Verlag, 1980), pp. 18-20, 29-30, 67-71, 75-85.

32. For an interpretation in terms of transcendental hermeneutics see *Die Idee der Sprache*, pp. 6-9 ("Vorwort zur zweiten Auflage"), also *Towards a Transformation of Philosophy*, pp. 100-101; for an emphasis on poetry see *Transformation der Philosophie* (Frankfurt-Main: Suhrkamp, 1973), vol. I, pp. 160-61.

33. Ricoeur, *The Rule of Metaphor*, p. 12. As he adds (p. 13): "Poetry does

not seek to prove anything at all: its project is mimetic; its aim . . . is to compose an essential representation of human actions; its appropriate method is to speak the truth by means of fiction, fable, and tragic *mythos*." For some comments regarding *On Interpretation* see Heidegger, *Unterwegs zur Sprache*, pp. 203-04.

34. Compare, e.g., Eugenio Coseriu, *Die Geschichte der Sprachphilosophie von der Antike bis zur Gegenwart: Eine Übersicht*, 2 vols. (Tübingen: Tübinger Beiträge zur Linguistik, 1970 and 1972).

35. As Aristotle writes: "It is a great thing, indeed, to make a proper use of the poetic forms, as also of compounds and strange words. But the greatest thing by far is to be a master of metaphor: this is the one thing that cannot be learnt from others; and it is also a sign of genius, since a good metaphor implies an intuitive perception of the similarity of dissimilars." *Poetics* 1459a 3-8.

36. See Marlies K. Danziger and Wendell S. Johnson, *The Critical Reader: Analyzing and Judging Literature* (New York: Ungar, 1978), pp. 8-14, 176. For a more elaborate breakdown of modes or perspectives compare Wilfred L. Guerin et al., *A Handbook of Critical Approaches to Literature* (2nd ed.; New York: Harper & Row, 1979): also M. H. Abrams, *The Mirror and the Lamp* (New York: Oxford University Press, 1953).

37. Hayden White, "The Absurdist Moment in Contemporary Literary Theory," in *Tropics of Discourse: Essays in Cultural Criticism* (Baltimore: Johns Hopkins University Press, 1978), pp. 263, 270-76.

38. Andrew Hacker, *Political Theory: Philosophy, Ideology, Science* (New York: Macmillan, 1961), pp. 13-20 (in the citation I have avoided the double use of "insight"); Hacker, "Capital and Carbuncles: The 'Great Books' Reappraised," *American Political Science Review*, vol. 48 (1954), pp. 775-86. See also Elizabeth M. James, *Political Theory: An Introduction to Interpretation* (Chicago: Rand McNally, 1976), pp. 10-15, 44-63.

Chapter 2: Empiricism and Behaviorism

1. To be sure, distrust of ordinary language was not invented during the "Heyday of Meanings." As Francis Bacon already observed in 1620 (in a passage quoted by Hacking): "Although we think we govern our words, . . . certain it is that words, as a Tartar's bow, do shoot back upon the understanding of the wisest, and mightily entangle and pervert the judgment. So that it is almost necessary, in all controversies and disputations, to imitate the wisdom of the mathematicians, in setting down in the very beginning the definitions of our words and terms, that others may know how we accept and understand them, and whether they concur with us or no." See Bacon, *The Advancement of Learning and Novum Organum*, ed. James E. Creighton (New York: Colonial Press, 1899), p. 324; more freely rendered in Ian Hacking, *Why Does Language Matter to Philosophy?* (Cambridge: at the University Press, 1975), p. 5.

2. Karl-Otto Apel, *Die Idee der Sprache in der Tradition des Humanismus von Dante bis Vico* (3rd ed., Bonn: Bouvier, 1980), p. 29.

3. William P. Alston, *Philosophy of Language* (Englewood Cliffs, N.J.: Prentice-Hall, 1964), pp. 12-13. As Hacking observes: "Whatever the merits of

the arguments, Russell unequivocally opts for what Alston calls a referential theory of meaning." *Why Does Language Matter to Philosophy?*, p. 72. One should note, however, that Russell construed "immediate objects" broadly enough to encompass general properties (like roundness or sweetness) and initially even numbers.

4. See Bertrand Russell, "On the Nature of Acquaintance" (1914) and "The Philosophy of Logical Atomism" (1918), in *Logic and Knowledge*, ed. Robert C. Marsh (London: Allen and Unwin, 1956), pp. 130, 201. In using phrases like "if I speak to myself" Russell seems to occupy a peculiar intermediary position between Hacking's periods of "ideas" and "meanings."

5. Russell, "The Philosophy of Logical Atomism," p. 204. Compare also Russell, *Our Knowledge of the External World as a Field for Scientific Method in Philosophy* (London: Allen and Unwin, 1926).

6. Hacking, *Why Does Language Matter to Philosophy?*, p. 75.

7. Russell himself was somewhat ambivalent about the virtues of a perfect logical language. "In a logically perfect language," he wrote, "there will be one word and no more for every simple object, and everything that is not simple will be expressed by a combination of words, by a combination derived, of course, from the words for the simple things that enter in, one word for each simple component. A language of that sort will be completely analytic, and will show at a glance the logical structure of the facts asserted or denied. The language which is set forth in *Principia Mathematica* is intended to be a language of that sort. It is a language which has only syntax and no vocabulary whatsoever. . . . Actual languages are not logically perfect in this sense, and they cannot possibly be, if they are to serve the purposes of daily life. A logically perfect language, if it could be constructed, would not only be intolerably prolix, but, as regards its vocabulary, would be very largely private to one speaker." See "The Philosophy of Logical Atomism," pp. 197-98.

8. Rudolf Carnap, *The Logical Structure of the World*, trans. Rolf A. George (Berkeley: University of California Press, 1967), pp. 5-7, 10.

9. *The Logical Structure of the World*, pp. 101, 127-28, 152-53, 288.

10. Carnap, *The Logical Syntax of Language*, trans. Amethe Smeaton (London: Routledge & Kegan Paul, 1964), pp. xiii-xv, 51-52.

11. See Carnap,"Pseudoproblems in Philosophy," in *The Logical Structure of the World*, pp. 301-343; "The Elimination of Metaphysics Through Logical Analysis of Language" (1932), in A. J. Ayer, ed., *Logical Positivism* (New York: Free Press, 1959), pp. 60-61.

12. "The Elimination of Metaphysics Through Logical Analysis of Language," pp. 76-77.

13. Moritz Schlick, "The Turning Point in Philosophy" (1930/31) and "Positivism and Realism" (1932/33), in Ayer, *Logical Positivism*, pp. 56,86. Regarding the verification criterion, the second essay continued (pp. 86-87); "It is the first step of any philosophizing, and the foundation of all reflection, to see that it is simply impossible to give the meaning of any statement except by describing the fact which must exist if the statement is to be true. . . . The meaning of a proposition consists, obviously, in this alone, that it expresses a definite

state of affairs. . . . The statement of the conditions under which a proposition is true is *the same* as the statement of its meaning, and not something different." Regarding metaphysical pseudo-statements the first essay observed (p. 57): "Thus metaphysics collapses not because the solving of its tasks is an enterprise to which the human reason is unequal (as for example Kant thought) but because there is no such task." Compare also his "Meaning and Verification" (1936), in Herbert Feigl and Wilfrid Sellars, eds., *Readings in Philosophical Analyses* (New York: Appleton-Century-Crofts, 1949), pp. 146-170.

14. See, e.g., Carl G. Hempel, "The Empiricist Criterion of Meaning" (1950), in Ayer, *Logical Positivism*, pp. 108-129; Peter Achinstein and Stephen F. Barker, eds., *The Legacy of Logical Positivism* (Baltimore: Johns Hopkins University Press, 1969).

15. See Karl Popper, *Logik der Forschung* (Vienna: Springer, 1935); Carnap, "Testability and Meaning" (1936/37), in Herbert Feigl and May Brodbeck, eds., *Readings in the Philosophy of Science* (New York: Appleton-Century-Crofts, 1953), pp. 47-92; Alfred J. Ayer, *Language, Truth and Logic* (first ed. 1936; 2nd ed., London: Gollancz, 1946), pp. 13, 38-39; Hacking, *Why Does Language Matter to Philosophy?*, p. 99. Still later Hempel reformulated the criterion by proposing to check sentences against the yardstick of a pure "empiricist language" whose descriptive terms are all experientially grounded; "The Empiricist Criterion of Meaning," pp. 116-118.

16. See Friedrich Waismann, "Verifiability," in G. H. R. Parkinson, ed., *The Theory of Meaning* (London: Oxford University Press, 1968), pp. 35-60; Hacking, *Why Does Language Matter to Philosophy?*, p. 99.

17. Wilfrid Sellars, "Empiricism and the Philosophy of Mind," in *Science, Perception, and Reality* (New York: Humanities Press, 1963), p. 169. For a critique of logical redescriptions or "re-identifications" see, e.g., Peter Strawson, *Individuals: An Essay in Descriptive Metaphysics* (London: Methuen, 1959), pp. 15-58.

18. Willard Van O. Quine, "Two Dogmas of Empiricism," in *From a Logical Point of View* (Cambridge: Harvard University Press, 1953), pp. 20, 39, 41-42. A consequence of this "counter-suggestion" was that "it is nonsense, and the root of much nonsense, to speak of a linguistic component and a factual component in the truth of any individual statement. Taken collectively, science has its double dependence upon language and experience; but this duality is not significantly traceable into the statements of science taken one by one" (p. 42). Quine's holism also carried pragmatic overtones — overtones which exceeded Carnap's "Principle of Tolerance." In repudiating the analytic-synthetic distinction, he stated (p. 46), "I espouse a more thorough pragmatism. Each man is given a scientific heritage plus a continuing barrage of sensory stimulation, and the considerations which guide him in warping his scientific heritage to fit his continuing sensory promptings are, where rational, pragmatic."

19. Michael Dummett, "What is a Theory of Meaning?" in Gareth Evans and John McDowell, eds., *Truth and Meaning: Essays in Semantics* (Oxford: Clarendon Press, 1976), pp. 81, 110-111, 126. For the notion of an "interpretative" semantics see also J. A. Foster, "Meaning and Truth Theory," in the same

volume, pp. 2-4. For a detailed review of the development of empiricism (and post-empiricism) in our century see Richard J. Bernstein, *Beyond Objectivism and Relativism: Science, Hermeneutics, and Praxis* (Philadelphia: University of Pennsylvania Press, 1983), esp. Chapter 3.

20. Michael J. Shapiro, *Language and Political Understanding: The Politics of Discursive Practices* (New Haven: Yale University Press, 1981), pp. 20, 92, 151. See also Karl-Otto Apel, "Analytic Philosophy of Language and the 'Geisteswissenschaften'," *Foundations of Language*, Suppl. Series, vol. 5 (Dordrecht: Reidel, 1967); and his "Heideggers philosophische Radikalisierung der 'Hermeneutik' und die Frage nach dem Sinnkriterium der Sprache," in *Transformation der Philosophie* (Frankfurt-Main: Suhrkamp, 1973), vol. 1, pp. 302-325.

21. See Russell, "On Propositions" (1919), in *Logic and Knowledge*, p. 293; Carnap, *The Logical Structure of the World*, p. 96. Compare also Russell, *The Analysis of Mind* (London: Allen and Unwin, 1921).

22. B. F. Skinner, *The Behavior of Organisms: An Experimental Design* (New York: Appleton-Century-Crofts, 1938). The study concentrated mainly on the effects of food deprivation and conditioning on the behavior of mature rats; subsequent works dealt also with pigeons pecking at a disk. The issue of reinforcement was further explored in Skinner and C. B. Ferster, *Schedules of Reinforcement* (New York: Appleton-Century-Crofts, 1957).

23. Skinner, *Verbal Behavior* (New York: Appleton-Century-Crofts, 1957); Morton Deutsch and Robert M. Krauss, *Theories in Social Psychology* (New York: Basic Books, 1965), p. 104.

24. See Noam Chomsky, "A Review of B. F. Skinner's *Verbal Behavior*," *Language*, vol. 35 (1959), pp. 28, 39, 57. My view on this matter tends to concur with Rorty's who writes: "The behaviorists gave up on the notion that 'nothing is better known to the mind than itself, but they kept the notion that some things were naturally knowable directly and others not, and the metaphysical corollary that only the first were 'really real'. This doctrine—that the most knowable was the most real— . . . added to the principle of the Naturally Given, produced either an idealistic or panpsychist reduction of the physical to the mental, or a behaviorist or materialist reduction in the other direction." *Philosophy and the Mirror of Nature* (Princeton: Princeton University Press, 1979), p. 105.

25. Hayden White, *Tropics of Discourse: Essays in Cultural Criticism* (Baltimore: Johns Hopkins University Press, 1978), pp. 270-271, 273.

26. George H. Sabine, "Preface to the First Edition," in *A History of Political Theory* (rev. ed.; New York: Holt, 1950), p. xi. Referring to himself as author Sabine added (p. xii): "So far as he can see, it is impossible by any logical operation to excogitate the truth of any allegation of fact, and neither logic nor fact implies a value. . . . As for values, they appear to the author to be always the reaction of human preference to some state of social and physical fact; in the concrete they are too complicated to be generally described even with so loose a word as utility. Nevertheless, the idea of economic causation was probably the most fertile suggestion added to social studies in the nineteenth century."

27. In the words of Raymond G. Gettell: "Ordinarily, political theories are the direct result of objective political conditions. They reflect the thoughts and inter-

pret the motives that underlie actual political development. . . . They indicate the conditions and the intellectual point of view of their age." See Getell's *History of Political Thought* (1924), ed. Lawrence C. Wanlass (2nd ed.; London: Allen and Unwin, 1953), p. 4; also William A. Dunning, *A History of Political Theories, Ancient and Medieval* (New York: Macmillan, 1902) and *A History of Political Theories from Rousseau to Spencer* (New York: Macmillan, 1920).

28. Andrew Hacker, "Capital and Carbuncles: The 'Great Books' Reappraised," *American Political Science Review*, vol. 48 (1954), pp. 777, 780-783.

29. B. F. Skinner, *Walden Two* (New York: Macmillan, 1962), pp. 260, 262; and *Beyond Freedom and Dignity* (New York: Random House, 1971), pp. 22-23. Without entering into a detailed assement of Skinner's proposals one may note the skewed character of his approach—the fact that behaviorism and "mentalism" do not exhaust possible alternatives. In a review of *Beyond Freedom and Dignity*, Paul Ricoeur has ably underscored this point. Countering Skinner's linkage of human autonomy with "mentalistic psychology" he observed: "My claim is that the ethical and political implications concerning freedom, dignity, value, autonomy etc., need not necessarily be conceived in terms of this psychology and that they are expressed better even in another language which has been explored during this last decade by phenomenologists and by the followers of Wittgenstein and Austin under the title of 'linguistic analysis' of action, or 'conceptual analysis in the theory of action.' According to conceptual analysis, the network of concepts which we use to speak of *human action* in ordinary language is not the conceptual framework of either behaviorism or mentalistic psychology." See "A Critique of B. F. Skinner's *Beyond Freedom and Dignity*," in Ricoeur, *Political and Social Essays*, ed. David Stewart and Joseph Bien (Athens, Ohio: Ohio University Press, 1974), p. 49.

30. Carnap, *The Logical Structure of the World*, pp. xviii, 297 (translation slightly altered).

31. Russell, "Philosophy and Politics," in Robert E. Egner and Lester E. Dennon, eds., *The Basic Writings of Bertrand Russell* (New York: Simon and Schuster, 1961), pp. 455, 462-464.

32. T. D. Weldon, "Political Principles," in Peter Laslett, ed., *Philosophy, Politics and Society* (New York: Macmillan, 1956), pp. 22-24, 33. With slight modifications Weldon accepted the logical-empiricist charge against traditional thought (p. 26): "It was that, since the philosophers had avowedly excluded all factual inquiries from their field of study, their investigations were either linguistic or 'metaphysical' and worthless. In the end, I think this criticism is justified, but the matter is not as simple as the early positivists supposed. As far as political philosophy is concerned, while it is true that this was generally regarded as an *a priori* inquiry, those who practised it certainly believed that they were somehow concerned with what goes on in human associations. They talked little about actual political institutions, but dealt with ghostly or abstract entities, the State, the Individual, Society, the General Will, the Common Good, and so on." See also Weldon, *The Vocabulary of Politics* (London: Penguin Books, 1953).

33. Joseph Margolis, "Difficulties in T. D. Weldon's Political Philosophy," *American Political Science Review*, vol. 52 (1958), p. 1114.

Chapter 3: Rationalism Old and New

1. Rudolf Carnap, *The Logical Structure of the World*, trans. Rolf A. George (Berkeley: University of California Press, 1967), p. 296. The opposition was formulated even more forcefully by Ayer who wrote: "The metaphysical doctrine which is upheld by rationalists, and rejected by empiricists, is that there exists a supra-sensible world which is the object of a purely intellectual intuition and is alone wholly real. . . . We showed that a proposition only had factual content if it was empirically verifiable, and, consequently, that the rationalists were mistaken in supposing that there could be *a priori* propositions which referred to matters of fact. . . . We admitted that there were propositions which were necessarily valid apart from all experience, and that there was a difference in kind between these propositions and empirical hypotheses. But we did not account for their necessity by saying, as a rationalist might, that they were speculative 'truths of reason'. We accounted for it by saying that they were tautologies." See Alfred J. Ayer, *Language, Truth and Logic* (New York: Dover Publications, 1952), pp. 134-135.

2. G. W. Leibniz, *New Essays Concerning Human Understanding*, trans. A. G. Langley (LaSalle, Ill.: Open Court, 1949), pp. 42-43, cited in Ian Hacking, *Why Does Language Matter to Philosophy?* (Cambridge: at the University Press, 1975), pp. 57-58.

3. Vincent Descombes, *Modern French Philosophy*, trans. L. Scott-Fox and J. M. Harding (Cambridge: at the University Press, 1980), p. 81. By "post-structuralism" I refer to the orientations of Foucault, Derrida, Deleuze, and others. The selected emphasis is supported by Ehrmann who writes: "What is structuralism? Before being a philosophy, as some tend to see it, it is a method of analysis. . . . (I)t is first of all, when applied to the sciences of man, a certain way of studying language problems and the problems of languages. Initially it was concerned with the structure of languages (*langues*), an area first explored by linguists whose interest developed the methods under study. It was then applied to anthropological inquiries, and in particular to the study of myths which are of the nature of language (*langage*)." See "Introduction" to *Structuralism*, ed. Jacques Ehrmann (Garden City: Anchor Books, 1970), p. ix. Compare also Lane's comments: "What, then, are the distinctive properties of structuralism? In the first place it is presented as a method whose scope includes all human social phenomena. . . . This is made possible by the belief that all manifestations of social activity, whether it be the clothes that are worn, the books that are written or the systems of kinship and marriage that are practiced in any society, constitute languages, in a formal sense. Hence their regularities may be reduced to the same set of abstract rules that define and govern what we normally think of as language." *Introduction to Structuralism*, ed. Michael Lane (New York: Basic Books, 1970), pp. 13-14.

4. Jean Piaget, *Structuralism*, trans. Chaninah Maschler (New York: Basic Books, 1970), pp. 4-5.

5. Ferdinand de Saussure, *Course in General Linguistics*, ed. Charles Bally and Albert Sechehaye, trans. Wade Baskin (New York: Philosophical Library, 1959), p. 16. As Richard and Fernande de George comment: "Not only did he significantly change the standard approach to linguistics, but his suggestion that

rites, customs, and similar social phenomena could be treated as systems of signs and studied in ways similar to the ways in which language is studied opened up an approach to the investigation of society which has been fruitfully mined by structuralists in many disciplines." *The Structuralists: From Marx to Lévi-Strauss*, ed. Richard T. and Fernande M. de George (Garden City: Anchor Books. 1970), p. xviii.

6. *Course in General Linguistics*, pp. 9, 11, 14.

7. *Course in General Linguistics*, pp. 15, 66, 107, 120 (translation slightly altered). Piaget lists three main reasons for the "predominantly synchronic emphasis in early linguistic structuralism": "The first of these reasons is of a very general order and relates to the relative independence of laws of equilibrium from laws of development. . . . The second reason, which was perhaps psychologically the primary one, was the desire to give oneself over to the study of the immanent character of language without being distracted by historical considerations." The third reason "relates to a circumstance peculiar to language, the arbitrariness of the verbal sign," a circumstance militating against an evolutionary teleology of signs. See *Structuralism*, p. 77.

8. *Course in General Linguistics*, pp. 81, 90, 95, 98-100 (translation slightly altered).

9. *Course in General Linguistics*, pp. 13-14, 77-78; Paul Ricoeur, "Structure and Hermeneutics," in *The Conflict of Interpretations: Essays in Hermeneutics*, ed. Don Ihde (Evanston: Northwestern University Press, 1974), p. 33. According to Ricoeur, this "Kantian unconscious" ultimately reflected a species-specific, genetic endowment. Thus, although unconcerned with empirical "reference," Saussurean linguistics acquired a kind of reference through the linkage of mind and nature: "This unconscious mind can be said to be homologous to nature; perhaps it even is nature." Regarding the position of language between rationality and arbitrary nonrationality compare also Saussure's statement (p. 133): "Everything that relates to language as a system must, I am convinced, be approached from this viewpoint which has scarcely received the attention of linguists: the limiting of arbitrariness. . . . In fact, the whole system of language is based on the irrational principle of the arbitrariness of the sign, which would lead to the worst sort of complication if applied without restriction. But the mind contrives to introduce a principle of order and regularity into certain parts of the mass of signs, and this is the role of relative motivation."

10. *Course in General Linguistics*, pp. 15, 22, 113, 122.

11. Louis Hjelmslev, *Prolegomena to a Theory of Language*, trans. Francis J. Whitfield (first publ. 1943; Madison: University of Wisconsin Press, 1961), pp. 5-6, 8-9, 13, 23-24, 47-48, 76. The formalist emphasis was also evident in the school of Prague—especially in the early work of Roman Jacobson who had been a leading figure in the "formalist" movement of literacy criticism in Moscow before becoming a co-founder of the Linguistic Circle of Prague in 1926. Together with N. S. Trubetzkoy, Jacobson was instrumental in inaugurating a structural analysis of phonology and in reducing structural phonemic correlations to binary or dichotomous oppositions—a reduction which exerted considerable impact on structural anthropology.

12. Claude Lévi-Strauss, *Structural Anthropology*, trans. Claire Jacobson and

Brooke G. Schoepf (first French ed. 1958; Garden City: Anchor Books, 1967), pp. 23, 31, 33, 45. Describing Lévi-Strauss's general outlook Claire Jacobson notes (pp. ix-x) that he "is primarily concerned with universals, that is, basic social and mental processes of which cultural institutions are the concrete external projections or manifestations. Anthropology should be a science of general principles; the theories which the anthropologist formulates should be applicable to all societies and valid for all possible observers. . . . His originality lies in the emphasis on form, on the primacy of relations over entities, and on the search for constant relationships among phenomena at the most abstract level." Piaget — who terms anthropology "the 'synoptic' social science" — presents Lévi-Strauss as "the very incarnation of the structuralist faith in the permanence of human nature and the unity of reason." *Structuralism*, p. 106.

13. *Structural Anthropology*, pp. 49, 60-61. See also Lévi-Strauss, *The Savage Mind* (Chicago: University of Chicago Press, 1966). As presented in the latter study, savage thought exhibits a quasi-logical order (though one unconscious of itself): an order operating at the "sensual" level and manifesting itself in kinship classifications, nomenclatures, totemic restrictions, and the like.

14. *Structural Anthropology*, pp. 67, 271. See also Lévi-Strauss, *Totemism*, trans. Rodney Needham (Boston: Beacon Press, 1963), pp. 90-91.

15. *Structural Anthropology*, pp. 19-22, 273.

16. *The Savage Mind*, pp. 258, 262. As he added, in a retort to Sartrean dialectics (p. 262): "We need only recognize that history is a method with no distinct object corresponding to it to reject the equivalence between the notion of history and the notion of humanity which some have tried to foist on us with the unavowed aim of making historicity the last refuge of a transcendental humanism: as if men could regain the illusion of liberty on the plane of the 'we' merely by giving up the 'I's that are too obviously wanting in consistency." The phrase "invariant diachronics" is Piaget's; see *Structuralism*, p. 108.

17. *The Savage Mind*, pp. 17-18, 130; see also Lévi-Strauss, *The Raw and the Cooked*, trans. John and Doreen Weightman (New York: Harper and Row, 1969), pp. 11, 14 (translation slightly altered). The sketched intermediary course or "bricolage" did not prevent Lévi-Strauss, on other occasions, from stressing the foundational character of the "unconscious activity of the mind" and its role in "imposing forms upon content"; to use the language of *The Savage Mind* (p. 30), the precarious "balance between structure and event, necessity and contingency, the internal and external" — quite apart from preserving traditional antinomies — tended to be tilted toward one side of the oppositional pairs.

18. See Noam Chomsky, *Current Issues in Linguistic Theory* (New York: Humanities Press, 1964), pp. 7-8; also "Persistent Topics in Linguistic Theory," *Diogenes*, No. 15 (Fall 1965), p. 13.

19. Chomsky, *Language and Mind* (New York: Harcourt, Brace and World, 1968), pp. 4, 17, 63. The same study contains a critique of Lévi-Strauss's writings (pp. 65-66). In Edie's words, "the notion of 'linguistic competence' which Chomsky is attempting to elaborate is based on the very straightforward linguistic fact that native speakers and hearers of a language can produce and recognize on the proper occasions an infinitely varied number of appropriate and new sentences for which their empirical linguistic habits and experience up to any given point

can have prepared them only in the most abstract and schematic manner." See James M. Edie, *Speaking and Meaning: The Phenomenology of Language* (Bloomington: Indiana University Press, 1976), p. 59.

20. See Chomsky, *Cartesian Linguistics: A Chapter in the History of Rationalist Thought* (New York: Harper & Row, 1966), pp. 13, 15, 20, 22; *Language and Mind*, pp. 22-23; also Piaget, *Structuralism*, p. 87. Piaget, who has developed his own version of generative or transformational analysis, is critical both of Chomsky's incipient biologism and his acceptance of Cartesian "innatism." On the controversy between the two see *Language and Learning: The Debate Between Jean Piaget and Noam Chomsky*, ed. Massimo Piattelli (Cambridge, Mass.: Harvard University Press, 1980).

21. See Chomsky, *Aspects of the Theory of Syntax* (Cambridge, Mass.: Harvard University Press, 1965), pp. 16-17; *Cartesian Linguistics*, pp. 33, 40, 42; *Language and Mind*, p. 15. The notion of "logical form" on the level of deep structure seems comparable to the empiricist distinction between logical-analytical and ordinary language; but in Chomsky's model, logical form is governed by grammatical and syntactical rules rather than by requirements of reference—which also explains why Chomsky maintains the traditional subject-predicate, substance-attribute mode of analysis. This point is downplayed by Ian Hacking, who writes: "Russell's idea of logical form as opposed to grammatical form is strikingly like Chomsky's idea of depth grammar as opposed to surface grammar. . . . (I)t is not monstrous to propose that first-order predicate logic is the core of a deep grammar of English." *Why Does Language Matter to Philosophy?* (Cambridge: at the University Press, 1975), p. 91.

22. *Cartesian Linguistics*, pp. 59-60; *Aspects of the Theory of Syntax*, pp. 30, 117; *Language and Mind*, pp. 24, 76.

23. *Cartesian Linguistics*, pp. 59-60, 63-64; *Aspects of the Theory of Syntax*, pp. 33, 58-59. The innatist thesis is again traced to Cartesianism and to romantic thought (and also to Platonism): "Thus, Wilhelm von Humboldt, who is now best remembered for his ideas concerning the variety of languages and the association of diverse language structures with divergent 'world-views', nevertheless held firmly that underlying human language we will find a system that is universal, that simply expresses man's unique intellectual attributes. For this reason, it was possible for him to maintain the rationalist view that language is not really learned—certainly not taught—but rather develops 'from within', in an essentially predetermined way, when the appropriate environmental conditions exist. . . . This Platonistic element in Humboldt's thought is a pervasive one; for Humboldt, it was as natural to propose an essentially Platonistic theory of 'learning' as it was for Rousseau to found his critique of repressive social institutions on a conception of human freedom that derives from strictly Cartesian assumptions regarding the limitations of mechanical explanation." *Language and Mind*, p. 67. For a further development of the "innateness" thesis (and its linkage with biological-genetic factors) see Chomsky, *Reflections on Language* (New York: Random House, 1975), pp. 3-35. On Chomsky's epistemology compare Emmon Bach, "Structural Linguistics and the Philosophy of Science," *Diogenes*, No. 15 (Fall 1965), pp. 111-127; and for a curious blending of empiricism and innatism Willard Van O. Quine, "Linguistics and Philosophy," in *Language and*

Philosophy, ed. Sidney Hook (New York: New York University Press, 1969), pp. 95-98.

24. Edmund Husserl, *Philosophie als strenge Wissenschaft* (2nd ed., Frankfurt-Main: Klostermann, 1971); "Philosophy as Rigorous Science," in *Phenomenology and the Crisis of Philosophy*, trans. Quentin Lauer (New York: Harper and Row, 1965), pp. 71-147. To be sure, a main difference resides in Husserl's linkage of consciousness with a "transcendental ego" as against the generally non-egological stance of structuralism.

25. Edie, *Speaking and Meaning*, pp. 45, 59, 62. "In order to avoid all misunderstanding," he elaborates further (p. 60), "when quoting Chomsky's psychologistic vocabulary we must emphasize the essential difference here between him and Husserl. We are attempting to give a 'transcendental' interpretation of his concept of 'linguistic competence'. There is no need to suppose that the structures by which a child comes to understand the grammar of his language, or to learn a new one, are *temporally* prior to this learning or somehow *innate in the organism prior to the acquisition of language*; a *logical priority* of the universal structures . . . is sufficient."

26. See Edmund Husserl, *Logical Investigations*, trans. J. N. Findlay (New York: Humanities Press, 1970), vol. 2, pp. 524-525 (translation slightly altered); also *Formal and Transcendental Logic*, trans. Dorion Cairns (The Hague: Martinus Nijhoff, 1969), pp. 18-19. The latter study firmly links thought and language (p. 19): "Now human thinking is normally done in language, and all the activities of reason are as good as entirely bound up with speech. Furthermore, so far as it is intersubjective, all the criticism from which the rationally true should emerge employs language and, in the end, leads always to statements." The connection of *langue* and *parole* in Husserl's presentation of "logos" is stressed by Edie, *Speaking and Meaning*, p. 16.

27. *Logical Investigations*, vol. 2, pp. 493, 510, 521, 525-526.

28. *Logical Investigations*, vol. 2, pp. 493, 517. For a detailed description of the "steps" involved in pure logical grammar see Edie, *Speaking and Meaning*, pp. 50-57.

29. As Edie writes: "There is . . . a sound motive for distinguishing the meaning of sentences and words from the physical occurrences themselves and thus designating the meaning of a sentence by the locution 'proposition' and the meaning of a word by the locution 'term'. Terms and propositions, unlike words and sentences, are indifferent to temporal and spatial locations, to tones of voice, to idiosyncrasies of accent, to whether they are spoken in one natural language or another. They are, in short, ideal types or 'meaning contents' which remain ideally the same each time they are 'cashed in' by producing their tokens in actual speech. . . . The important thing here is that what we *mean* by a language, that is, a system of linguistic signs proper (*Ausdrücke*), is that it enables us to entertain and express meanings which are experienced as ideally independent of the physical sounds or marks which are nevertheless their necessary embodiment. . . . Primarily we must distinguish the ideality of the 'intended sense' from the ideality of the linguistic structures which enable us to intend such an ideal sense." *Speaking and Meaning*, pp. 18, 20-22.

30. Ricoeur, *The Conflict of Interpretations*, pp. 40, 83-84. As he adds (p.

51), in its customary form "structural thought remains a thought which does not think itself. In return, it is up to a reflective philosophy to understand itself as a hermeneutics, so as to create the receptive structure for a structural anthropology. In this respect, it is the function of hermeneutics to make the understanding of the other—and of his signs in various cultures—coincide with the understanding of the self and of being." One might mention here that, within structural linguistics, a certain shift of attention to interpretative semantics has been noticeable during recent decades—with some linguists going as far as to insist that exploration of semantic meaning is a precondition of syntactical analysis; see, e.g., Emile Benveniste, *Problems in General Linguistics*, trans. Mary E. Meek (Coral Gables: University of Miami Press, 1971).

31. Clifford Geertz, *The Interpretation of Cultures* (New York: Basic Books, 1973), pp. 6, 24, 350-351, 355-357. As he elaborates (p. 20): "To set forth symmetrical crystals of significance, purified of the material complexity in which they are located, and then attribute their existence to autogenous principles of order, universal properties of the human mind, or vast, a priori *Weltanschauungen*, is to pretend a science that does not exist and imagine a reality that cannot be found. Cultural analysis is (or should be) guessing at meanings, assessing the guesses, and drawing explanatory conclusions from the better guesses, not discovering the Continent of Meaning and mapping out its bodiless landscape." A more radical critique of structural anthropology has been developed by Jacques Derrida who distinguishes between two types of structuralism: an objectivist or "centered" type stressing oppositions between conceptual entities, and a free-moving type reflecting the ontological "play" of "difference" (between "absence and presence"); see his "Structure, Sign and Play in the Discourse of the Human Sciences," in *Writing and Difference*, trans. Alan Bass (Chicago: University of Chicago Press, 1978), pp. 278-293.

32. Jurgen Habermas, "Towards a Theory of Communicative Competence," *Inquiry*, vol. 13. (1970), pp. 361-363; see also Karl-Otto Apel, "Noam Chomsky's Theory of Language and Contemporary Philosophy: A Case Study in the Philosophy of Science," in *Towards a Transformation of Philosophy*, trans. Glyn Adey and David Frisby (London: Routledge and Kegan Paul, 1980), pp. 180-224.

33. George Steiner, *Extraterritorial: Papers on Literature and the Language Revolution* (New York: Atheneum, 1971), pp. ix-xi. "Let me go further," he adds (p. 124): "The linguistics of Noam Chomsky *could* account, and could account with beautiful economy and depth, for a world in which men would all be speaking *one* language, diversified at most by a moderate range of dialects. The fact that generative and transformational grammar would be beautifully concordant with such a result, that such a result is in some manner both natural and obvious to Chomsky's postulates, seems to me to cast serious doubts on the whole model." For a more empiricist-linguistic critique see Charles F. Hockett, *The State of the Art* (The Hague: Mouton, 1968).

34. Maurice Merleau-Ponty, "On the Phenomenology of Language," in *Signs*, trans. Richard C. McCleary (Evanston: Northwestern University Press, 1964), p. 84; Ricoeur, *The Conflict of Interpretations*, pp. 8-9. "Of course," Ricoeur adds (p. 15), "Husserl would not have accepted the idea of meaning as ir-

reducibly nonunivocal. He explicitly excludes this possibility in the First Investigation, and this is indeed why the phenomenology of the *Logical Investigations* cannot be hermeneutic." A more radical critique has been articulated, again, by Derrida who views Husserl's dichotomies—between meaning and usage, between essential and actual language—as an outgrowth of traditional metaphysics or a metaphysical epistemology. The distinction between ideality and reality in particular, he notes, echoes "the opposition between form and matter—which inaugurates metaphysics." For Husserl, he elaborates, "everything that constitutes the effectiveness of what is uttered, the physical incarnation of the meaning, the body of speech . . . is, if not outside discourse, at least foreign to the nature of expression as such, foreign to that pure intention without which there could be no speech. . . . (Thus) in spite of all the themes of receptive or intuitive intentionality and passive genesis, the concept of intentionality remains caught up in the tradition of a voluntaristic metaphysics—that is, perhaps, in metaphysics *as such*." See Jacques Derrida, *Speech and Phenomena, and Other Essays on Husserl's Theory of Signs*, trans. David B. Allison (Evanston: Northwestern University Press, 1973), pp. 6, 34.

35. Hayden White, *Tropics of Discourse: Essays in Cultural Criticism* (Baltimore: Johns Hopkins University Press, 1978), pp. 273-274.

36. *Tropics of Discourse*, pp. 272-274. See also T. S. Eliot, *The Sacred Wood: Essays on Poetry and Criticism* (London: Methuen, 1920); John Crowe Ransom, *The New Criticism* (New York: New Directions, 1941); Cleanth Brooks, *The Well Wrought Urn: Studies in the Structure of Poetry* (rev. ed.; London: Dobson, 1968). For a more detailed discussion of the New Criticism, as example of a "formalistic approach" to exegesis, see Wilfred L. Guerin et al., *A Handbook of Critical Approaches to Literature* (2nd ed.; New York: Harper and Row, 1979), pp. 69-118; and on the structuralist approach Robert Scholes, *Structuralism in Literature: An Introduction* (New Haven: Yale University Press, 1974).

37. Eric D. Hirsch, *Validity in Interpretation* (New Haven: Yale University Press, 1967), pp. 26-27, 45-46, 134, 218. As Hirsch adds (pp. 3, 244), the author as "determiner of his text's meaning" is not simply "identical with the subjectivity of the author as an actual historical person," but may rather "be defined as the final and most comprehensive level of awareness determinative of verbal meaning." See also his *The Aims of Interpretation* (Chicago: University of Chicago Press, 1976); and for a critical assessment David C. Hoy, *The Critical Circle: Literature, History, and Philosophical Hermeneutics* (Berkeley: University of California Press, 1978), pp. 11-40.

38. Leo Strauss, *What Is Political Philosophy? and Other Studies* (Glencoe: Free Press, 1959), pp. 11-12, 34. Strauss, it is true, toned down the rationalist flavor of the postulated "knowledge" by stating that "philosophy is essentially not possession of the truth, but quest for the truth" and by distinguishing this quest from a mathematical knowledge of "homogeneity" (pp. 11, 39). Yet elsewhere, appealing to the "full and original meaning" of the term "philosophy," he suggested that "to say that the whole is knowable or intelligible is tantamount to saying that the whole has a permanent structure or that the whole as such is unchangeable or always the same." *Natural Right and History* (Chicago: University

of Chicago Press, 1953), pp. 30-31. The indebtedness to Husserl was acknowledged by Strauss in "Philosophy as Rigorous Science and Political Philosophy," *Interpretation*, vol. 2 (1971), pp. 1-9.

39. *What Is Political Philosophy? and Other Studies*, pp. 39, 56-57. The bent toward a canonical-receptive or "reproductive" interpretation (stressing the primacy of the *interpretandum*) is noted by Hwa Yol Jung, *The Crisis of Political Understanding: A Phenomenological Perspective in the Conduct of Political Inquiry* (Pittsburgh: Duquesne University Press, 1979), p. 159.

40. Strauss, *What Is Political Philosophy? and Other Studies*, pp. 66-67; *Persecution and the Art of Writing* (Glencoe: Free Press, 1952), p. 25. In the words of one of his students, Strauss's exegetic concern was with "what is written as opposed to its historical, economic, or psychological background"; but the "written" was for Strauss a reflection of an underlying intent, for "he had liberated himself and could understand writers as they understood themselves." Allan Bloom, "Leo Strauss," *Political Theory*, vol. 2 (1974), p. 385. For a debate on the merits of hidden authorial intent see Harvey C. Mansfield, Jr., "Strauss's Machiavelli," and John G. A. Pocock, "Prophet and Inquisitor: Or, A Church Built Upon Bayonets Cannot Stand: A Comment on Mansfield's 'Strauss's Machiavelli'," in *Political Theory*, vol. 3 (1975), pp. 372-384 and 385-401.

41. John G. Gunnell, *Political Theory: Tradition and Interpretation* (Cambridge, Mass.: Winthrop Publishers, 1979), p. 59. For an epilogue to the New Criticism see Frank Lentricchia, *After the New Criticism* (Chicago: University of Chicago Press, 1980); and for a critique of structuralism and formalism Fredric Jameson, *The Prison-House of Language: A Critical Account of Structuralism and Russian Formalism* (Princeton: Princeton University Press, 1972).

42. Strauss, *What Is Political Philosophy? and Other Studies*, pp. 36, 40; also "Political Philosophy and the Crisis of Our Time," in George J. Graham, Jr. and George W. Carey, eds., *The Post-Behavioral Era: Perspectives on Political Science* (New York: McKay, 1972), pp. 217-242. Elsewhere he spoke more judiciously of "the political question par excellence, of how to reconcile order which is not oppression with freedom which is not license." *Persecution and the Art of Writing*, p. 37.

43. Enzo Paci, *The Function of the Sciences and the Meaning of Man*, trans. Paul Piccone (first Italian ed. 1963; Evanston: Northwestern University Press, 1972). "I would like to think," Husserl stated in his "Vienna Lecture" of 1935, "that I, the supposed reactionary, am far more radical and far more revolutionary than those who in their words proclaim themselves so radical today." As he added: "Because of the requirement to subject all empirical matters to ideal norms, i.e., those of unconditioned truth, there soon results a far-reaching transformation of the whole praxis of human existence, i.e., the whole of cultural life. . . . There is a tendency, then, for more and more still nonphilosophical persons to be drawn into the community of philosophers." See Husserl, *The Crisis of European Sciences and Transcendental Phenomenology*, trans. David Carr (Evanston: Northwestern University Press, 1970), pp. 287, 290. The potential radicalism of philosophy was acknowledged by Strauss when he noted that "moderation is not a virtue of thought"; *What Is Political Philosophy? and Other Studies*, p. 32.

44. As one recent study points out: "Although existentialism and structuralism are based on very different assumptions about the nature of man and society, many of the Marxist attitudes toward economic justice and social change appear in the theories of various existentialists, structuralists and semiologists. . . . In addition to its impact on a number of intellectual disciplines, structuralism, in the beginning, supplied the French Left with a pseudopolitical theory that did not negate their Socialist leanings, but removed them from the direct involvement with Marxism." The same study also hints at a curious blending of radicalism and conservatism: "Those who drifted into the structuralist debates found a means to deradicalize themselves without abandoning their humanist convictions. The very complexities of structuralist methods obscured the fact that structuralism would become the new conservatism of the Left." See Edith Kurzweil, *The Age of Structuralism: Lévi-Strauss to Foucault* (New York: Columbia University Press, 1980), pp. 2-4.

45. Noam Chomsky, "Science and Ideology," in P. M. S. Blackett el al., eds., *Jawaharlal Nehru Memorial Lectures 1967-72* (Bombay: Bharan, 1973), p. 207; *For Reasons of State* (New York: Random House, 1973), pp. 374-375, 379.

46. Chomsky, *Problems of Knowledge and Freedom* (New York: Random House, 1972), pp. vii, ix, 49-50. In a similar vein, the connection between politics and epistemology is underscored in the essay on "Language and Freedom": "A vision of a future social order is in turn based on a concept of human nature. If in fact man is an indefinitely malleable, completely plastic being, with no innate structures of mind and no intrinsic needs of a cultural or social character, then he is a fit subject for the 'shaping of behavior' by the state authority, the corporate manager, the technocrat, or the central committee." *For Reasons of State*, p. 404.

47. Geoffrey Sampson, *Liberty and Language* (Oxford: at the University Press, 1979), pp. 7-8, 87-88. Sampson challenges more broadly Chomsky's rationalist commitments (p. 77): "A rationalist may be largely in agreement with liberals as to the values which society ought to promote; but the rationalist rejects the empiricist premises from which a liberal infers that an unplanned society will best promote those values. The case of liberalism depends on the belief that humans are incurably ignorant, and the rationalist does not accept this."

48. Sampson, *Liberty and Language*, p. 119; Steiner, *Extraterritorial*, p. 125. As Steiner adds: "To me, man looks a queerer, more diverse beast than Chomsky would have him. And Nimrod's tower lies broken still." Compare also Hannah Arendt, *The Human Condition* (Garden City: Anchor Books, 1959), pp. 11-12.

Chapter 4: Ordinary Language and Existentialism

1. Leo Strauss, *What Is Political Philosophy? and Other Studies* (Glencoe: Free Press, 1959), pp. 12, 82-83; Hannah Arendt, *The Life of the Mind*, vol. I: *Thinking* (New York: Harcourt Brace Jovanovich, 1977), pp. 80, 121. For the rapprochement between philosophy and rhetoric see, e.g., I. A. Richards, *The Philosophy of Rhetoric* (New York: Oxford University Press, 1936); Henry W. Johnstone, Jr., *Philosophy and Argument* (University Park: Pennsylvania State

University Press, 1959); Don M. Burks, ed., *Rhetoric, Philosophy, and Literature: An Exploration* (West Lafayette, Ind.: Purdue University Press, 1978); Ernesto Grassi, *Rhetoric as Philosophy: The Humanist Tradition* (University Park: Pennsylvania State University Press, 1980).

    2. Michael J. Shapiro, *Language and Political Understanding: The Politics of Discursive Practices* (New Haven: Yale University Press, 1981), p. 21. Shapiro finds the linkage between ordinary language philosophy and existentialism (or existential phenomenology) in their common reliance on rhetoric (p. 27): "In developing the alternative perspective that language is better understood from a rhetorical than a logical frame of reference, Wittgenstein and Austin are supported by developments in continental philosophy."

    3. Shapiro, *Language and Political Understanding*, p. 50; Ludwig Wittgenstein, *Philosophical Investigations*, trans. G. E. M. Anscombe (Oxford: Blackwell, 1953), §§ 7, 23, 43. Delineating the Cambridge and Oxford schools or "philosophical groups," Chappell includes among Wittgensteinians philosophers like Wisdom, Malcolm, Waismann, and Anscombe, while listing in the second group—next to Austin and Gilbert Ryle—such thinkers as Strawson, Hart, Hampshire, Hare, and Warnock; see V. C. Chappell, ed., *Ordinary Language: Essays in Philosophical Method* (Englewood Cliffs, N.J.: Prentice-Hall, 1964), pp. 2-3.

    4. J. L. Austin, *How To Do Things With Words*, ed. J. O. Urmson (first publ. 1962; New York: Oxford University Press, 1965), pp. 1-4, 100.

    5. *How To Do Things With Words*, pp. 3, 5-6, 14, 60. The study subdivided infelicities further into "misfires" and "abuses," and the former into "misinvocations" and "misexecutions" (pp. 16-18). Regarding the "first person" moorings of performatives Austin added (p. 61): "The 'I' who is doing the action does thus come essentially into the picture. An advantage of the original first person singular present indicative active form ... is that this implicit feature of the speech-situation is made *explicit*."

    6. *How To Do Things With Words*, pp. 67, 73, 98-99, 135, 144-146. As a third component of speech acts the study listed "perlocutions" or "perlocutionary acts" whose performance entailed "certain consequential effects upon the feelings, thoughts, or actions of the audience, or of the speaker, or of other persons" (p. 101). Concentrating on the linguistic ingredients of utterances or speech acts, the study further differentiated between "phonetic," "phatic," and "rhetic" acts (and correspondingly between "phones," "phemes," and "rhemes")—the first denoting the uttering of noises, the second the uttering of vocables and words, and the third the use of words for discursive purposes. In stressing the "rhetic" (or rhetorical) element, Austin in a sense inverted the priority scheme of structural linguistics (p. 98): "The pheme is a unit of *language*. . . . But the rheme is a unit of *speech*."

    7. *How To Do Things With Words*, pp. 73, 100, 144, 150-151. "Truth and falsity," the study added (p. 148), "are (except by an artificial abstraction which is always possible and legitimate for certain purposes) not names for realities, qualities, or what not, but for a dimension of assessment—how the words stand in respect of satisfactoriness to the facts, events, situations, etc., to which they refer. By the same token, the familiar contrast of 'normative or evaluative' as opposed to the factual is in need, like so many dichotomies, of elimination."

8. John R. Searle, *Speech Acts: An Essay in the Philosophy of Language* (Cambridge: at the University Press, 1970), pp. 4, 12, 16-17.

9. *Speech Acts*, pp. 17-19, 23-25, 62-68. Regarding "expressibility," Searle went so far as to assert (p. 20) that "cases where the speaker does not say exactly what he means—the principal kinds of cases of which are nonliteralness, vagueness, ambiguity, and incompleteness—are not theoretically essential to linguistic communication." The epistemological legacy reverberates also in the study's methodology or "method of investigation" which is described (p. 4) as "empirical and rational rather than *a priori* and speculative." Venturing into a broader historical overview, Searle found it "possible to distinguish at least two strands in contemporary work in the philosophy of language—one which concentrates on the uses of expressions in speech situations and one which concentrates on the meaning of sentences. . . . Thus, for example, Wittgenstein's early work, which falls within the second strand, contains views about meaning which are rejected in his later work, which falls within the first strand. But although historically there have been sharp disagreements between practitioners of these two approaches, it is important to realize that the two approaches . . . are complementary and not competing" (pp. 18-19).

10. Searle, *Expression and Meaning: Studies in the Theory of Speech Acts* (Cambridge: at the University Press, 1979), pp. vii, 10-12, 135. To some extent, the reliance on intentionality was already present in *Speech Acts* which stated (p. 16): "When I take a noise or a mark on a piece of paper to be an instance of linguistic communication, as a message, one of the things I must assume is that the noise or mark was produced by a being or beings more or less like myself and produced with certain kinds of intentions."

11. *Expression and Meaning*, pp. 2-6, 12-19. In developing his taxonomy Searle still expressed allegiance to empiricist methodology, stating (p. viii) that "the method I use in this essay is in a sense empirical. I simply look at uses of language and find these five types of illocutionary point, and when I examine actual discourse I find, or at least claim, that utterances can be classified under these headings."

12. For a general comparison of the two perspectives see Stanley Cavell, "Existentialism and Analytical Philosophy," *Daedalus*, vol. 93 (Summer 1964), pp. 946-974.

13. Jean-Paul Sartre, *Being and Nothingness: An Essay on Phenomenological Ontology*, trans. Hazel E. Barnes (New York: Philosophical Library, 1956), pp. 514-515.

14. *Being and Nothingness*, pp. 515-516 (translation slightly altered).

15. *Being and Nothingness*, pp. 515-518.

16. Georges Gusdorf, *Speaking (La Parole)*, trans. Paul T. Brockelman (Evanston: Northwestern University Press, 1965), pp. 3-4, 7-10.

17. *Speaking*, pp. 35-36, 69-71.

18. *Speaking*, pp. 49-51, 61. Although acknowledging the rarity of both alternatives in their pure form, the study (pp. 52-53, 81) discovered approximations in prominent philosophical and sociological writings. Thus, the "thought of Bergson" was claimed to put "in opposition the superficial self, contaminated by language which makes it a thing among other things, and the profound self, an

inexpressible incantation, the authenticity of a thought resisting all formulation, a mystical effusion, a pure poetry." Similarly, both Kierkegaard and Karl Jaspers were found to insist "that the activity of speaking brings about the replacement of each of the speakers in dialogue by a kind of savage, impersonal individual." In stark antithesis to this "condemnation of the established language," Emile Durkheim affirmed "the authority of common meaning as it is formalized within various collective phenomena"—on the premise that "the community causes us to be: with language and in language it gives us concepts and moral rules."

19. *Speaking*, pp. 56-57, 62-63.

20. Maurice Merleau-Ponty, *Phenomenology of Perception*, trans. Colin Smith (London: Routledge & Kegan Paul, 1962), pp. 183, 193. James Edie describes Merleau-Ponty's early language theory as "a 'gestural' theory of expression," adding: "The body is expressive of meaning in many ways more fundamental than speaking; speaking is but the refinement, specification, and extension of preverbal behaviors which already bestow a human sense on the world." See his *Speaking and Meaning: The Phenomenology of Language* (Bloomington: Indiana Unversity Press, 1976), pp. 77-78.

21. *Phenomenology of Perception*, pp. 177-179.

22. *Phenomenology of Perception*, pp. 181-183, 187-188. Merleau-Ponty in this context criticized also the notion of the purely arbitrary character of the sign function or of the relation between "signifier"and "signified" (p. 187). "If we consider only the conceptual and delimiting meaning of words, it is true that the verbal form . . . appears arbitrary. But it would no longer appear so if we took into account the affective content of the word, which we have called above its 'gestural sense'. . . . It would then be found that the words, vowels and phonemes are so many ways of 'singing' the world, and that their function is to represent things not, as the naive onomatopoeic theory had it, by reason of an objective resemblance, but because they extract, and literally express their affective essence."

23. *Phenomenology of Perception*, pp. 193-194. The difference between constituted meanings and meaning-constitution was related by Merleau-Ponty to the distinctions between *langue* and *parole* or between *parole parlée* and *parole parlante* (pp. 196-197): "It might be said, restating a celebrated distinction, that *languages* or constituted systems of vocabulary and syntax—as empirically existing 'means of expression'—are both the repository and residue of acts of *speech* in which unformulated significance not only finds the means of being conveyed outwardly, but moreover acquires existence for itself and is genuinely created as significance. Or again one might draw a distinction between the *word in the speaking* (or speech act) and the *spoken word*."

24. Edie, *Speaking and Meaning*, pp. 86-87; Merleau-Ponty, *Consciousness and the Acquisition of Language*, trans. Hugh J. Silverman (Evanston: Northwestern University Press, 1973), pp. 31, 50. Edie divides Merleau-Ponty's reflections on language into three periods: the first marked by the emphasis on gestural expression, the second by the confrontation with structural linguistics, and the last by more broadly ontological concerns. In this scheme, *Consciousness and the Acquisition of Language* stands at the threshold of the second phase which includes primarily such writings as *The Prose of the World* and the language essays

in *Signs*, while the last phase is captured in *The Visible and the Invisible*.

25. Jürgen Habermas, *Theorie des kommunikativen Handelns* (Frankfurt-Main: Suhrkamp, 1981), vol. I, pp. 433-435.

26. Searle's reliance on subjectivity is evident in a statement like the following: "If we adopt illocutionary point as the basic notion on which to classify uses of language, then there are a rather limited number of basic things *we do* with language: we tell people how things are, we try to get them to do things, we commit ourselves to do things, we express feelings and attitudes and we bring about changes through our utterances." *Expression and Meaning*, p. 29 (italics mine).

27. Jacques Derrida, "Signature Event Context," *Glyph*, vol. 1 (Baltimore: Johns Hopkins University Press, 1977), pp. 187-188, 192. As he added (p. 192), the broader, decentered conception of language introduces into speech "a dehiscence and a cleft which are essential. The 'non-serious', the *oratio obliqua* will no longer be able to be excluded, as Austin wished, from 'ordinary' language . . . . Above all, this essential absence of intending the actuality of utterance, this structural unconsciousness, if you like, prohibits any saturation of the context. In order for a context to be exhaustively determinable, in the sense required by Austin, conscious intention would at the very least have to be totally present and immediately transparent to itself and to others, since it is a determining center of context. The concept of — or search for — the context thus seems to suffer from the same theoretical and practical uncertainty as the concept of the 'ordinary', and from the same metaphysical source: the ethical and teleological discourse of consciousness." Searle wrote a rejoinder entitled "Reiterating the Differences: A Reply to Derrida" in the same volume, pp. 198-208, to which Derrida in turn replied in "Limited Inc," *Glyph*, vol. 2 (Baltimore: Johns Hopkins University Press, 1977), pp. 162-254.

28. Hans-Georg Gadamer, *Philosophical Hermeneutics*, trans. David E. Linge (Berkeley: University of California Press, 1976), pp. 64-65, 79.

29. Martin Heidegger, *Unterwegs zur Sprache* (Pfullingen: Neske, 1959), pp. 14, 31, 250, 254. For an English version see "Language" in Heidegger, *Poetry, Language, Thought*, trans. Albert Hofstadter (New York: Harper and Row, 1971), pp. 192, 208; and "The Way to Language" in Heidegger, *On the Way to Language*, trans. Peter D. Hertz (New York: Harper and Row, 1971), pp. 120, 124. Merleau-Ponty's early "gestural" theory of expression has been criticized by Paul Ricoeur for shortchanging both linguistic-semiological issues and philosophical reflexivity, in *The Conflict of Interpretations: Essays in Hermeneutics*, ed. Don Ihde (Evanston: Northwestern University Press, 1974), pp. 247-254.

30. Gusdorf, *Speaking*, p. 73; Searle, *Expression and Meaning*, pp. 65-66. The level of intention which, in Searle's view, may perhaps be bypassed concerns the "author's ulterior motives."

31. Hayden White, *Tropics of Discourse: Essays in Cultural Criticism* (Baltimore: Johns Hopkins University Press, 1978), p. 275. For Sartre's own literary theory see, e.g., his *What is Literature?*, trans. Bernard Frechtman (New York: Philosophical Library, 1949).

32. P. D. Juhl, *Interpretation: An Essay in the Philosophy of Literary Criticism* (Princeton: Princeton University Press, 1980), pp. 10, 13, 47. Juhl differentiates his approach expressly from Hirsch's more speculative-normative

focus on intentionality, stating (p. 12): "Whereas Hirsch is more or less explicitly offering a recommendation as to what critics *ought* to do in interpreting a text — namely, try to ascertain the author's intention — my view is that they are necessarily doing so already, in virtue of what it is for a literary work to have a certain meaning." The study treats contextual factors and linguistic rules as corroborating evidence for gauging authorial intent. Relatively little attention, however, is given to the question how authorial intent is accessible to a reader or interpreter presumably guided by a distinct intentionality, that is, to the relation between author's and reader's intent (although the Appendix offers a critique of the "hermeneutic circle," pp. 239-300).

33. Quentin Skinner, "Meaning and Understanding in the History of Ideas," *History and Theory*, vol. 8 (1969), pp. 28, 48-49. See also his "Conventions and the Understanding of Speech Acts," *Philosophical Quarterly*, vol. 20 (1970), pp. 118-138; "On Performing and Explaining Linguistic Actions," *Philosophical Quarterly*, vol. 21 (1971), pp. 1-21; "Some Problems in the Analysis of Political Thought and Action," *Political Theory*, vol. 2 (1974), pp. 277-303; and "Hermeneutics and the Role of History," *New Literary History*, vol. 7 (1975), pp. 209-232. Skinner's exegetic views are concretely applied to his *The Foundations of Modern Political Thought*, 2 vols. (Cambridge: at the University Press, 1978), which contains a section on "Rhetoric and Liberty" (vol. I, pp. 23-48).

34. J. G. A. Pocock, *Politics, Language and Time: Essays on Political Thought and History* (New York: Atheneum, 1973), pp. 15, 25, 28; John G. Gunnell, *Political Theory: Tradition and Interpretation* (Cambridge, Mass.: Winthrop Publishers, 1979), pp. 135, 138 (and for an assessment of Skinner's and Pocock's arguments, pp. 98-103). Pocock (p. 17) closely relates political utterance with "rhetoric," that "language in which men speak for all the purposes and in all the ways in which men may be found articulating and communicating as part of the activity and the culture of politics." Compare also John Dunn, "The Identity of the History of Ideas," *Philosophy*, vol. 43 (1968), pp. 85-104, and his *The Political Thought of John Locke* (Cambridge: at the University Press, 1969).

35. See John Searle, *The Campus War: A Sympathetic Look at the University in Agony* (New York: World Publishing Co., 1971); Gunnell, *Political Theory*, pp. 135-136; Philip Thody, *Jean-Paul Sartre: A Literary and Political Study* (New York: Macmillan, 1961); Wilfrid Desan, *The Marxism of Jean-Paul Sartre* (Garden City, N.Y.: Anchor Books, 1966); Barry Cooper, *Merleau-Ponty and Marxism: From Terror to Reform* (Toronto: University of Toronto Press, 1979); Sonia Kruks, *The Political Philosophy of Merleau-Ponty* (Atlantic Highlands, N.J.: Humanities Press, 1981); and Mark Poster, *Existential Marxism in Postwar France: From Sartre to Althusser* (Princeton: Princeton University Press, 1975).

36. Paulo Freire, *Pedagogy of the Oppressed* (New York: Seabury Press, 1970), pp. 11, 75-76, 88, 119. For a similar emphasis on linguistic and political "expressiveness" (but from a more romantic, Humboldtian vantage point) see Charles Taylor, *Language and Human Nature* (Alan B. Plaunt Memorial Lectures, Carleton University, 1978).

Chapter 5: Transcendental Hermeneutics and Universal Pragmatics

1. John R. Searle, *Expression and Meaning: Studies in the Theory of Speech Acts* (Cambridge: at the University Press, 1979), p. viii; Peter Strawson, *Individuals: An Essay in Descriptive Metaphysics* (London: Methuen, 1959) and *The Bounds of Sense: An Essay on Kant's Critique of Pure Reason* (London: Methuen, 1966). The phrase "minimalist interpretation of the transcendental" is used by Jürgen Habermas in *Communication and the Evolution of Society*, trans. Thomas McCarthy (Boston: Beacon Press, 1959), p. 21.

2. Martin Heidegger, *Being and Time*, trans. John Macquarrie and Edward Robinson (New York: Harper and Row, 1962), section 34, pp. 203-204, 208-209 (in these and subsequent citations the translation has been slightly altered for purposes of clarity). The basic approach of the study is aptly characterized by Kockelmans who writes: "Heidegger's original point of departure was an analytic of man's being taken as *Da-sein, lumen naturale*—that is, as ek-sistence, standing out, and thus as being-in-the-world. He used phenomenological and hermeneutic methods in order to let the 'things themselves' become manifest, interpreting them from the preontological understanding of Being which is inherent in man's being as such. Heidegger hoped that a careful analysis of man's being would help him find a way to make our preontological understanding of Being explicit." See Joseph J. Kockelmans, ed., *On Heidegger and Language* (Evanston: Northwestern University Press, 1972), p. xi.

3. *Being and Time*, pp. 204-206. Regarding the speaker-addressee relationship the section stated (p. 205): "Communication (*Mitteilung*) is never anything like a conveying of experiences, such as opinions or wishes, from the interior of one subject into the interior of another. Co-being (or being with another *Dasein*) is essentially manifest in an initial co-disposition and co-understanding; in speech co-being is 'explicitly' shared." The four-dimensional structure of speech is noted by several commentators, but regularly without an allusion to parallels with speech-act theory; see, e.g., Jan Aler, "Heidegger's Conception of Language in *Being and Time*," and Walter Biemel, "Poetry and Language in Heidegger," in Kockelmans, *On Heidegger and Language*, pp. 53-54, 72.

4. *Being and Time*, pp. 206, 208. On the role of silence in existential phenomenology see, e.g., Bernard P. Dauenhauer, *Silence: The Phenomenon and Its Ontological Significance* (Bloomington: Indiana University Press, 1980). Compare also George Steiner, *Language and Silence* (New York: Atheneum, 1967).

5. *Being and Time*, pp. 209-210. With regard to the overall development of Heidegger's thoughts on language, Kockelmans distinguishes between two basic phases (before and after the so-called *"Kehre"*), while Biemel differentiates between three periods (*Being and Time*, texts of the 1930's, and postwar writings); see Kockelmans, *On Heidegger and Language*, pp. xi-xii, 68. The general development is succinctly pinpointed by Kockelmans in these terms (p. xii): "In Heidegger's later works his attention turns from a concern for language from the viewpoint of man's speech to a concern for language's essential contribution to the very possibility of man's speech." Concerning the notion of "topology" com-

pare Otto Pöggeler, "Heidegger's Topology of Being," in the same volume, pp. 107-146.

6. *Being and Time*, pp. 61-62; Paul Ricoeur, "Existence and Hermeneutics," in *The Conflict of Interpretations: Essays in Hermeneutics*, ed. Don Ihde (Evanston: Northwestern University Press, 1974), pp. 3, 6-11. Despite the distinction between two routes, Ricoeur (p. 6-7) claims to "fully accept the movement toward this complete reversal of the relationship between understanding and being" and even depicts the two approaches as less antithetical than complementary: "If I begin by giving due consideration to Heidegger's philosophy, it is because I do not hold it to be a contrary solution; that is to say, his analytic of *Dasein* is not an alternative which would force us to choose between an ontology of understanding and an epistemology of interpretation. The long route which I propose also aspires to carry reflection to the level of an ontology, but it will do so by degrees, following successive investigations into semantics and reflection."

7. *The Conflict of Interpretations*, pp. 12-13, 15. In addition to Husserlian phenomenology Ricoeur also links semantic analysis with "other currently viable philosophies" of language (p. 15): "Of course, the semantics of multivocal expressions opposes the theories of metalanguage which would hope to remake existing languages according to ideal models. . . . On the other hand, this semantics enters into a fruitful dialogue with the doctrines arising from Wittgenstein's *Philosophical Investigations* and from the analysis of ordinary language in the Anglo-Saxon countries."

8. *The Conflict of Interpretations*, pp. 16-19.

9. *The Conflict of Interpretations*, pp. 17, 20-21. In addition to Freudian "archaeology," Ricoeur also mentions Hegel's "teleology" (of spirit) and religious "eschatology" as possible avenues toward an existential ontology—the latter seen only as a distant "promised land for a philosophy that begins with language and with reflection" (p. 24).

10. See Jürgen Habermas, *Strukturwandel der Öffentlichkeit: Untersuchungen zu einer Kategorie der bürgerlichen Gesellschaft* (Neuwied: Luchterhand, 1962); *Theory and Practice*, trans. John Viertel (Boston: Beacon Press, 1973); *Knowledge and Human Interests*, trans. Jeremy J. Shapiro (Boston: Beacon Press, 1971). To some extent, language also was relevant under the auspices of the "technical interest": as medium in a (Peircean) "community of investigators" or scientists. In his lecture on "Knowledge and Human Interests" (1965) Habermas summarized the three dimensions somewhat schematically by stating that cognitive or "knowledge-constitutive interests take form in the medium of work, language, and power"—adding that "the human interest in autonomy and responsibility is not mere fancy, for it can be apprehended a priori. What raises us out of nature is the only thing whose nature we can know: language." *Knowledge and Human Interests*, pp. 313-314.

11. See Habermas, "Introduction: Some Difficulties in the Attempt to Link Theory and Practice," in *Theory and Practice*, pp. 18-19. The distinctions between valid knowledge and everyday cognitive pursuits, and also between "rational reconstruction" and pure self-reflection or "self-critique" were further

outlined in 1973 in Habermas's "A Postscript to *Knowledge and Human Interests*," *Philosophy of the Social Sciences*, vol. 3 (1975), pp. 157-189.

12. Habermas, "On Systematically Distorted Communication," *Inquiry*, vol. 13 (1970), pp. 205-208. Habermas relied at this point chiefly on Alfred Lorenzer, especially his subsequently published *Über den Gegenstand der Psychoanalyse, oder: Sprache und Interaktion* (Frankfurt-Main: Suhrkamp, 1973).

13. Habermas, "On Systematically Distorted Communication," pp. 210-216. On the level of normal speech, the essay (pp. 210-211) invoked the Saussurean distinction of "signifier" and "signified" (language-sign and significative content) and the Fregean polarity of *Sinn* and *Bedeutung* (*significatum* and *denotatum*). On the same level, "intersubjectivity" basically denoted an aggregate of egos or subjects: "The one being (ego) asserts his absolute non-identity in relation to the other being (alter ego); at the same time, however, both recognize their identity inasmuch as each acknowledges the other as being an ego, that is, a non-replaceable individual who can refer to himself as 'I'."

14. Habermas, "Towards a Theory of Communicative Competence," *Inquiry*, vol. 13 (1970), pp. 360-361. Proceeding to a more detailed critique, the paper advanced three main points (which I have mentioned in chapter 3 and thus can briefly summarize here): namely, that generative grammar reflects the principles of *"monologism," "a priorism,"* and *"elementarism"*—that is, the tenets that meaning components are lodged in solitary organisms, that they precede or antedate possible experience, and that the semantics of natural languages are derived from these components (p. 363).

15. "Towards a Theory of Communicative Competence," pp. 363-366.

16. "Towards a Theory of Communicative Competence," pp. 366-369. As he added (p. 369), the "idealization" in this context resided basically in the fact "that we suppose an exclusively linguistic organization of speech and interaction." For a detailed review of the arguments supporting the concept of "communicative competence" see Thomas McCarthy, "A Theory of Communicative Competence," *Philosophy of the Social Sciences*, vol. 3 (1973), pp. 135-156.

17. "Towards a Theory of Communicative Competence," pp. 369-371. As Habermas added (p. 372): "These three symmetries represent, incidentally, a linguistic conceptualization of what are traditionally known as the ideas of truth, freedom, and justice." The labels "constatives," "representatives," and "regulatives" were actually used in the (longer) German version of the essay, entitled "Vorbereitende Bemerkungen zu einer Theorie der kommunikativen Kompetenz," in Habermas and Niklas Luhmann, *Theorie der Gesellschaft oder Sozialtechnologie—Was leistet die Systemforschung?* (Frankfurt-Main: Suhrkamp, 1971), pp. 101-141, at 111-112. In the same context Habermas mentioned a fourth type of linguistic acts, termed "communicatives," having to do with the purely linguistic-grammatical sense of an utterance.

18. "What Is Universal Pragmatics?", in Habermas, *Communication and the Evolution of Society*, trans. Thomas McCarthy (Boston: Beacon Press, 1979), pp. 1-3 (in these and subsequent citations I have slightly altered the translation for purposes of clarity).

19. "What Is Universal Pragmatics?", pp. 5-6, 9, 12-14. As Habermas added

(p. 14): "When the pretheoretical knowledge to be reconstructed expresses a universal capability, a general cognitive, linguistic, or interactive competence (or subcompetence), then what begins as explication of meaning aims at the reconstruction of species competences."

20. "What Is Universal Pragmatics?", pp. 14, 19-20, 26-29. "By 'communicative competence'," Habermas stated (pp. 28-29), "I understand the ability of a speaker oriented to mutual understanding to embed a well-formed sentence in relations to reality" in a three-fold way, namely, in relations to "(1) the external reality of what is supposed to be an existing state of affairs; (2) the internal reality of what the speaker would like to express before a public as his intentions; and finally (3) the normative reality of what is intersubjectively recognized as a legitimate interpersonal relationship."

21. "What Is Universal Pragmatics?", pp. 25, 42-43, 49, 53-55, 57. Strictly speaking, speech-act theory was relevant mainly for the "regulative" (or normative) use of language, while the "cognitive" and "expressive" uses were the province of formal semantics and the analysis of intentionality. However, as Habermas stated (p. 34): "For a theory of communicative action the third aspect of utterances, namely the establishment of interpersonal relations, is central; I shall therefore take the theory of speech acts as my point of departure."

22. "What Is Universal Pragmatics?", pp. 61-64.

23. "What Is Universal Pragmatics?", pp. 65-67. Regarding the status of language the section added (p. 68): "Language also appears in speech, for speech is a medium in which the linguistic means that are employed instrumentally are also reflected. In speech, speech sets itself off from the regions of external nature, society, and internal nature, as a reality *sui generis*, as soon as a sign-substrate, meaning, and denotation of a linguistic utterance can be distinguished."

24. "What Is Universal Pragmatics?", pp. 21-25. Despite the previously stressed contrast between reconstruction and empiricism, methodological differences were said to be insufficient "to banish linguistics, for example, from the sphere of empirical science." The study at this point (p. 25) invoked chiefly the works of Chomsky and Piaget to vindicate reservations regarding transcendental inquiry: "The paradigms introduced by Chomsky and Piaget have led to a type of research determined by a peculiar connection between formal and empirical analysis rather than by their classical separation. The expression *transcendental*, with which we associate a contrast to empirical science, is thus unsuited to characterizing, without misunderstanding, a line of research such as universal pragmatics."

25. Karl-Otto Apel, "Sprechakttheorie und transzendentale Sprachpragmatik zur Frage ethischer Normen," in Apel, ed., *Sprachpragmatik und Philosophie* (Frankfurt-Main: Suhrkamp, 1976), pp. 16, 18-19, 24. Compare also his *Towards a Transformation of Philosophy*, trans. Glyn Adey and David Frisby (London: Routledge and Kegan Paul, 1980); the original German version appeared in two volumes under the title *Transformation der Philosophie* (Frankfurt-Main: Suhrkamp, 1973).

26. "Sprechakttheorie und transzendentale Sprachpragmatik," pp. 87, 92-93. This universal quality of language rules, Apel adds (pp. 82, 84), is particularly important for the grounding of ethical norms; thus, "the circumstance that the performance of a promise implies an obligation has to be traced to universal rules

of language and not to their conventional implementation in natural languages." More generally, it is chiefly the field of ethics which corroborates "the possibility and necessity of a transcendental interpretation of speech-act theory."

27. "Sprechakttheorie und transzendentale Sprachpragmatik," pp. 94, 96-97, 117. "The beginning of ethics," another passage states (p. 122), "cannot be the recourse to a *fact* no matter how universal, but only the demonstration, accomplished through *reflective argumentation*, that every possible interlocutor (everyone who raises the question of a possible grounding or justification of norms) has already necessarily recognized the universal-pragmatic norms of ethics (namely, as conditions of possibility of meaningful argumentation)."

28. For a general examination of Ricoeur's work see Don Ihde, *Hermeneutic Philosophy: The Philosophy of Paul Ricoeur* (Evanston: Northwestern University Press, 1971); and for a detailed assessment of Apel's perspective my "Sinnerlebnis und Geltungsreflexion: Apels Transformation der Philosophie," *Philosophische Rundschau*, vol. 25 (1978), pp. 1-42. For a broad overview of contemporary hermeneutical thought, including Heidegger's *Being and Time*, Ricoeur's "phenomenological hermeneutic," Gadamer's "philosophical hermeneutic," and the "critical hermeneutics" of Apel and Habermas, compare Josef Bleicher, *Contemporary Hermeneutics: Hermeneutics as Method, Philosophy and Critique* (London: Routledge and Kegan Paul, 1980).

29. Anthony Giddens, *Central Problems in Social Theory: Action, Structure and Contradiction in Social Analysis* (Berkeley: University of California Press, 1979), p. 120. For Lacan's stance regarding linguistics and language theory see Anika Lemaire, *Jacques Lacan*, trans. David Macey (London: Routledge and Kegan Paul, 1977), pp. 38-64. Ricoeur elsewhere differentiates between a critical-reductive and a "restorative" depth psychology; see his *Freud and Philosophy: An Essay on Interpretation*, trans. Denis Savage (New Haven: Yale University Press, 1970).

30. Habermas, "Towards a Theory of Communicative Competence," p. 366; Apel, "Sprechakttheorie und transzendentale Sprachpragmatik," p. 94.

31. Habermas, "What Is Universal Pragmatics?", pp. 2-3, 42, 68. With regard to the demarcation from "internal nature" Habermas suggests vaguely (p. 67) that "it is precisely in this expressive attitude that the 'I' knows itself not only as subjectivity but also as something that has always already transcended the bounds of mere subjectivity, in cognition, language, and interaction simultaneously"; but the comment is not further clarified. The conception of intersubjectivity relates also to the meaning of "discourse" and the "ideal speech situation"; for some critical comments on the latter notions see Steven D. Ealy, *Communication, Speech, and Politics: Habermas and Political Analysis* (Washington, D.C.: University Press of America, 1981), pp. 212-215, 226-231; J. Donald Moon, "Political Ethics and Critical Theory," in Daniel R. Sabia and Jerald Wallulis, eds., *Changing Social Science: Critical Theory and Other Critical Perspectives* (Albany: State University of New York Press, 1983), pp. 171-188; and John B. Thompson, "Universal Pragmatics," in Thompson and David Held, eds., *Habermas: Critical Debates* (Cambridge, Mass.: MIT Press, 1982), pp. 116-133.

32. Some of the quandaries or shortcomings of Habermas's conception of language are discussed in Oliva Blanchette, "Language, the Primordial Labor of

History," *Cultural Hermeneutics*, vol. 1 (1974), pp. 325-382.

33. Kockelmans, "Language, Meaning, and Ek-sistence," in Kockelmans, *On Heidegger and Language*, p. 31. Aler, I believe, overstates his case when (in the same volume, p. 59) he presents authentic insight in *Being and Time* as essentially "wordless" or "speechless": "This *logos*, the genuine *logos*, is wordless. . . . The authentic mode of *logos* thus does not properly belong to language." For Heidegger's views on interpretation (*Auslegung*) see *Being and Time*, pp. 188-195.

34. Ricoeur, *The Conflict of Interpretations*, pp. 13, 15, 23. The stress on the interpreter's role is particularly clear in these comments on "the deepest wish of hermeneutics" (pp. 16-17): "The purpose of all interpretation is to conquer a remoteness, a distance between the past cultural epoch to which the text belongs and the interpreter himself. By overcoming this distance, by making himself contemporary with the text, the exegete can appropriate its meaning to himself: foreign, he makes it familiar, that is, he makes it his own. . . . Every hermeneutics is thus, explicitly or implicitly, self-understanding by means of understanding others." See also Ricoeur, *Interpretation Theory: Discourse and the Surplus of Meaning* (Fort Worth, Tex.: Texas Christian University Press, 1976).

35. Habermas, "On Systematically Distorted Communication," pp. 205-206, 208-209, 216-217. The postulated distinction between ordinary hermeneutics and systematic explanatory depth understanding has been a main bone of contention between Habermas and Hans-Georg Gadamer, a controversy which is ably reviewed in Thomas McCarthy, "Rationality and Relativism: Habermas's 'Overcoming' of Hermeneutics," in Thompson and Held, eds., *Habermas: Critical Debates*, pp. 57-78, and in Dieter Misgeld, "Critical Theory and Hermeneutics: The Debate between Habermas and Gadamer," in John O'Neill, ed., *On Critical Theory* (New York: Seabury Press, 1976), pp. 164-183.

36. Habermas, "What Is Universal Pragmatics?", pp. 11-13. For a presentation of (depth) exegesis in terms of the interpreter's assessment of the validity claims raised in a text see Habermas, *Theorie des kommunikativen Handelns* (Frankfurt-Main: Suhrkamp, 1981), vol. I, pp. 190-195. In Apel's writings, the role of the interpreter—and especially the question whether the interpreter can understand an author "better" than the latter understood himself—is discussed in his "Einleitung" to *Transformation der Philosophie*, vol. I, pp. 45-51. For examples of a reader-centered approach in contemporary literary theory see Wolfgang Iser, *The Implied Reader: Patterns of Communication in Prose Fiction from Bunyan to Beckett* (Baltimore: Johns Hopkins University Press, 1974); and Jane P. Thompson, ed., *Reader-Response Criticism: From Formalism to Post-Structuralism* (Baltimore: Johns Hopkins University Press, 1980).

37. Heidegger, *Being and Time*, pp. 158-159; Ricoeur, *The Conflict of Interpretations*, pp. 10, 20; Habermas, "Towards a Theory of Communicative Competence," pp. 372-374, and "Vorbereitende Bemerkungen zu einer Theorie der kommunikativen Kompetenz," p. 141.

38. Habermas, *Toward a Rational Society: Student Protest, Science, and Politics*, trans. Jeremy J. Shapiro (Boston: Beacon Press, 1970), pp. 118-119 (translation slightly altered). For a similar orientation see Karl-Otto Apel, "The Conflicts of Our Time and the Problem of Political Ethics," in Dallmayr, ed.,

From Contract to Community: Political Theory at the Crossroads (New York: Marcel Dekker, 1978), pp. 81-101.

Chapter 6: The Rule of Metaphor

*"What rousing call does the bugler's/Silver horn cast in the tangle/Of the Saga's deep slumber?" (Stefan George)

1. The German original reads: "Wunder von ferne oder traum/Bracht ich an meines landes saum/Und harrte bis die graue norn/Den namen fand in ihrem ´ born—/Drauf konnt ichs greifen dicht und stark/Nun blüht und glänzt es durch die mark . . . /Einst langt ich an nach guter fahrt/Mit einem kleinod reich und zart/Sie suchte lang und gab mir kund:/'So schläft hier nichts auf tiefem Grund'/Worauf es meiner hand zerrann/Und nie mein land den schatz gewann. . . . /So lernt ich traurig den verzicht:/Kein ding sei wo das wort gebricht." The English translation is by Peter Hertz and can be found in Martin Heidegger, *On the Way to Language*, trans. Peter D. Hertz (New York: Harper and Row, 1971), p. 60. (The translation of the preceding motto is taken from the same volume, p. 89.)

2. Martin Heidegger, "Das Wesen der Sprache" and "Das Wort," in his *Unterwegs zur Sprache* (Pfullingen: Neske, 1959), pp. 157-216 and 217-238. For a translation see "The Nature of Language" and "Words" in Heidegger, *On The Way to Language*, pp. 57-108 and 139-156. For commentaries on Heidegger's comments on the poem compare Walter Biemel, "Poetry and Language in Heidegger," in Joseph J. Kookelmans, ed., *On Heidegger and Language* (Evanston: Northwestern University Press, 1972), pp. 83-91; and Peter J. McCormick, *Heidegger and the Language of the World: An Argumentative Reading of the Later Heidegger's Meditations on Language* (Ottawa: University of Ottawa Press, 1976), pp. 9-16.

3. See Aristotle *Poetics* 1457b 6-9, and 1459a 3-8. Aristotle also dealt with metaphorical language in his *Rhetoric*; but there he took over the definition of metaphor offered in *Poetics*.

4. Thomas Hobbes, *Leviathan* (New York: Dutton, 1953), Part I, Chapters 4 and 5, pp. 16, 18, 21. For a detailed historical account of the relation between philosophy and metaphor see James D. Edie, *Speaking and Meaning: The Phenomenology of Language* (Bloomington: Indiana University Press, 1976), pp. 161-180.

5. Rudolf Carnap, *Philosophy and Logical Syntax* (London: Kegan Paul, Trench, Trubner, 1935), p. 29. See also Gottlob Frege, "On Sense and Reference" (1892), in *Translations from the Philosophical Writings of Gottlob Frege*, ed. Max Black and Peter Geach (Oxford: Blackwell, 1952), pp. 56-78.

6. Gilbert Ryle, *The Concept of Mind* (New York: Barnes and Noble, 1949), pp. 266-267; Susanne K. Langer, *Philosophy in a New Key: A Study of the Symbolism of Reason, Rite, and Art* (2nd ed.; New York: New American Library, 1951), p. 125. As Langer added (p. 124): "In a genuine metaphor, an image of the literal meaning is our symbol for the figurative meaning, the thing

that has no name of its own. . . . Since the *context* of an expression tells us what is its sense—whether we shall take it literally or figuratively, and how, in the latter case, it is to be interpreted—it follows that the context itself must always be expressed literally, because it has not, in turn, a context to supplement and define its sense. Only the novel predication can be metaphorical."

7. Jean Cohen, *Structure du langage poétique* (Paris: Flammarion, 1966), p. 212; Northrop Frye, *Anatomy of Criticism: Four Essays* (Princeton: Princeton University Press, 1957), pp. 73-74, 76, 79. "In other words," Frye added (pp. 86-87), "a poet's intention is centripetally directed. It is directed towards putting words together, not towards aligning words with meaning. . . . What the poet meant to say, then, is, literally, the poem itself." For comments on metaphor see pp. 122-125.

8. Philip Wheelwright, *Metaphor and Reality* (Bloomington: Indiana University Press, 1962), pp. 16, 20, 37-39, 71; Colin M. Turbayne, *The Myth of Metaphor* (rev. ed.; Columbia, S.C.: University of South Carolina Press, 1970), pp. 11, 17, 22, 26-27, 51-52. Ricoeur's comments on Turbayne's study are, in my view, directly to the point: "In the first place, the author installs himself in an order of reality homogeneous with that of the positivism criticized by his thesis. The concern is always with 'facts' and therefore also with truth in the verificationist sense. . . . The question is precisely whether poetic language does not break through to a pre-scientific, onto-predicative level, where the very notions of fact, object, reality, and truth, as delimited by epistemology, are *called into question* by this very means of the vacillation of literal reference. Furthermore, the author speaks of a mastery of models that is not to be found in poetic experience, where something other than the poet speaks even as he speaks, and where, beyond the control of the poet, a reality comes to language." See Paul Ricoeur, *The Rule of Metaphor: Multi-Disciplinary Studies of the Creation of Meaning in Language*, trans. Robert Czerny (Toronto: University of Toronto Press, 1977), pp. 253-254.

9. Ferdinand de Saussure, *Course in General Linguistics*, ed. Charles Bally and Albert Sechehaye, trans. Wade Baskin (New York: Philosophical Library, 1959), pp. 122-127; Claude Lévi-Strauss, *The Savage Mind* (Chicago: University of Chicago Press, 1966), pp. 105-106 (also pp. 204-207 and 224-228 for "metaphorical" treatments of the relations between human society and birds and dogs, and between totemism and sacrifice); Roman Jacobson, "Closing Statements: Linguistics and Poetics," in T. A. Sebeok, ed., *Style in Language* (Cambridge, Mass.: MIT Press, 1960), pp. 356, 358. In the meantime a structuralist and formalist theory of poetry has been developed chiefly by Todorov and Culler; see Tzvetan Todorov, *Introduction to Poetics*, trans. Richard Howard (Minneapolis: University of Minnesota Press, 1981), and Jonathan Culler, *Structuralist Poetics: Structuralism, Linguistics and the Study of Literature* (Ithaca, N.Y.: Cornell University Press, 1975).

10. Max Black, *Models and Metaphors: Studies in Language and Philosophy* (Ithaca, N.Y.: Cornell University Press, 1962), pp. 229, 236-239; Mary B. Hesse, *Models and Analogies in Science* (Notre Dame: University of Notre Dame Press, 1966), pp. 157, 176-177.

11. John R. Searle, *Expression and Meaning: Studies in the Theory of Speech*

Acts (Cambridge: at the University Press, 1979), pp. 60, 65, 77, 85-86, 92-93. Regarding the endorsement of the interaction model by Black and Hesse see *Models and Metaphors*, pp. 38-47, and *Models and Analogies in Science*, pp. 162-166.

12. Edie, *Speaking and Meaning*, pp. 164-166, 186-187. Like Gusdorf and the early Merleau-Ponty, Edie links human intentionality with "expressiveness" (p. 152): "From the point of view of phenomenological analysis, language appears as one aspect of a total, contextual, human activity of 'expressing' which cannot be studied in isolation from man's existential insertion in his life-world. If man *as a unitary whole* is intentional of the world, it is impossible to isolate the study of language from the study of man as a world-intending organism, a dynamic experiencer who structures his experience by *expressing* its *meaning*. . . . Another way of saying the same thing is to say that man is essentially expressive."

13. *Speaking and Meaning*, pp. 189-190. Stressing the speaker's purposive role, Edie insists (p. 188) that "a word becomes a metaphor when it is used to refer with a new purpose, *with a new intention*, to a previously disclosed aspect of experience in order to reveal a hitherto unnamed and indistinct experience of a different kind. The metaphorical use of words thus brings about a reorganization, a refocusing of experience, which continues to grow in complexity with each new *purpose*."

14. Ricoeur, *The Rule of Metaphor*, p. 221 (italics added).

15. *The Rule of Metaphor*, pp. 224, 230-231, 239.

16. *The Rule of Metaphor*, pp. 236, 239, 244-245, 247.

17. *The Rule of Metaphor*, pp. 247-248, 255 (translation slightly altered).

18. Martin Heidegger, *Der Satz vom Grund* (Pfullingen: Neske, 1957), pp. 86-87, 89; "The Nature of Language," in Heidegger, *On the Way to Language*, pp. 99-100 (for the German version see *Unterwegs zur Sprache*, pp. 206-207). Elaborating on the passages in *Der Satz vom Grund* Ricoeur writes that the argument "suggests that the trans-gression of a meta-phor and that of meta-physics are but one and the same transfer. Several things are implied here: first, that the ontology implicit in the entire rhetorical tradition is that of Western 'metaphysics' of the Platonic or neo-Platonic type where the soul is transported from the visible world to the invisible world; second, that metaphorical means transfer from the proper sense to the figurative sense; and finally, that both transfers constitute one and the same *Über-tragung*." *The Rule of Metaphor*, p. 280.

19. Ricoeur, *The Rule of Metaphor*, pp. 282, 284-286; Jacques Derrida, "White Mythology: Metaphor in the Text of Philosophy," trans. F. C. T. Moore, in *New Literary History*, vol. 6 (Autumn 1974), pp. 11, 25. As Derrida adds (p. 6): "Metaphor seems to bring into play the use of philosophical language in its entirety, nothing less than the use of what is called ordinary language in philosophical discourse, that is to say, of ordinary language *as* philosophical language."

20. Metaphysical truth, he writes at one point, "is merely the truth about 'what-is' or being; metaphysics is the history of this truth. It tells us what being is by conceptualizing the 'is-ness' or 'beingness' of beings. In the beingness of being metaphysics thinks the thought of Being, but without being able to reflect on

the truth of Being with its particular mode of thought. Metaphysics moves every-where in the realm of the truth of Being, which truth remains the unknown and unfathomable ground." See Heidegger, "Postscript" (1943) to "What is Meta-physics?" in Walter Kaufmann, ed., *Existentialism: From Dostoevsky to Sartre* (New York: New American Library, 1975), p. 258 (translation slightly altered). Compare also Heidegger's "The Way Back into the Ground of Metaphysics" (1949), in the same volume, pp. 265-279; and his "Überwindung der Meta-physik," in *Vorträge und Aufsätze*, vol. I (Pfullingen: Neske, 1967), pp. 63-91.

21. Ricoeur, *The Conflict of Interpretations: Essays in Hermeneutics*, ed. Don Ihde (Evanston: Northwestern University Press, 1974), pp. 12, 28, 60.

22. Heidegger, *Der Satz vom Grund*, p. 89.

23. Heidegger, *Unterwegs zur Sprache*, pp. 21, 25, 193. For English versions see Heidegger,*Poetry, Language, Thought*, ed. Albert Hofstadter (New York: Harper and Row, 1971), pp. 198-199, 202; and *On the Way to Language*, p. 88.

24. Heidegger, "The Origin of the Work of Art," in *Poetry, Language, Thought*, pp. 49-50, 53-54, 65-66, 73-74 (translation slightly altered). Regard-ing the differential relation between presence and absence Heidegger adds (p. 53): "Beyond beings, not away from them but before them, there is still something else that happens: in the midst of beings as a whole an open place oc-curs. There is a clearing—which, from the vantage point of beings, is more full of being than they are. This open place, therefore, is not enclosed by beings; rather, the clearing itself—just like the 'nothing' which we scarcely know—encircles all that is. . . . Thanks to this clearing, beings are disclosed in certain changing degrees; at the same time, they are also concealed in the sphere of the clearing. Each being we encounter sustains this curious opposition of presencing by simultaneously retreating into concealment." For the German version see Heidegger, *Holzwege* (Frankfurt-Main: Klostermann, 1950), pp. 39, 41-43, 53,60-61.

25. Maurice Merleau-Ponty, *The Visible and the Invisible*, ed. Claude Lefort, trans. Alphonso Lingis (Evanston: Northwestern University Press, 1968), pp. 125, 221-222; Michel Foucault, *Language, Counter-Memory, Practice*, ed. Donald F. Bouchard, trans. Donald F. Bouchard and Sherry Simon (Oxford: Blackwell, 1977), p. 36. With specific reference to language Foucault adds (pp. 41-42): "In a language stripped of dialectics, at the heart of what it says but also at the root of its possibilities, the philosopher is aware that 'we are not everything'; he learns as well that even the philosopher does not inhabit the whole of his language like a secret and perfectly fluent god. Next to himself, he discovers the existence of another language that also speaks and that he is unable to dominate, one that strives, fails, and falls silent and that he cannot manipulate, the language he spoke at one time and that has now separated itself from him, now gravitating in a space increasingly silent."

26. Hans-Georg Gadamer, *Truth and Method* (New York: Seabury Press, 1975), pp. 230, 262-263, 272-273, 331, 341 (translation slightly altered).

27. Gadamer, *Truth and Method*, pp. 260, 264, 321, 340-341, 345-346, 360. Regarding the role of subject matter Gadamer goes so far as to assert (p. 238) that "the hermeneutical task turns automatically into a substantive (or object-oriented) question and is always co-determined by it; thereby, herme-

neutical inquiry gains a firm footing." On the other hand, the rapprochement to Heidegger is evident in the statement (p. 228): "Heidegger's thesis was that Being itself is time—a thesis which exploded the entire subjectivism of modern philosophy and, in fact (as was soon to appear), the whole range of questions posed by traditional metaphysics revolving around being as a form of presencing. That *Dasein* is concerned about its being, that it is distinguished from all other beings by its understanding of being—these points do not constitute (as it might seem in *Being and Time*) a final foundation supporting a transcendental approach. Rather, there is a very different kind of grounding or reason sustaining all understanding of being, and this is that there is a 'there' or a clearing in Being, that is, a difference between beings and Being." For more detailed discussions of Gadamer's hermeneutics see Richard Palmer, *Hermeneutics: Interpretation Theory in Schleiermacher, Dilthey, Heidegger, and Gadamer* (Evanston: Northwestern University Press, 1969), pp. 162-217; David C. Hoy, *The Critical Circle: Literature and History in Contemporary Hermeneutics* (Berkeley: University of California Press, 1978), pp. 41-72; John G. Gunnell, *Political Theory: Tradition and Interpretation* (Cambridge, Mass.: Winthrop Publishers, 1979), pp. 110-118.

28. Henri Birault, "Thinking and Poetizing in Heidegger," in Joseph J. Kockelmans, ed., *On Heidegger and Language* (Evanston: Northwestern University Press, 1972), p. 157. See also Heidegger, *Unterwegs zur Sprache*, pp. 17-18, 28; and for an English version *Poetry, Language, Thought*, p. 195.

29. Hayden White, "The Absurdist Moment in Contemporary Literary Theory," in his *Tropics of Discourse: Essays in Cultural Criticism* (Baltimore: Johns Hopkins University Press, 1978), pp. 263, 278. "In the thought of Bataille, Blanchot, Foucault, and Jacques Derrida," he adds polemically (p. 262), "we witness the rise of a movement in literary criticism which raises the critical question only to take a grim satisfaction in the contemplation of the impossibility of ever resolving it or, at the extreme limit of thought, even of asking it. Literature is reduced to writing, writing to language, and language in a final paroxysm of frustration, to chatter about silence." For a more balanced assessment see his "Foucault Decoded: Notes from Underground" in the same volume, pp. 230-260.

30. Harold Bloom, Paul de Man, Jacques Derrida, Geoffrey H. Hartman, and J. Hillis Miller, *Deconstruction and Criticism* (New York: Continuum, 1979), pp. vii-viii, 83-84. On the topic of difference Harold Bloom adds in a Nietzschean vein (p. 5): "Only the agon is of the essence. Why? Is it merely my misprision, to believe that good poems must be combative?" On the relation between Gadamer and Derrida see Hoy, *The Critical Circle*, pp. 77-84.

31. Michael Oakeshott, *Rationalism in Politics, and Other Essays* (New York: Basic Books, 1962), pp. 127, 129; William E. Connolly, *The Terms of Political Discourse* (Lexington, Mass.: Heath and Co., 1974), pp. 6, 10, 40.

32. John G. Gunnell, *Political Philosophy and Time* (Middletown, Conn.: Wesleyan University Press, 1968), pp. 258-259. Regarding the dismantling of traditional dualisms he elaborates (pp. 257-258): "Heidegger's project for the destruction or overcoming of Western metaphysics, the avowed return to the pre-Socratic understanding of being, is actually neither a 'destruction' nor a 'return' in any usual sense of the word any more than Plato undertook to destroy the

philosophy of his predecessors and to return to the myth. . . . His destruction of metaphysics is not a renunciation of philosophy, but the rejection of the old truth, the old symbols, that no longer conform to experience or provide a medium for the movement of the creative mind." For a critical analysis of more "destructive" or "deconstructive" tendencies in Gunnell's subsequent writings see John S. Nelson, "Destroying Political Theory in Order to Save It," in Nelson, ed., *From Epistemology to Action: Essays on Theory and Politics in America* (forthcoming).

33. Hannah Arendt, *The Life of the Mind*, vol. I: *Thinking* (New York: Harcourt Brace Jovanovich, 1977), pp. 10-12. At a later point Arendt adds in a more personal vein (p. 212): "I have clearly joined the ranks of those who for some time now have been attempting to dismantle metaphysics, and philosophy with all its categories, as we have known them from their beginning in Greece until today. Such dismantling is possible only on the assumption that the thread of tradition is broken and that we shall not be able to renew it. Historically speaking, what actually has broken down is the Roman trinity that for thousands of years united religion, authority, and tradition. . . . What you then are left with is still the past, but a *fragmented* past, which has lost its certainty of evaluation." As she continues, however: "If some of my listeners or readers should be tempted to try their luck at the technique of dismantling, let them be careful not to destroy the 'rich and strange', the 'coral' and the 'pearls' which can probably be saved only as fragments."

34. *The Life of the Mind*, vol. I: *Thinking*, pp. 103-104, 106, 108-110. The ambiguity is manifest in her frequent reference to the "thinking ego" and in her claim (p. 103) that "the metaphor achieves the 'carrying over' — *metaphorein* — of a genuine and seemingly impossible *metabasis eis allo genos*, the transition from one essential state, that of thinking, to another, that of being an appearance among appearances, and this can be done only by *analogies*."

Chapter 7: Language and Politics

* ". . . to a child belongs the kingdom." (Heraclitus)

1. Richard Rorty, *Philosophy and the Mirror of Nature* (Princeton: Princeton University Press, 1979), pp. 371-373, 378.

2. Michael Oakeshott, "The Voice of Poetry in the Conversation of Mankind," in *Rationalism in Politics, and Other Essays* (New York: Basic Books, 1962), p. 197.

3. "The Voice of Poetry in the Conversation of Mankind," pp. 198-200. In the essay, philosophy — seen as "the impulse to study the quality and style of each voice, and to reflect upon the relationship of one voice to another"— was treated not so much as a separate idiom but as "a parasitic activity; it springs from the conversation, because this is what the philosopher reflects upon, but it makes no specific contribution to it" (p. 200). For a stronger appreciation of the role of "theory" or "theorizing" see Oakeshott, *On Human Conduct* (Oxford: Clarendon Press, 1975), pp. 1-31.

4. "The Voice of Poetry in the Conversation of Mankind," p. 198, 201-203.

5. Rorty, *Philosophy and the Mirror of Nature*, pp. 360, 370, 388-389. As

Rorty admits (p. 370): "The notion of an edifying philosopher is, however, a paradox. For Plato defined the philosopher by opposition to the poet."

6. Paul Ricoeur, *The Rule of Metaphor: Multi-Disciplinary Studies of the Creation of Meaning in Language*, trans. Robert Czerny (Toronto: University of Toronto Press, 1977), pp. 293, 296, 300-301. Referring to the "speculative *logos*," Ricoeur notes (p. 302): "Because it forms a system, the conceptual order is able to free itself from the play of double meaning and hence from the semantic dynamism characteristic of the metaphorical order."

7. *The Rule of Metaphor*, pp. 309-313.

8. Heidegger, *What is Philosophy?*, trans. William Kluback and Jean T. Wilde (New Haven: College and University Press, 1956), p. 95; "The Nature of Language," in *On the Way to Language*, trans. Peter D. Hertz (New York: Harper and Row, 1971), pp. 70, 90. For the German version see Heidegger, *What is Philosophy?*, p. 94; *Unterwegs zur Sprache* (Pfullingen: Neske, 1959), pp. 173, 195-196. Compare also David Halliburton, *Poetic Thinking: An Approach to Heidegger* (Chicago: University of Chicago Press, 1981). As it seems to me, Ricoeur correctly captures the thrust of Heidegger's comments by noting that "the poem does not serve as an ornament to the philosophical aphorism, and . . . the latter does not constitute the poem's translation. Poem and aphorism are in a mutual accord of resonance that respects their difference. To the imaginative power of thought-full poetry, the poet replies with the speculative power of poeticizing thought." *The Rule of Metaphor*, p. 310.

9. *The Rule of Metaphor*, pp. 302, 306, 308, 313. Ricoeur seeks to avoid the reductive consequence of rational analysis by noting (p. 303) that "destruction of the metaphorical by the conceptual in rationalizing interpretations is not the only outcome of the interaction between different modalities of discourse. One can imagine a hermeneutic style where interpretation would conform both to the notion of concept and to that of the constitutive intention of the experience seeking to be expressed in the metaphorical mode." But the latter "style" points again in the vicinity of poetic thinking.

10. Jürgen Habermas, *Philosophisch-politische Profile* (Frankfurt-Main: Suhrkamp, 1971), pp. 82-83, 85. For a broader critique of "post-modernist" trends see Habermas, "Modernity versus Post-Modernity," *New German Critique*, No. 22 (Winter 1981), pp. 3-14.

11. Heidegger, "The Origin of the Work of Art," in his *Poetry, Language, Thought*, trans. Albert Hofstadter (New York: Harper and Row, 1971), pp. 66, 68, 75, 79 (translation slightly altered); for the German version see "Der Ursprung des Kunstwerkes," in *Holzwege* (Frankfurt-Main: Klostermann, 1950), pp. 54, 56, 62, 66. Regarding the notion of "world-play" see Heidegger, "The Nature of Language," in *On the Way to Language*, p. 106; "Das Wesen der Sprache," in *Unterwegs zur Sprache*, p. 214. For a differentiation of Heidegger's conception of art and poetry from both aesthetic "formalism" and reductive "historicism" see Michael Murray, "The New Hermeneutic and the Interpretation of Poetry," in *Contemporary Literary Hermeneutics and Interpretation of Classical Texts*, ed. S. Krésic (Ottawa: University of Ottawa Press, 1981), pp. 53-73; also Edward G. Lawry, "The Work-Being of the Work of Art in Heidegger," *Man and World*, vol. 11 (1978), pp. 186-198.

12. Heidegger, "Letter on Humanism," in *Martin Heidegger: Basic Writings*, ed. David F. Krell (New York: Harper and Row, 1977), pp. 194-206; "Language," in *Poetry, Language, Thought*, p. 198; and "The Nature of Language," in *On the Way to Language*, pp. 58-59. For the German versions see Heidegger, *Über den Humanismus* (Frankfurt-Main: Klostermann, 1949), pp. 5, 16; *Unterwegs zur Sprache*, pp. 20, 160-161. For a portrayal of Heidegger's thoughts on language in terms of a path leading from the "liberation of grammar from logic" to the "liberation of language from logic and from grammar," see Michael Murray, *Modern Critical Theory: A Phenomenological Introduction* (The Hague: Nijhoff, 1975), pp. 143-202.

13. Ricoeur, "Naming God," *Union Seminary Quarterly Review*, vol. 34 (1979), p. 217, and "The Model of the Text," in *Hermeneutics and the Human Sciences*, ed. John B. Thompson (Cambridge: Cambridge University Press, 1981), pp. 201-202; Donald Davidson, "On the Very Idea of a Conceptual Scheme," in *Relativism: Cognitive and Moral*, eds. Jack W. Meiland and Michael Krausz (Notre Dame: University of Notre Dame Press, 1982), p.79.

14. Rorty, *Philosophy and the Mirror of Nature*, p. 252; Ricoeur, "Philosophy and Religious Language," *The Journal of Religion*, vol. 54 (1974), p. 74; James Edie, *Speaking and Meaning: The Phenomenology of Language* (Bloomington: Indiana University Press, 1976), p. 184. The stress on a priori structures does not prevent Edie from noting (p. 153): "It is necessary to suppose that even in the communication of mathematical concepts or logical 'truths' there lies beneath the threshold of what is, strictly speaking, communicated differences of meaning both for the 'communicator' and for the 'receiver' that are remarkable. In the highly formalized and abstract forms of communication with which formal logicians are content, such differences of meaning are 'negligible', but in other forms of communication they become less and less negligible as we proceed from the derived and abstract schemata of mathematics to the lived experience which is their source."

15. Rorty, *Philosophy and the Mirror of Nature*, pp. 380, 382; Heidegger, "Language," in *Poetry, Language, Thought*, p. 208; *Unterwegs zur Sprache*, p. 31; "Letter on Humanism," in *Martin Heidegger: Basic Writings*, pp. 232-236; *Über den Humanismus*, pp. 38-42. Regarding the relation of "ethos" and ethics see also my *Twilight of Subjectivity: Contributions to a Post-Individualist Theory of Politics* (Amherst: University of Massachusetts Press, 1981), p. 254.

16. Oakeshott, "The Voice of Poetry in the Conversation of Mankind," pp. 213-216.

17. Ibid., pp. 206, 208-212.

18. Ibid., pp. 217-221, 223-224, 234. Commenting on traditional metaphysics, Oakeshott voices the belief (p. 224, note 1) "that what Plato described as *theoria* is, in fact, aesthetic experience but that he misdescribed it and attributed to it a character and a supremacy which it is unable to sustain." In a phrase reminiscent of Heidegger's portrayal of "artworks," the essay affirms at another point (p. 218) that poetry "does not use, or use up or wear-out its images, or induce change in them: it rests in them, looking neither backwards nor forwards."

19. Hannah Arendt, *The Life of the Mind*, vol. I: *Thinking* (New York: Har-

court Brace Jovanovich, 1977), pp. 14-15, 58-59.

20. The assessment of "judging" is complicated by the fact that the projected third volume dealing with this faculty was not completed. The above association with commonsense reasoning (or *phronesis*) derives from Arendt's stress on "particularity." As she writes at one point: "Judgment deals with particulars, and when the thinking ego moving among generalities emerges from its withdrawal and returns to the world of particular appearances, it turns out that the mind needs a new 'gift' to deal with them." According to another passage, the "faculty of judgment" may be called "with some reason the most political of men's mental abilities. It is the faculty that judges *particulars* without subsuming them under general rules which can be taught and learned until they grow into habits that can be replaced by other habits and rules." See *The Life of the Mind*, vol. I: *Thinking*, pp. 192-193, 215. I am aware that, in some respects, judging is also akin to aesthetics and thus to "poetic thinking."

21. *The Life of the Mind*, vol. I: *Thinking*, pp. 8, 57, 62, 76-77, 129. The notion of "absence," one should add, is balanced in the study by an equal emphasis on presence and "difference." Thus, while at one point (p. 199) the thinking ego "moving among invisible essences" is said to be "strictly speaking, nowhere," another passage links thinking with the medieval *nunc stans* or eternal present (p. 210): "Using a different metaphor, we call it the region of the spirit, but it is perhaps rather the path paved by thinking, the small inconspicuous track of non-time beaten by the activity of thought within the time-space given to natal and mortal men." Arendt incidentally establishes a particularly intimate connection between thinking and language, arguing (p. 121) that thinking "needs speech not only to sound out and become manifest; it needs it to be activated at all. And since speech is enacted in sequences of sentences, the end of thinking can never be an intuition; nor can it be confirmed by some piece of self-evidence beheld in speechless contemplation."

22. Oakeshott, "The Voice of Poetry in the Conversation of Mankind," p. 202, note 1; Arendt, *The Human Condition* (Garden City: Anchor Books, 1959), pp. 4, 175-176.

23. As Heidegger writes at one point: "The essence of freedom is originally not connected with the will and particularly with the causality of human willing. Freedom reigns in the domain of free openness seen as a clearing, that is, as unconcealment (of Being). . . . The freedom of openness consists neither in unfettered arbitrariness nor in the constraint of mere laws: freedom is the clearing which also conceals." See "The Question Concerning Technology," in *Martin Heidegger: Basic Writings*, p. 306, "Die Frage nach der Technik," in *Vorträge und Aufsätze*, vol. I (Pfullingen: Neske, 1967), pp. 24-25. Arendt's thoughts on the political relevance of "truth" and morality are developed in her essays "Truth and Politics," in *Philosophy, Politics, and Society*, Third Series, eds. Peter Laslett and W. G. Runciman (New York: Barnes and Noble, 1976), pp. 106-133; and "Thinking and Moral Considerations," *Social Research*, vol. 38 (1971), 414-447. On "judging" and politics see her *Between Past and Future: Six Exercises in Political Thought* (New York: Meridian Books, 1963), pp. 219-224.

24. Heidegger, "What Are Poets For?", in *Poetry, Language, Thought*, pp. 94, 141 (translation slightly altered); also "Building Dwelling Thinking," in the

same volume, p. 148. For the German versions see "Wozu Dichter?" in *Holzwege*, pp. 250-251, 294; "Bauen Wohnen Denken," in *Vorträge und Aufsätze*, vol. 2 (Pfullingen: Neske, 1967), p. 22.

25. Oakeshott, "The Voice of Poetry in the Conversation of Mankind," pp. 235, 244. Regarding the Hölderlin passage see Heidegger, ". . . Poetically Man Dwells . . . ," in *Poetry, Language, Thought*, pp. 228-229 (translation slightly altered); ". . . Dichterisch Wohnet der Mensch . . .," in *Vorträge und Aufsätze*, vol. 2, pp. 77-78. Regarding the notion that poetic giving is animated by the "simplest and most gentle of all laws," see "The Way to Language," in *On the Way to Language*, p. 128; "Der Weg zur Sprache," in *Unterwegs zur Sprache*, p. 259.

Index